SOME TROUBLE WITH COWS

SOME TROUBLE WITH COWS

Making Sense of Social Conflict

BETH ROY

University of California Press

Berkeley   Los Angeles   London

University of California Press
Berkeley and Los Angeles, California

University of California Press, Ltd.
London, England

© 1994 by
The Regents of the University of California

An earlier version of part of chapter 9 was published as "Of
Cabbages and Kings and Why the Sea Is Boiling Hot: How
Communities Decide to Fight," *International Journal of the
Sociology of Law* 20 (1992): 285–93. Reprinted by permission
of the Academic Press Ltd.

Library of Congress Cataloging-in-Publication Data

Roy, Beth.
    Some trouble with cows : making sense of social conflict /
Beth Roy.
        p.   cm.
    Includes bibliographical references and index.
    ISBN 0-520-08341-5 (alk. paper).—ISBN 0-520-08342-3
(pbk. : alk. paper)
    1. Communalism—Bangladesh.   2. Hindus—
Bangladesh.   3. Muslims—Bangladesh.   I. Title.
DS393.8.R69   1994
303.6'23'095492—dc20   93-25761
                                                                        CIP

Printed in the United States of America
9   8   7   6   5   4   3   2   1

The paper used in this publication meets the minimum
requirements of American National Standard for Information
Sciences—Permanence of Paper for Printed Library
Materials, ANSI Z39.48-1984. ♾

Contents

I became a university student at the same time Tuhin matriculated. A grey-haired woman with an evolved and busy life, I
longed for the luxury of fighting necessity back far enough to think
a thought through to its conclusion. The notion of being a student
again after years of teaching delighted me. I wanted to sit at the
feet of a mentor, to learn new skills of scholarship, and to widen my
intellectual community. I felt too comfortable in my own; I wanted
the challenges of disagreement and of fresh points of view.

At the same time, I was crusty and opinionated, and I felt some
skepticism about what I'd find in that bastion of establishment, The
Academy. In the event, I was surprised and gratified. During my
first semester in the sociology department at Berkeley, I headed for
a class on race in America, because I figured I'd meet people there
who shared a certain set of social concerns. The strategy paid off
handsomely, for Bob Blauner taught that course. I quickly came to
value highly both his principles and his approaches to scholarship.
Among many other contributions, Bob pioneered oral history as a
method for academic research. Talking with "real" people is a
touchstone, and time and again Bob has helped to bring me back
from flights of rhetoric to the position of careful attention to what
people say and do that (I hope) characterizes this study. His critical
questions, always so respectful, helped me to focus my interests,
and his encouragement of oddball ways of thinking and working
has cheered me on throughout the years I've spent on this project.

At the same time that Bob helped me to find my methodological
feet, Sandria Freitag became my link to South Asian scholarship.
To find Sandy, a historian of India, when I crossed the bridge to
Berkeley was a stroke of unbelievably good luck. She is a superb
craftsperson of the historiographic art and a keen and creative
thinker about questions of central interest to me. Not only did
Sandy introduce me to the Subalternists, a group of South Asian
historians doing some of the most exciting scholarship of the day,
but she consistently encouraged me to go ever more deeply into
questions about which I naively thought I understood something.
Over and over, she posed a question that opened the lid to another
whole level of inquiry, and she always did it with charm, goodwill,
and a generosity of time and spirit that in itself was inspirational.

Kim Voss was the first sociologist before whom I laid my agenda
for this study. In her own work, she combines sociological inquiry

with historical method, and she brought her rigorous mind and enormous energy to the considerable task of making order out of my woolly agenda. At first I regarded her methods with suspicion, peppering her with abuse when she posed questions in terms taken from the physical sciences. But her kindness and patience eased me past that reaction, I'm glad to say, because what I met on the other side were hard questions of purpose and belief that had to be confronted and answered. With her unusual analytic capacity to take apart a question and construct means for answering it, Kim gently pushed me into a new precision which made my investigations enormously more meaningful.

Other faculty members at Berkeley also have won my gratitude. Jyoti Das Gupta, whose work on language conflict in India formed a conceptual backdrop to my study, gave me encouragement and assistance. Neil Smelser helped me think through some of my theoretical premises in a jolly process of friendly contention. Michael Burawoy saw me through a close reading of Gramsci that proved deeply satisfying in part because of Michael's erudite guidance and the thoughtful controversies he raised in our discussions.

In South Asia I was overwhelmed with kindness. First, I want to thank all the friends who housed me and fed me, who took messages and made travel arrangements and suffered through endless changes of itinerary. Chander Chopra in New Delhi is one of my dearest friends and a constant source of engagement both of the heart and of the mind. Govind Chopra, too, tolerated my endless comings and goings, always with good humor and generous hospitality. The Chakravartis in Calcutta are kin, a legal bond made actual over years of friendship. Smriti Misra in North Bengal is my sister and Mahamaya Roy my mother; without the interludes they afforded me for rest and restoration I could never have finished this, or many other, projects. Prodyot Misra spent long hours poring over tapes and translations with me, only the latest episodes in a years-long dialogue about history and ideas, a conversation that leaps over great expanses of time and distance to pick up exactly where it left off.

In Bangladesh, my newer friends, Ataur and Sultana Rahman, and their family and colleagues were indispensable to this project; many of their endless contributions are specified throughout the story that follows. In addition to what they did for me, their lives

are an inspiration. In the work to which they have dedicated themselves and the diverse community they have constructed around
them, they embody the spirit of respectful peace-making that this
study is all about.

Not the least of what the Rahmans did for me was to introduce
me to many, many people who helped more generously than I can
say. Staff people at Gono Unnayan Prochesta—Reza, Provash,
Kamrul, Anima, and on and on—mobilized numbers of people to
meet with me. They cloaked my enterprise in their good reputa-
tions, giving me that invaluable quality, trustworthiness, which I
had as yet done nothing to deserve. Then there was Mukta, who
drove me up one side of Bangladesh and down the other, contributing along the way some of the most pithy commentaries I heard.
Other friends also emerged from the wide circle of the Rahmans:
Fuzlul Huq in Madaripur, Delwar in Gopalganj, the Hudas in
Jamalpur and Rafique, Samir Ghosh in Kishorganj, Dr. and Mrs.
Hossein in Mymensingh—the list is so long that I am bound to have
omitted worthy names; I assure those people that I do so from
disorganization, not disrespect.

Then there were the people who assisted me directly in the
research. Dilruba Haider abandoned her own life with no advance
notice, to travel with me throughout Bangladesh. She translated for
hour upon hour, her attention never wandering; often when my
brain had gone blank from exhaustion, Dilruba was ready with the
next question, remembered the critical piece of information from
an earlier interview, and was still capable of exercising the intelligent charm that made her such a pleasure to work with, both for
me and for our interviewees. Meanwhile, back in Dhaka, another
assistant, Rina, was spending hours in the archives searching out
press reports and noting their absences.

In Calcutta, Bela Bandyopadhyaya suffered the extreme dis-
tresses of work in the West Bengal State Archives, sorting through
mountains of materials tattered by the elements and eaten by
"white ants." On her own initiative, she found and interviewed
migrants from Bangladesh in Calcutta, providing me with a fascinating dimension I would otherwise have entirely missed. Finally,
she and her daughter Durba agonized over the transcription and
translation of interviews, spending hours in the dark of Calcutta's
power outages running machines on stacks of batteries and some-

how finding a way to translate the spirit as well as the letter. Bela was more than "assistant" to me. A fine scholar in her own right, she fed me intellectually as well as literally, frequently pulling delicious meals, as if by magic, out of packets and parcels in the most unlikely places. In addition to all her other contributions, Bela introduced into my world of friends her wonderful husband, Nripen, whose ever-inquiring mind and enthusiastic encouragement delighted me and buoyed me through arduous moments in Calcutta.

Then there are the scholars who extended support of various kinds: Sumit Sarkar and Sekhar Bandyopadhyay, who sponsored me (I read Sumit's work on the Swadeshi movement early in the project with great appreciation, and I discovered Sekhar's study of Namasudras late in the project at a most opportune and fruitful moment); Barun De, who gave me encouragement and help in the formulation of the study; Surinjan Das, who made available to me his excellent, thorough study on communal riots in Bengal; Adrian Cooper in London, whose work on the Tebagha Movement opened new dimensions to my thinking; Salahuddin Ahmed in Dhaka, whose oral history project inspired me to believe in my own; John Broomfield, a noted scholar of Bengal whom I discovered just up the street from my home in San Francisco and who generously opened his personal library to me; and many others who helped to guide me through sources and possibilities.

Some key friends read the manuscript at various stages and gave me wonderful feedback. Matthew Hallinan, an activist with a mind that is never still and a capacity to connect from the heart that suggests the true meaning of *spiritual*, talked through some of the most central ideas with me and expanded my understandings. A. B. Siddique checked my accuracy and engaged me in debate about some of my political positions. Mariah Breeding read the manuscript with care and imagination, bringing to bear her keen analytic abilities and ringing clarity about how people work. Shelby Morgan reflected back to me the core of my ideas at a time when I was groping for focus.

Throughout the formulation and writing of this work in its first incarnation as a dissertation, I met with other students of Bob Blauner in a seminar. The personnel changed as others finished their writing and went on to greener pastures, but everyone involved added to the gestalt of support and good debate that made the seminar so special an assistance.

For almost twenty years an important part of my identity has been constituted by my participation in the Bay Area Radical Therapy Collective, an exceptional group of talented therapists who consistently theorized and practiced on the cutting edge. To many of them I am indebted for their coverage of my practice when I was away. The working theory I've drawn on in my research is very much our collective creation, although I don't hold my colleagues responsible for the ways I've transformed and used it here.

My work in India and Bangladesh was funded by the National Science Foundation, to whom I am most grateful, and the analysis and writing of the dissertation by the Fund for Research in Dispute Resolution, a group which supports a range of very worthy work and was generous enough to extend that range to include my project. Juliana Birkhoff and her staff at the Fund went beyond the financial to contribute a spirit of supportiveness and interest that I greatly appreciate. Finally, I consider this project to be the first in what is destined to become a body of work sponsored by the Village Scholars' Program of Shanti Kendra, the Peace Center of Gono Unnayan Prochesta.

Map 1. Asia and environs

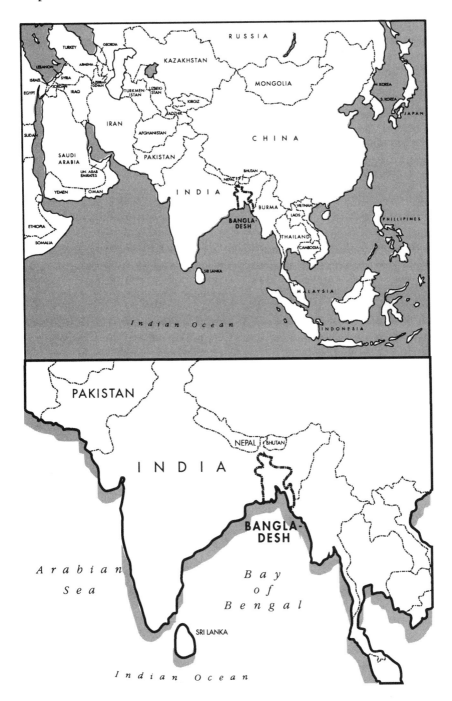

Map 2. South and Southeast Asia

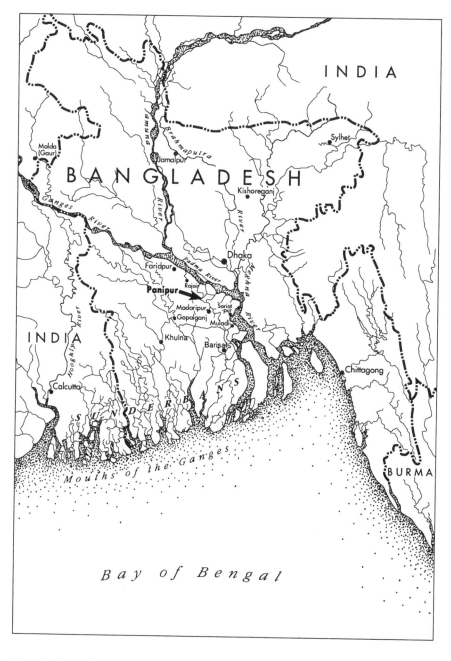

Map 3. Bangladesh

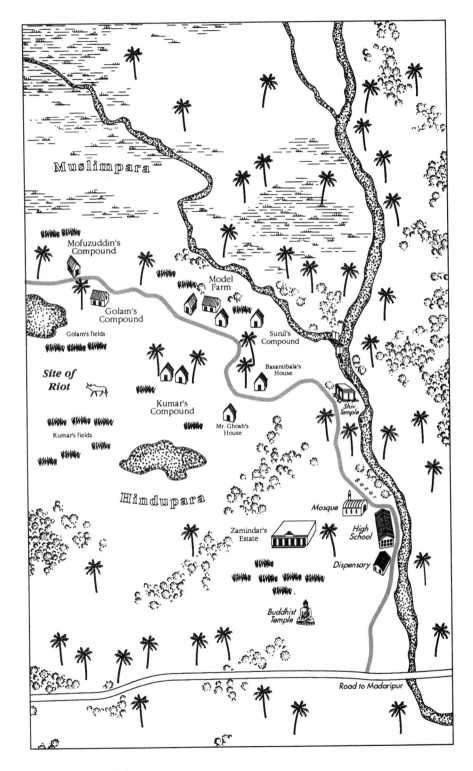

Map 4. The village of Panipur

The Cast of Characters

(presented in order of appearance)

Basantibala Majumdar	The widow of a cousin of the *zamindar* of Panipur; matriarch of a large, extended Hindu family, the poor gentility of the village
Sujit Ghosh	Basantibala's neighbor, a small landowner and a caste Hindu
Altaf-uddin	The elected chairman of Panipur Union, a Muslim and a major player in the riot
Sunil Mondal	A middle-aged Namasudra (low-caste Hindu) farmer, owner of land sufficient to necessitate hired help and lucrative enough to enable him to send his sons to university
Raghu Nandan	A Hindu police officer who fought in the riot
Mofizuddin	A Muslim farmer with holdings roughly comparable to Sunil's; an old man who fought in the riot and is now a *matabbar* of the village
Nayeb Ali	Mofizuddin's friend, also a Muslim, a little older and of comparable worth and status
Kumar Tarkhania	Appearing only by reputation, the Namasudra farmer whose crop was eaten; he subsequently migrated to India and died there

xvii

The Cast of Characters

Golam Fakir A Muslim farmer with small holdings, the owner of the wayward cow

Jogendra Pal A Hindu elder who tried to intervene in the riot

Bhupendranath An educated Namasudra man living at Pani- pur

Sidheshwar Tarkhania A Muslim who participated in the riot

Sona Miah A retired Muslim government officer and amateur historian from a northern district

Introduction

In a remote village somewhere in South Asia, someone's cow ate someone else's crop. Within two days, tens of thousands of men were ranged against each other, armed, hostile, righteous.

Who those men were, how they chose sides, the symbolic choreography of their fight, were all particular to that village. But an inclination to confrontation is widespread. Social conflict is a durable fact of life throughout the world, from the back alleys of Belfast to the urban canyons of New York City, from the dusty pathways of Israeli settlements to the public squares of Lithuania.

The need to understand why some groups of people define others as Other, how enemies are made, why conflicts often turn so brutal, is not politely academic. As, I suspect, with most enduring questions of scholarship, the personal and the political merge urgently in these questions. Born an American Jew during the Holocaust, reared on the Korean War and the McCarthy hearings, come to adulthood in a segregated southwestern city during the first throes of the civil rights movement, I, like most citizens of this century, experienced conflict as an assumed part of life. Perhaps it was no accident that I chose mediation as a career, nor that I came to wonder more and more, as the years of helping people resolve conflict rolled on, about the nature of animosity.

So much enmity appears in the modern world that it is tempting to ascribe it to human nature and let it go at that. But I could not work as a mediator if I truly believed that conflict emerges from some dark, inescapable side of the human psyche. To help people solve problems, I must believe in the existence of solvable prob-

lems, and, sure enough, that belief has led to the identification and
resolution of many conflicts over the years.

But do lessons learned in practice with individuals and small
groups apply to conflicts among much larger—and perhaps more
resistant—masses of people? Had my colleagues and I learned
anything, I wondered, over the years of practice that had theoretical significance on the level of collectivities, and, if so, how could
we turn theories into tools for understanding, and perhaps helping
to solve, those intractable struggles?

Before I became a mediator in the United States, I lived in India,
and there I encountered a dramatic example of community conflict,
the longtime struggle between Hindus and Muslims that cul-
minated, in 1947, in the radical reorganization of the subcontinent.* I determined to start my project there.

Communalism (as such friction between communities is labeled
in South Asia) has been studied and theorized abundantly, for
obvious reasons. Ethnic, racial, religious, and other sorts of community conflicts interlace so much of modern history with thick lines
of intransigence that their understanding is a high priority for
peacemakers and politicians alike. In India, communalism runs like
a pulsating vein through the body politic of modern times. Every
account from whatever perspective, whether nationalist, colonial-
ist, or popular, must contend with questions of community conflict.
Too often such "disturbances" are dismissed as aberrations of
human nature. But to do so is to relinquish any possible response
beyond brute repression, and that response has again and again
proven inadequate. More to the point, tensions between Hindus
and Muslims have taken many forms in different places and at
different moments, suggesting causes and dynamics that beckon to
be understood in specific terms rather than universals.

If we avoid the temptation to lump together every instance of
strife between communities inhabiting common borders—those

*To Western consciousness, the word *India* defines an area coincident with the
British Empire in the region. In fact, that Empire has now become half a dozen
more or less independent nations. My study is set in what today is Bangladesh.
At the time of the events I describe it was Pakistan, a nation that had come into
being only a few years before with the Independence of India. When writing of
the area as a whole, I try to use the more precise designations *South Asia* or *the
subcontinent*. I beg the reader's indulgence for my occasional lapses into the
colloquial *India* to mean the region rather than the current nation-state.

sorts of conflicts called communal, nationalist, ethnic, and so on—
then we can begin to ask a set of questions that are otherwise
meaningless. What were the motivations of people who at one
moment lived peacefully side by side, yet at another came to
blows? What was happening to induce animosity, and what happened at the moment of conflict that decided them to mobilize and
fight? What events, both in the large frame of their lives as occu-
pants of a land experiencing historic changes and in the small frame
of their day-to-day world, combined to inspire their acts of conten-
tiousness? In particular, how did they comprehend and interpret
those experiences, and translate them, both as individuals and as
communities, into the dramas they enacted?

It is this space between the most private of experiences and the
most public of actions that especially interests me in my study of
community friction.[1] When I consider stories of village communalism, I want to know how people saw their world, how they placed
their own desires within it, and how their sense of political possibility was influenced by distant winds of change. It has become
common to assert that the most intimate domestic behaviors are in
fact socially constructed. Collective experience is translated into
psychological reality through a web of ideas internalized as invisible assumptions about the world. To unravel the psychological
realities of collective behavior, I believe we must look to shared
areas of understanding and social location. For instance, group
actions are formulated from the experience of identity, that is, the
complex construction of an individual's location in the community
and her ties with others. Similarly, the will to action is born of
detailed ideologies that often are experienced as common sense or
unexamined assumptions about rights and powers. Both identity
and ideology-making draw deeply at the well of community memories, those shared histories constructed through storytelling that
serve to define memberships within groups and relations among
them, and that bound the formulation of protest.

Adventures in Methodology

To learn something of life on the level of internal experience (internal both to the individual and to the community), I determined to
study cases of communalism through face-to-face encounters with

participants. For my study I chose a northeastern area of the South
Asian subcontinent called Bengal, specifically, the portion that is
modern-day Bangladesh.* (I'll say more later about how and why
I happened to choose that precise spot.)

Hindu-Muslim "communal disturbances" (an expression that
illustrates the inimitable British knack for understatement) first
became noteworthy elsewhere in India during the nineteenth century, but they came later to Bengal, starting in 1907 and spreading
throughout the century.[2] All these incidents involved hostilities
between peoples of the two communities, but there were actually
very important differences among them. Some sprang from political disagreements, others from economic protest or neighborly disputes, still others from a host of creative causes. All drew in some
fashion on people's identities as Muslims or Hindus, yet most were
sparked by some clearly defined problem to which religion was not
intrinsic.

The mystery that engaged me was why these struggles became
defined as communal. Recent discussions have historicized the very
definitions of *communalism*, calling attention to the role of British
colonialists in conceptualizing and imposing a monolithic definition
upon very complex happenings.[3] Was that label indeed an imposition by outsiders? If the concept of communalism was a construct
of the British policy of divide and rule, why, I wondered, did it
work? Why did the people involved allow their troubles to be
divisively defined in terms of Hindus and Muslims, considering the
multiplicity of issues involved? Or did they? Were all these struggles about so many different things formulated by the fighters
themselves as hostilities between the communities, and, if so, how
did that come to be?

Having selected an area of study, I searched the archival record
to catalog instances described as communal.[4] From that list I selected six localities: three appeared frequently in the historical
record as sites of contention (Kishoreganj, Gopalganj, and Jamalpur), and three were noteworthy for the absence of mention
(Faridpur, Madaripur, and Sariatpur), because I thought it was as

*The history of the creation of Bangladesh in the wash of colonialism and
international politics is complex. A brief chronology is given in Appendix A, and
I discuss the details as they are relevant to what follows.

important to know why communities remained peaceful as why they came to blows.

I went next to visit those locations and began interviewing people, starting with the elderly, moving on to conversations with the young about the stories they had heard, asking people about relations between the communities in their towns and villages. Very soon it became apparent that I had made a mistake; I had assumed those localities not identified as contentious in official reports had been peaceful. While interviewing, I came by chance upon an event totally absent from any written record I had found: a riot in an out-of-the-way place. It had been blacked out of the press and recorded, if at all, only in governmental files currently inaccessible.[5] I was thus offered the serendipitous opportunity to construct a history of an event solely from firsthand accounts. Although I went on to interview people in each of my selected sites, this riot became the focus of my study. The lack of a paper trail, which might have been a serious handicap, was in fact a blessing, for I was thoroughly constrained to do what my theory dictated: to build a history out of the subjective versions of those who participated in it.

Why was that a useful thing to do? After all, subjective accounts are just that: piecemeal approaches to a shared reality. Some thinkers argue that you cannot know "what really happened" by listening to the distorted memories of the players, many of whom in any case are now dead or dwelling in the hazy mists of old age. Instead, you must employ more objective reflections of events—documents or indices of material consequence.

It is true that the stories I heard in that Bangladeshi village were not about "what happened" (itself a questionable concept). What I heard was how people *saw* what happened, or, rather, how people *remembered* what they saw, or, rather, how they *talked* about what they remembered, or, rather, how they talked *to me* about what they remembered—or, rather, what I *heard* people say to me about what they remembered.

I was well aware that what I learned from my informants engaged my own history at every step of the process and was transformed in that interaction. "There is a relation between angles and attitudes. Where I look from is tied up with how I see."[6] Perhaps those angles are a problem. We could talk about them in terms of distortions and biases and blind spots. But we can equally embrace them as the point of the exercise. After a lifetime of engagement with other people's stories, with a strong sense of gratitude for the ways I have been shaped by those I supposedly influenced, I have come to suspect that all human understanding takes the form of conversation. I have a hard time believing in the myth of the lone thinker receiving enlightenment in grand isolation.

In this view, the "problems" of memory distortion, selective telling, and biased hearing become sources of understanding. What sticks in people's memories, what they choose to say and when they choose to remain silent, how they distort what they know to be their experience, and, overarching all, what I notice and what I overlook are all intensely informative. The selection of truths-to-tell constitutes a story within a story, or, more accurately, the context for the story itself.[7] By looking at forms of discourse as well as content, we can learn much about individuals' relationships to institutions, about their experience of economic and political changes, about conflicts of tradition they are experiencing as social transformation takes place, for all these dynamics interweave in the manner of expression characterizing a story.

True, we cannot learn everything. Not every question is best answered by an oral-history approach. If you want to know what social and economic conditions are associated with protest and rebellion, for instance, you might well compare examples from varied places and moments in history rather than listening to the stories of ordinary folk.[8] But the questions that most interest me— why people live harmoniously together at one time and at another do not, or, more fundamentally, how people decide to form groups and act to change their world—can be well illuminated by asking the players. If the realm of inquiry is, as I've said, the intersection between individual and collective experience, then the perceptions of the individuals who compose that collectivity are very important.

The division between structural forces and psychological ones is, to me, a false one. How are we to comprehend a Bangladeshi farmer's understanding of his times if we do not hear his story in the context of a material, structural reality? No individual's psychology is divorced from the real conditions of her life, and those conditions are historical. Whereas a developmental Freudian view contends that individual psychology is formed in early childhood, I believe that people are responsive to change throughout life—not, to be sure, in some simple and linear way, but richly, complexly, informatively. Material conditions are inherent in every formulation of personal conflict, in ordinary people's grievances and quarrels and decisions to protest or to stay quiet. To lend a keen ear to the specifics of each incident of community conflict, then, leads us back to the general, but in another way and on another level. We cannot generalize reasons for each individual's actions, but by studying a given individual's personal story we can understand generalized relationships between individual and society, between personal decisions and public forces. Those abstract relationships are useful, not to explain why people have done what they did, but to raise a different set of questions. Rather than asking, for instance, what lapse of controls allowed aggression to emerge? we are led to ask, what goals did these people formulate at that historic moment, in response to what external events, and how did they come to mold their strategies in the form of community conflict?

To make such delineations requires considerable interpretation, and here again the position of the analyzer enters in. My own position was an odd one. When I began the study, I trusted that it would be informative, but I also expected that most of my information would be, at best, secondhand. What, after all, would induce people who had come to blows with each other to tell me about it? In earlier, more casual conversations with people of the region, I had often been told hearsay tales. But everyone always insisted that *he* took no part in combat; he personally would never do such a thing. I knew something similar would be likely to happen in my own world if I were interviewing people about incidents of racial tension, or anti-Semitism, or any of the other common forms of intergroup hostility. People feel frightened to confess contentious activities, or they are ashamed or ambivalent. People are intuitive and likely to pick up my biases against such means of working out differences, and they understandably protect themselves from censure, through the simple expedient of secrecy.[9] It is a supreme act of trust and respect to talk openly about these things.

But my experience interviewing in Bengal was a very different matter. Sometimes I met the expected reticence. As often, though, people lavished on me their stories with openness and goodwill. Why they did so may have had less to do with me than with their need to tell their stories, to reflect upon and continuously reconstruct their own histories.

Honesty was also aided by the company I kept. In 1988, the year before my study, Bangladesh had endured terrible floods. Because I had lived across the border in Indian West Bengal for some years long before and as a consequence have a fair command of the Bengali language, I volunteered to help the relief effort if I could. To tell the truth, I thought it unlikely that anyone would accept my offer. As I was quick to confess, I could do little that was useful; I had few skills that would help repair damaged homes or heal damaged bodies.

To my surprise and eventual delight, I was wrong. A highly respected organization working in the rural hinterland of Bangladesh needed a literary person, ideally someone with a sociological perspective and experience in organizational consulting, to help them remedy a serious lack of documentation for their program. So overwhelmed had they been for two years in saving lives from floods that they had allowed their budgeting and planning and report-writing to fall far behind. Some of their funders were upset, and they were prepared to pay my fare to help their Bangladeshi colleagues clean their paper house. I went, worked harder than I ever had in my life, made friends, and was inspired and astonished by the capacities of these village-level workers, by their ingenuity and perseverance and optimism in the face of enormous odds.

When I returned, eighteen months later, to conduct my own research, which by then was refocused in Bangladesh, I found my friends there fully prepared to return the favor. Three of the sites I had selected to study fell within the work area of the organization; the other three were some distance away. The staff, however, was drawn from all over Bangladesh, so each of the sites either was the birthplace of a staff member or hosted an affiliated organization. All these people introduced me, helped to arrange interviews, spread the word that I was trustworthy. And so people talked with me. Over and over, someone would say, "You'll be careful how you use this, won't you? I'm only telling you because I've known and trusted So-and-so for years."*

This, then, is a study of discord facilitated by an act of cooperation. Never was an altruistic impulse more fully rewarded. What follows is a joint effort, one that has indebted me to all my hosts and facilitators, as well as to the women and men who shared their histories and their ideas so openly and so warmly with me.

*All names in the account that follows, including that of the village, are pseudonyms, an attempt to preserve some measure of anonymity.

Part One

Making Trouble

Chapter One

The Quarrel

Cows, Crops, and Communities

"There was trouble with cows," said the farmer. "I tied my cow and went home. But the cow got loose and ate the [plants] in their field."

By the time the "trouble" was over, masses of men had mobilized, several people had died, many were injured, and life in the village was altered forever after.

The problem, it seems, was that the cow belonged to a Muslim and the crop to a Hindu.

I first heard about the incident from an old woman named Basantibala Majumdar. Her family were acquaintances of mine, and I had come to pay her a condolence call, for her husband, a well-loved and ancient man, had died since my last visit to Bangladesh.[1] The monsoon season had made travel slow and wet. A village boat, rowed, poled, and pulled by a bare-chested, bearded man, had transported us* through winding channels and flooded paddy fields to a muddy embankment not far from Basantibala's home.

*Our party included a young woman who assisted me in most of the interviews with interpretation and questions, and a staff member from the development organization hosting me, who happened to live in the village. Throughout my account I use "I" or "we" not quite indiscriminately; sometimes I mean to suggest the importance of the entourage (as in this scene in Basantibala's house) or some question that evolved from a discussion between my assistant and me. I use "I" when an exchange was truly between me and the respondent.

13

The house was one of the few in the village built of brick and plaster. The Majumdars were Hindus, poor relations of the local *zamindar*, or large landlord. Their two spacious rooms were crammed with possessions. Old blankets hung from rafters; age-faded *sarees* and *dhotis*° and children's clothing were draped over lines crisscrossing the moldy walls. Life filled the rooms. Women stood about the perimeter, briefly smiling at us, then drifting away to rejoin the endless flow of domestic activities we could glimpse within. Everywhere children peered from behind doorways, edging out into the adult spaces with growing boldness as my visit lost its novelty. A naked boy about ten, clearly retarded, lay on the floor playing with motes of dust in a shaft of sunlight and singing quietly to himself. People glanced benignly at him from time to time but paid him no real attention.

Over tea and biscuits, I told Basantibala that I had come back to her village to study conflicts. I didn't happen to mention to her that I was especially interested in conflicts between Hindus and Muslims or that my study was designed to include places with no history of communal conflict as well as those known for overt fighting. Her village, Panipur, and Faridpur, the district in which it is located, fell into the "no conflict" category. So far, everyone I'd spoken to had confirmed that view:

[A Hindu woman:] No, we never had any communal disturbances. . . . Communal harmony was very much prevalent throughout the Faridpur area, even when there was trouble in Dhaka, Khulna, and many other places in Bengal. . . . Our Muslim neighbors, especially those who were highly respected people, used to assure us that they would not allow any such trouble here. They said that the Hindus should not be afraid of their Muslim neighbors.

[A Hindu man:] We [Hindus and Muslims] were good friends. We played together. We read in the same schools together. We were on the same football teams.

[A Muslim man:] Nothing happened here in 1946 [when there were massive riots in Calcutta and elsewhere]. In [1950, when major riots

°A *dhoti* is the male equivalent of a *saree;* it is an unstitched piece of fabric worn draped as pants. Clothing signifies community; only Hindus, and upper-caste ones at that, wear *dhotis.*

occurred in Barisal, near here] there were some little incidents. . . . It was not a plan. There were just some people, a few people. . . . We Hindus and Muslims were together.

[A Muslim man:] In childhood, I had many friends, both Hindu and Muslim. We made no distinction. We freely visited each other's houses, took food with no problem.

Were there ever any communal riots around here?

No. . . . The Namasudras [low-caste Hindu farmers] and the Muslims were both cultivators, they worked side by side, so there was no animosity between them.

When I asked Basantibala whether there had ever been fighting in her village, therefore, I was making conversation rather than expecting news. To my surprise, she answered:

Oh yes, there was, so many times. There were riots. Then all the Hindu people left.

I was flustered. "Oh, really? When?" I stuttered.

Spilling the Beans

The room full of people suddenly became quiet, and then it erupted into chaotic debate. Several men first denied that anything had happened, but when Basantibala persisted, everyone began trying to place "oh-*that*-riot" in time, a creative process involving big storms, dates in the Bengali calendar nobody quite knew how to translate into English equivalents, disagreements over who got married when, and so on. Basantibala insisted that the biggest riot had happened in the British period, when she was newly married and had no children. She guessed her own age to be about seventy, so that would have placed the incident in the mid-1930s, a time, I knew, of considerable upheaval in other rural parts of East Bengal. I was surprised, but the news was believable.

By this time neighbors had begun to drift in. With helpful enthusiasm they muddied the waters even further. Mr. Ghosh, an unassuming, immediately likable man in his sixties who lived next door, reeled off a whole list of riots:

Which riot are you asking about? At the time of Pakistan, do you mean? Do you mean the one at the temple with the Buddha priest? Or do you mean at Partition [in 1947]?°

My head was spinning with this proliferation of mayhem. It didn't help that everyone was talking at once, adding to the list, placing events in other towns at different times, and generally being most unhelpfully helpful. At last a young man quietly brought some order to the proceedings with authoritative hearsay:

I heard from my father that there was this trouble.

What did you hear?

There was some *kheshari dal* [a variety of lentil] planted in a field, and someone's cows ate it. The fighting went on for two or three days. . . .

Hindus supported each other, and Muslims supported each other. Then the police came and made a temporary camp over there to stop it. It was at the time of British Empire, not after Independence. Both Hindus and Muslims participated.

Here we had a nicely objective statement. It was nobody's fault: some cows ate some plants; the cows happened to belong to a member of one community, the plants to another; people fought, as people do over banal village disputes; the police came and stopped it. The young man had given us a skeleton of a tale. It was an incident that had happened many times in many places in India. But there were some tantalizing hints of bigger drama: the fighting went on for two or three days; the police not only came, they camped out.

Mr. Ghosh now took up the tale and began to hang flesh on the skeleton. Still contesting the dates, he nonetheless now understood that I was truly interested in this particular riot, and he set about covering the bare bones with tough sinews of intent and responsibility:

It was a very recent riot. . . .

Side by side were a Hindu piece of land and a Muslim piece of land. In both fields, *dal* [lentil crop] was growing. The Muslim farmer kept his cow so that it could eat a little bit from the Hindu field too. A few hours

°When India became independent from the British and was simultaneously divided to form Pakistan, of which this area was a part.

later, the Hindu farmer came and saw that some of his plants had been eaten by the Muslim cow.

So the Hindu man went to the Muslim's house and said, "Your cow has eaten my *dal*. So I'm going to call a *matabbar* [village headman] and see what he has to say about it."

The Muslim was not happy about that, so he put his cow where it could eat more plants. When the Hindu came to his field and saw more plants had been eaten, he became angry. So he took the Muslim cow, and the owner saw his cow was taken and he got a *lathi* [stick] and he ran after him and beat him. In the Hindu's hand there was no weapon [he was unarmed]. So the Muslim beat him, then left his cow and rushed to his house.

After that, Hindu people took up *koch* [a fishing spear] and *lathi* and swords and rushed to that field. And Muslims, too, came armed with the same things to the field. They fought each other for a few hours.

Then night came, and they went home. It became too dark for them to see who they were fighting, at whom they were throwing the stick. Also local leaders came and stopped the fight.

The Caste Hindus

It was clear where Mr. Ghosh's loyalties lay: it was the Muslim's fault. The Muslim meant his cow (a "Muslim" cow) to eat the Hindu's crop. The Hindu was innocent. All he did was to make a just complaint. Very reasonably, he proposed that the village authority adjudicate the dispute. The Muslim retaliated with more of the same injustice. Only then did the Hindu take matters into his own hands, seizing the cow. But then the Muslim escalated the fight to violence, attacking the unarmed Hindu. Outrageously provoked, the Hindus, now multiplied, took up weapons and fought, until night and local leadership intervened.

Mr. Ghosh was a Hindu. It made sense that he would line up with the Hindu protagonist. Mr. Ghosh himself was not a central actor in the Panipur riot, a fact established by his description of the morning after:

The next morning, I was going to the *bazar* [market] to buy milk. People were sitting and talking about the fighting the day before. So I stopped to hear what they were saying.

Were they Hindus?

No, they were Muslims. I heard them say, "We'll fight." I said, "No, why is it necessary to quarrel? It's better to compromise. Local people, the *matabbar*, and the chairman° will decide it." They said, "Don't talk to us. Go and do your work."

Then I saw that in the Namasudra area, at some distance, there was another group sitting together. I thought, "It will not stop; there will be another fight." So I hurried to my house.

Just as I reached my house, I could hear the fight begin. The two groups were running after each other with knives and other weapons. But we were neutral, so we stayed at home. From a distance we observed the fight. One side ran at the other, and when they had a chance, they ran at the other side.

All this time Mr. Ghosh had been speaking in an even tone, while the roomful of people listened politely. Basantibala, thoroughly upstaged, slipped out to arrange another round of refreshments, since our visit was clearly taking on major proportions.

Castes, Fixed and Mobile

As he described how the fight escalated and the sides arranged themselves for combat, Mr. Ghosh introduced a significant distinction: "Then I saw that in the Namasudra area, at some distance, there was another group sitting together." This was the first time he had mentioned that the Hindus involved were Namasudras. They were "at some distance," and Mr. Ghosh hurried to distance himself even further: "I thought, 'It will not stop; there will be another fight.' So I hurried to my house."

As a metaphor for relations between high- and low-caste Hindus, Mr. Ghosh's description was perfect. He both identified with the warriors as Hindus and at the same time distinguished himself decisively: "[W]e were neutral, so we stayed at home. From a distance we observed the fight." *We* in this case clearly did not mean *Hindu* but *caste* Hindu.

Mr. Ghosh was delineating distinctions of caste, class, and culture so complex they intertwine like columbines climbing an ancient wall. He and the man with the cow-ravished plant were and

°The elected head of Panipur Union. A union is roughly equivalent to a city ward; a cluster of villages, it is the level at which effective rural electoral power is brokered.

were not of the same group. Caste is easy to deplore, difficult to understand. Its complexities are legendary. Nehru repeated a popular conception of caste when he likened it to the medieval trade guilds of Europe.[2] But to imagine that caste is simply a hierarchy of occupations is soon to become bewildered by modern-day exceptions. Indeed, exception was probably the rule even historically. To describe caste by economic function is to fail to describe much that is important about it. Caste is a rich mixture of ideology, ritual, highly internalized group identity and aversion, and practical community association.[3]

Of all that might be said about caste, three qualities are especially important to the Panipur story. First of all, caste is a paradox. It describes crystal-clear distinctions, and also a strong generic unity. At one and the same time it defines social distance and religious association. Almost everything about daily life signifies distinctions of caste identity: names (most surnames are caste identifiers); adornment (Brahmin men, for instance, wear a thread around their chests; certain painted marks on faces, or bracelets, or styles of draping clothing connote caste membership); food habits (what people eat and with whom); protocols of touch and proximity. The number of these signposts to membership in a caste testifies to the seriousness with which caste identity is taken.

But caste is more than distinction. It is also hierarchy. Caste is an endless ranking of status, Brahmins at the top, Untouchables (renamed *harijans*, or "children of god," by Gandhi, but more commonly known by their post-Independence bureaucratic designation, Scheduled Caste) at the bottom. When Mr. Ghosh separated himself from the plans of the Namasudras, he not only distinguished activities suitable for his caste from theirs but also implied some disapproval.

Nonetheless, there is also a strong sense of an overarching bond among castes. Even as Mr. Ghosh disassociated himself (in the plural, "we"), he expressed a strong bias in favor of a fellow Hindu done wrong.

The second characteristic of the caste system significant in the Panipur drama is status mobility. As fixed as caste delineation is, as infinitely often described and thoroughly legislated by myriad details of ritual and universally understood distinctions, it is also changeable. Castes have throughout the centuries sought to up-

grade their status. Western stereotypes of fatalistic Hindus passively accepting their plight in the lower reaches of an oppressive
status map are simply untrue.

Finally, caste continues to have strong associations with economic privilege, even if it does not coincide with precise occupations. In East Bengal until 1947, when the British left and Pakistan
was formed, landlords, moneylenders, professionals, educated people in general—a category know as *bhadralok*, literally "gentlefolk," an ill-defined word which every Bengali understands precisely—tended to be upper-caste Hindus, whereas peasants,
artisans, serving people were Muslims or low-caste Hindus. To be
sure, the correspondence was not one to one: "In East Bengal, the
landlords . . . consisted of a few big zamindars and numerous petty
talukdars.° Most of them belonged to the upper Hindu castes,† but
there were also a handful of Muslims."[4] In his autobiography the
East Bengali writer Nirad Choudhury mentions a Muslim *zamindar* and a low-caste Hindu *zamindar* who figured large in his
turn-of-the-century rural world.[5] Nor were these relationships
static. Throughout the twentieth century changes were afoot as the
upper classes were threatened by economic reversals and Muslims
campaigned for improvements in their status. But the majority of
big landlords continued to be upper-caste Hindus, and the majority
of poor cultivators were Muslims and Namasudras.

The coincidence of caste and class produces an overdetermined
set of social relationships. The gulf between poor, low-caste cultivators and economically advantaged, high-caste Hindus is enormous. The latter constitute a little world of their own. In a village
they enjoy an easy social familiarity, even though they may individually belong to different castes or occupations. Mr. Ghosh is a
Kayashtha; Basantibala's family, the Majumdars, are Brahmins.‡

°*Zamindars* are, roughly, big landlords or estate holders, and *talukdars* are
intermediary landholders. For a thorough discussion of the *zamindari* system in
Bengal I recommend Partha Chatterjee's book *Bengal 1920–1947* (1984).

†The 1881 census showed only 12.8 percent of the Bengali Hindu population
as belonging to the three highest castes: Brahmin, Baidya, and Kayashtha (Rafiuddin Ahmed, *The Bengal Muslims 1971–1906* [1981], p. 192 n. 9). In Faridpur
district, which includes Panipur, there were about 150,000 Brahmins and Kayashthas in 1931 (Government of Bengal, *Bengal District Gazetteer, B. Volume, Faridpur District, Statistics, 1921–1922 to 1930–1931* [1933], p. 6).

‡These are the two major castes in Faridpur district. Brahmins were tradition-

The Majumdars are small landlords and schoolteachers, the Ghoshes small landlords and merchants. They are near neighbors and are in and out of each other's houses—witness Mr. Ghosh's arrival during my visit. The friendliness of the two caste-Hindu families is bounded by the many ways in which they maintain caste distinction. I do not know the Majumdars' practices specifically, but Brahmin families commonly keep separate cups and silverware for other-caste visitors, and it would not be unusual for a Brahmin woman like Basantibala to refuse food and drink in Mr. Ghosh's house even though she serves him freely in her own.

Social Location

This endless delineation of relations and distinctions among groups of people reflects a very important aspect of an agricultural society like Bengal. Knowing exactly how your group, be it caste or community or class, is expected to behave vis-à-vis every other group establishes your own social location, a process which in the industrialized world is to a much larger extent left to each individual to accomplish. Indeed, the defining social transformation wrought by industrialization is precisely this dislocation of working individuals from their groups, their "liberation" into a wage economy. Each one, with an emphasis on the word *one*, must establish her own status and interactions with others, and the field on which that happens is believed to be primarily economic.*

But in an agricultural society economic position is far more fixed—although, as I've commented, not exactly cemented. The process of determining where people fit in is therefore given over to a much greater extent to groups. There is a common understanding of where any given group stands in relation to every other, and once an individual's membership in a group or a series of groups is ascertained, so also is her place in society. When changes happen, often they are group changes, not individual ones. Of course, individual lives do change, sometimes every bit as dramatically as in

---

ally priests, and Kayashthas were scribes and clerks (*Bangladesh District Gazetteers: Faridpur* [1977], p. 68).

*In actuality, social location in the industrialized world is more truly bounded by group factors—race, gender, class at birth, and so on—but that observation is obscured by myths of individualism.

American mythology. Rags-to-riches stories are not unknown, and twentieth-century upward mobility has become a prospect in the consciousness of modern-day citizens of the Indian subcontinent, if not a very common event. But the more usual and historic route to change, both economic and social, is through the group. One's group identity, the group that claims one and with which the world identifies one, is therefore very central to one's sense of self and treatment in the world. People in every agricultural society experience some variation on this same theme, however different the particularities may be.

The group defines for an individual not only how to behave, as the Panipur story well illustrates, but often how to feel and think as well. If life is to improve, the group as a whole must participate both in the process of gain and in the fruits thereof. It is in the nature of societies newly industrializing that this group-based mobility mixes with an individualized derivative. In Bengal during the 1950s the newly won independence of the country, combined with the formation of the entirely new nation-concept of Pakistan, unsettled old economic and power relations and opened up unfamiliar prospects. But people at one and the same time attended to their personal fortunes and experienced change in terms of their place in a group. Caste was an element in the definition, but the Panipur riot demonstrated how it intersected other identities, both economic and religious.

Bias and Loyalty

When the gauntlet was down, for instance, Mr. Ghosh's allegiance to his fellow Hindus won out over any class or caste estrangements. Even from a distance, he unselfconsciously revealed his affinities:

So many people gathered that each party had about two or three thousand people. The Muslims said, "We won't allow any Hindus to stay here." The Hindus were also saying, "We won't let any Muslims stay on this side of the river. We'll push them to the other side of the river." . . .

The Namasudras were greater in number, and they were more courageous. They had a lot of food. But the Muslims, they didn't have much— only some *chal* [uncooked rice]. They would eat a handful of *chal* and some water. Since the Namasudras had plenty of food, they had plenty of courage.

Food weighs heavily in the scales of significance in many cultures, and especially in South Asia. Over and over, people expressed distinctions of status and nuances of respect through food, not to mention using it as a material demarcation of position. To eat uncooked rice is unthinkable to a Hindu. From Mr. Ghosh's tone of voice, I inferred that the Muslims eating it were, to him, inferior beings, a theme he elaborated as he continued his story:

The Muslims fell back a little, and the Namasudras advanced. Then Raghu Nandan [a Hindu police officer] said to the S.D.O. [subdivisional officer, a civil official], Raghu*babu* said, "Sir, this is the time to give the order to fire. Otherwise there will be a lot of bloodshed."

So the S.D.O. said, "Inform both sides, if they don't stop, we'll fire."

Then Raghu Nandan rode his horse and went to both sides and told them of the S.D.O.'s decision, and said, "I'll raise a flag, and as soon as I raise it, you all leave this place. Otherwise we will fire." As soon as the flag was raised, the Namasudras left. But the Muslims attacked. And the police fired. One or two—I'm not sure how many—were killed.

Not only had the police come and camped and stopped the fight, they had fired on the mob and killed people. Suddenly the stakes had risen dramatically. Mr. Ghosh's point of view continued to be woven into his historic memory. The only named official was not the high-ranking S.D.O., but a Hindu policeman who played the active role. Mr. Ghosh called him Raghu*babu*, a familiar and respectful form of address to a Hindu *bhadralok*, thus suggesting that they were acquainted, that this man of power was on his side. The Hindus, in Mr. Ghosh's account, continued to behave lawfully. They were stronger, more courageous; they advanced, but when the police told them to retreat they did so. The Muslims, on the other hand, disobeyed, moving forward, and so more of them were killed when the police fired. Mr. Ghosh managed to convey the notion that there was justice in their disproportionate slaughter. At first he seemed unsure just how many had died, but when pressed he gave us exact figures and an amazing interpretation:

Two Muslims were killed, and one Hindu. Since two men were killed on the Muslim side, they had to kill one more on the Hindu side. Otherwise it would look as though the police were partial. So the police later ran and killed a man on the Hindu side, to make it even.

Mr. Ghosh was clearly a reasonable and respect-worthy individual. Yet his construction of events seemed improbable. Biased accounts, memories at variance depending on the allegiances of the storyteller, were only to be expected. Who among us has ever engaged in contentious activity, from a fight with one's mate to a union battle or a campaign for a favored political candidate, without skewing reality toward our own perspective? But bias is more than false representation. If we take seriously the accounts of those involved, what emerges is a history of differing realities. Not only did people remember differently, or report differently; they actually lived the experience differently.[6]

To understand an event, not to mention a phenomenon, we must encompass the varying experiences of that event, even though we must understand that what we understand is only an approximation. That the approximation departs from the experience of the actor is not a problem; it is the point. How experience is experienced is one topic of importance. But how that experience is formulated, remembered, and retold tells the hearer something beyond "what happened," which we cannot in any case know and which did not in any case happen, since what happened happened to many different people differently. To add to the fun, what happened also changed as it happened and went on changing later. Memory is formed by past knowledge and experience, but it is also altered by the future. Each new experience, including each telling, changes the tale. The telling itself is part of the experience, for what we live combines with what we think to construct what we do, and all three in constant interplay define experience. When the experience is a social one, when the telling is done by members of a group about a group event, the history of memory sheds light on the history of events. Collective memory is social action in its own right, and it is part and parcel of every historical act.[7]

The Muslims

Riveted by Mr. Ghosh's honest and forthright one-sidedness, I didn't immediately register the arrival of a newcomer. He was hard to miss, though, an imposing presence in the crowded room. He was the elected chairman of Panipur Union, Altaf-uddin, the very man to whom Mr. Ghosh had referred a little earlier. He wore a long white beard, the long white shirt and *lungi*, or ankle-length skirt, favored by Muslim men, and an Islamic cap. Our guide to this village had scheduled us to interview him first, at his home. I had, it seemed, upset social protocol by dropping in before that to see Basantibala. Word spreads quickly in a village, and when he had heard we were there, talking in the Majumdar house, Altaf-uddin had determined to right the situation by bringing himself to us.

He also brought a marked change to the tone of the discussion. Once Altaf was settled, I turned back to Mr. Ghosh and asked him what his reactions had been to the battle. There had been a decided shift in Mr. Ghosh's sails:

We had no adverse reaction.

Why not?

[With a sideways glance at Altaf:] Because there were influential elders in this area. So whenever there were tensions among us, they would intervene. So we lived as brothers.

Altaf, as influential elder, promptly agreed:

There were some small incidents [before the riot], but they were smoothed over quickly. . . . Once an incident began, all the Hindus would take the side of the Hindus and all the Muslims would take the side of the Muslims. The influential people, both Muslims and Hindus, would come forward to solve the problem.

I already knew that Hindus talked differently in the presence of Muslims, and the tension in this case was tangible. So I eased Mr. Ghosh off the hook, turning to Altaf and asking for his version of the story.

I got the news at night that there was a little conflict between Hindus and Muslims, and that the Hindus were already out organizing a riot for the next day. The reason was that a cow ate the lentils in one field. A Muslim's cow ate the *kheshari* in a field of a Hindu. It was a very petty thing. For that, they had some chase and counter-chase in the late afternoon. A little fighting, too. Now the Hindus were out with their horses to inform the other Hindus to come next day, to riot.

Where before Muslims plotted in the *bazar*, now Hindus rode the countryside mobilizing warriors. If Mr. Ghosh spoke for caste Hindus, I thought, Altaf-uddin was about to give me the version of the Muslims.

Muslims in Bengal

Islam became a factor in the life of the subcontinent very early: Arab traders journeyed there within a few years of the death of Muhammad in 632. However, the Muslim community in India traces its roots to Moghul conquests much later, in the twelfth century. The first sultanate in India was established in Bengal, at Gaur in the district of Malda, in the early thirteenth century, and Moghul rule was consolidated elsewhere in the subcontinent only four hundred years later.[8]

The earliest Bengali Muslims were immigrants from central Asia, Afghanistan, Persia, Arabia, and northern India,[9] but only a tiny minority of the subcontinent's Muslim population today can trace their ancestry to immigration. Most are converts.* Until the British government's first census of the area in 1872, Bengal was considered to be a Hindu domain. What that census revealed shocked both rulers and indigenous elites: Muslims constituted very close to half the population, and in some areas they were an imposing majority.[10] Their distribution was uneven: some western districts, including those that had housed the earliest Muslim administrations, showed them in the minority. But in the east, around Dhaka, the capital of Moghul Bengal from 1612 on, Muslims constituted 60 percent of the population.[11]

Within that community there were vast distinctions. If the gulf separating high- from low-caste Hindus was enormous, that between upper- and lower-class Muslims was in some respects even greater. Class tended to coincide with origins. Upper-class Muslims traced their heritage to immigrants and claimed membership in a group called the *ashraf*. Converts, or the *atrap*, were drawn from the most oppressed among the population. While they were theoretically united by common worship and a theology lacking the

---

*Some Bangladeshis oppose conversion theories, arguing instead for the more prestigious notion of immigration. Tamizuddin Khan, a founding father of Pakistan, wrote in his memoirs: "But immediate conversion does not seem to be a full explanation for the preponderance of Muslims in Bengal, where the caste system was far less rigorous than in South India, which saw no large scale conversions. There is reason to believe that in Bengal an additional cause for such a large concentration of Muslims was the fact that millions of Muslim[s of the] disintegrated Moghul Empire and of the innumerable provincial satraps and chieftains settled in the fertile soil of Bengal and most of them took to the cultivation of the land" (*The Test of Time*[1989], p. 51).

sorts of rigid distinctions Hindus suffered through caste, *ashraf* and *atrap* Muslims were nonetheless severely alienated by culture and language. The *ashraf* prided themselves on their knowledge and use of Urdu, the language of the Moghul court at Delhi, which is spoken widely by Muslims in the northwestern parts of the subcontinent. To the *ashraf* in Bengal, Bengali was a crude and unworthy tongue. They especially disdained the dialects most common among the rural masses. Upper-class names, such as Syed and Shaikh, were similar to those current in Arabia and Persia. In fact, not all people with these names could claim direct descent from Arabian or Persian immigrants; high-caste Hindus who converted tended to be awarded these honorifics. People with Bengalified names, such as Mandal, Pramanik, Sarkar, were common among the peasantry and were held in contempt.[12] So, too, were those Muslims who practiced despised occupations—weavers, shoemakers, barbers, and the like—all of whom, had they been Hindus, would have been Untouchables.

Between those who made clear claim to the distinction of *ashraf* and those who were *atrap* was a very small rural gentry. Although they occupied somewhat the same economic position as the Hindu *bhadralok*, and although they contributed some superb and beloved literary figures, they asserted far less cultural influence, for their numbers were minute. In the 1881 census, for example, only 0.92 percent of Bengali Muslim workers were listed as professionals, in contrast to 2.09 percent of Hindus. The commercial classes included only 2.55 percent of Muslims, 4.76 percent of Hindus. Fully 90 percent of Muslims were agricultural workers or laborers, compared to 76 percent of Hindus.[13] But according to Rafiuddin Ahmed, a historian of Bengali Muslims, "numbers alone do not explain the insignificant role played by the middle income group and . . . their failure to act as a 'link.' " The entire consciousness of these people yearned for acceptance by the *ashraf*. Among Hindus, the *bhadralok* may have shared with their Islamic counterpart a hearty contempt for manual labor. But they could speak with other Hindus, however low-class, in Bengali, a language to which they were all loyal and that was embedded in a mutually understood cultural history. Many socially ambitious Bengali Muslims, however, revered a culture from another land, using a language wholly unknown to their lower-class neighbors. As Ahmed put it,

"No effective leadership could be expected from a group striving hard to adopt a class culture totally alien to the common man."[14]
    Sitting in Basantibala's front room, however, Altaf-uddin seemed distinctly non-alien, a thoroughly Bengalicized version of Muslim gentry. Here he was, ensconced in powerful but friendly stature amid the beds and clothing of his Hindu neighbors. The scene before me could stand as a metaphor for Hindu-Muslim relations in the modern period: culturally both similar and different, socially both friendly and distant, historically both joined and antagonistic.

Culture and Community

When the British conquered India, the Muslim upper classes turned their backs pridefully on English education. Hindus, by contrast, and especially Bengalis, embraced it. Education was the entryway to middle-class life, and education in English, the language of the state, was most important. Before long, therefore, Muslims found themselves excluded from new arenas in which economic power was to be found within colonial power relations.[15] This principled refusal to accept positions as agents of foreign rule further increased the class divide within the Islamic community. By the close of the nineteenth century, Muslims in Bengal accounted for half of the population, but only for 29 percent of those in schools. Among college students the picture was even more polarized: 93.9 percent were Hindus, only 5.4 percent Muslims.[16]
    At the same time that the Muslim middle class turned away from British education, they sought to distinguish themselves culturally from their Hindu neighbors. "What is it that makes you as a Muslim different from Hindus?" I asked a religious man. He replied, in English:

Religious performances are quite different. We go to the mosque, wearing caps, saying prayers there. They go to the *puja* [ritual celebration] in the Kalibari [temple of the goddess Kali], beating the drums, et cetera, et cetera.
    There are people who are very conservative in both communities. . . . In general, either a Muslim or a Hindu, they strictly follow the rules, the instructions of the religion, [which makes] differences come up. A Hindu makes water standing, and a Muslim just, what should I

say . . . The Hindu is not wearing [a] cap, the Muslim is wearing a cap. Just see it, that I am wearing a cap.
Nowadays there is some slackness in the customs. I cannot find a Muslim or a Hindu out by what they wear. Now they are all alike. They are not wearing beards now. They are not wearing caps.

This man moved quickly from a consideration of religious ritual to very personal habits such as urination. With great seriousness he bemoaned the inclination of youth to blur distinctions of attire. At the turn of the century, those very distinctions had been adopted with great deliberateness by his forefathers:

Ibn Maazuddin Ahmad . . . [in 1914] found his Muslim identity totally incompatible with local symbols, dress, and language. He . . . dismissed *dhoti* and *chadar* [a shawl] as explicitly Hindu. To him a Muslim attired in *dhoti-chadar* was as distasteful as the Sanskritized Bengali of the Hindus. Ironically enough, his own [writing] style was highly Sanskritic whenever he was not watching himself. [17]

Rafiuddin Ahmed writes that the change away from such "everyday Bengali wear" happened over a period of two decades. Seventy-five years later, it was still effective. Muslim men quite universally wore *lungis*, and friends noted in casual commentary that the choice of attire was deliberate and politically motivated. Yet although Muslim men may not wear *dhoti*, Hindu men—all the men in Basantibala's front room, for instance—do wear *lungi* for working or lounging. Sartorial differentiation, while significant, is not absolute.

Often people commented on the importance of being able to tell the affiliation of a stranger. "My identity as a Muslim was quite visible," Altaf told us. "I wore this long *kurta* [knee-length shirt] and *toupee* [cap] and beard." But identification is often not so easy. "I cannot find a Muslim or a Hindu out by what they wear," as the religious man quoted above complained.

Among women, too, distinctions are common but not universal. Some Muslim women observe *purdah*, wearing the characteristic robes and face masks in public. The veil is limited to Muslim women, so its presence is a clear statement. Its absence, however, is not; many Muslim Bengali women move freely outdoors dressed in *sarees*. Similarly, a vermilion mark in the part of a woman's hair tells you definitively she is Hindu, but since only married women wear it, its absence does not prove a woman is not Hindu. And some modern married Hindu women eschew the vermilion mark, so its absence is no longer even a conclusive sign of marital status among Hindus. East Bengali women of both communities are likely to wear costumes common among Pakistani women, or women in the western regions of India, where the Moghul Empire was centered in its later years. *Kurta*, *salwar*, and *kameez*, a loose-fitting tunic, baggy pants, and flowing scarf, are common both in the countryside and among modern city women.

Although in theory costumes identify religious affiliation, in fact dress is often influenced by class and function as well. Peasant women, for instance, often wear *sarees* without blouses, but Basantibala would not present herself to us blouseless, for it is improper to her station. Some among the younger women working in the Majumdar inner courtyard, however, wore no blouse, for comfort while doing domestic work in hot weather.

Many details of daily life are more alike across community lines than different. All Bengalis' diet relies on rice, fish, and lentils; preparations may vary slightly, but often don't. But Hindu and Muslim women concoct distinctly different sweets, and they revel in those differences and respect each other's contributions. It is hard to distinguish a Muslim cultivator's homestead from a Hindu's, except by specifically religious signifiers such as altars. Relationships among both Muslim and Hindu family members are characterized by norms of generational and gender hierarchy, with decision-making dominated by elders and with men clearly ascendant.

Yet on the gender front important differences derive from religious practice, too. Islamic polygamy (now limited to two wives per Muslim man) combines with ease of divorce to disadvantage women decidedly. Muslim women, more influenced by rules of *purdah* to begin with (although many do not observe it, and some Hindu women, especially upper-class ones, are effectively confined to the home by tradition as well), are vulnerable to abuses from which Hindu women have greater (albeit not adequate) social protection.

People tend to socialize within religious boundaries. Everyone had stories of inter-religious friendships, yet such relationships were noteworthy as exceptions. Neighborhoods are organized by community. When a Muslim family moved into a Hindu neighborhood recently, their arrival was heartily resented. "They are so loud," said the Hindu woman next door. "They quarrel and yell at each other, so we get no peace." It is a stereotype that Muslims are more combative at home, one that would not stand up to detailed investigation, but this woman drew on it to express her social discomfort over her new neighbors' proximity.

Underlying overt cultures and religious practices are personal habits that give people a meaningful sense of distinction, such practices as standing versus squatting to urinate. Hindus bathe midday before their major meal, Muslims may bathe any time it is convenient. While all Bengalis share many cultural attributes, these matters of personal habit are very influential. They cause people to "feel" their identities on a noncognitive level, and when people have contact within the other community it is often these details on which they comment most profoundly.

Nationalism and Partition

Through all such details of differentiation there nonetheless was created by British rule a strong impetus for unity. The two themes, of shared and competing interests, run richly through the experience of nationalist protest. It is perhaps a popular Western misconception of European colonialism in India that its rule went unchallenged for two hundred years. In fact, direct rule was established only after a serious rebellion in 1857 of Indian troops against the British army in which they were employed. The Indian National Congress, parent organization to resistance against imperial domination, was founded in 1885, and from the beginning of the twentieth century the British were faced with militant opposition.

At first, the Congress remained politely upper-class. In Bengal, though, other, more militant forces were brewing, especially in the eastern parts of the province. In 1905 Lord Curzon, then governor-general of India, partitioned Bengal into two provinces. Overtly, his reasoning was administrative; the existing united province included an enormous area, part of it non–Bengali-speaking. But in fact the motivation was political. "Bengal united is a power," wrote the home secretary. "Bengal divided will pull several different ways . . . one of our main objects is to split up and thereby to weaken a solid body of opponents to our rule."[18]

When the division came, it reflected the lines of religious community. East Bengal was formed of Muslim-majority districts, combined with Assam and Burma; West Bengal contained the Hindu-majority areas, with Orissa and other Hindi-speaking regions. The eastern districts were especially mistrusted, "a hotbed of the purely Bengali movement, unfriendly if not seditious in character and dominating the whole tone of Bengal administration."[19]

Partition evoked the first mass-based revolt. Called the Swadeshi (or Homeland) movement, it used the tactic of boycotting everything British: goods, education, offices, courts. Most students and officeholders, however, were Hindus, since the Muslims had eschewed British-tainted institutions from the start. But in East Bengal many merchants were Muslims. To refuse to purchase, indeed often to burn, British-made goods economically disadvantaged those shopkeepers. Muslims, moreover, appreciated Partition, because it gave them far greater access to power in East Bengal than they had had in Hindu-dominated united Bengal. It was a fact not lost upon subsequent historians that the first massive uprising against the British contained within it such powerful elements of hostility between Muslims and Hindus. "Divide and rule" could not have been more blatant. The British revoked Partition in 1911, but they had succeeded in heightening bitter rivalry between the communities.

Paradoxically, the first national campaign to challenge British rule was built on the cornerstone of Hindu-Muslim unity. The Congress was largely a Hindu organization, because at first it excluded all who were not English-educated and sought merely to negotiate more respect and privileges from the foreign rulers. With the introduction of Gandhi to leadership in the early 1910s, however, the Congress determined to move into the public domain. Gandhi set about building a controversial alliance with an Islamic movement called Khilafat. An international campaign was under way to restore the caliph, head of the Muslim world, to power in the aftermath of the destruction of the Ottoman Empire during the First World War, and Khilafat was its Indian arm, led by two dynamic brothers named Ali.[20]

Despite this auspicious early alliance, relations between Hindu and Muslim nationalists grew increasingly stormy. The Congress movement had notable Muslim leaders—Abul Kalam Azad, for instance, who was president of the organization during the final negotiations with the British—but many Muslims resented and resisted the Congress and eventually organized an independent movement under the aegis of the Muslim League. Although the League's agenda was the protection of Muslims' rights during the process of dismantling the Empire, only late in the struggle, in 1940, was the demand raised for a separate Muslim state.

It succeeded. Seven years later, when the British quit India, Pakistan was formed from the western and eastern Muslim-majority areas of the subcontinent, the two wings separated by fifteen hundred miles of India. East Bengal became East Pakistan.* Born in an explosion of communal bloodshed and bitterness, both wings of Pakistan were soon faced with the necessity of replacing the educated Hindus, who fled to India in great numbers. In Bengal, changes had been afoot throughout the twentieth century. The founding of Islamic schools was an important theme in Muslim nationalism. More and more Muslims were becoming educated. Responding to nationalist movements and negotiations, the British had granted, piece by piece, some elements of representational government. But still, newly independent Pakistan, especially East Bengal, had to rely on a grossly insufficient pool of Muslims trained for administrative or professional service. Those few who were educated passed into the period of Independence with distinct advantage.

Politics in Panipur

Altaf-uddin was one of the advantaged few, a local man whose father before him had been the elected chairman of the Union and who had himself succeeded to that position in the Pakistani period. In 1971, a quarter-century after Pakistan was formed, the Bengalis rebelled against exploitation and formed the independent nation of Bangladesh. Throughout these changes, Altaf remained in office.

*For the East Bengalis, Pakistan was both a triumph and a tragedy. Bengal was one of two states cut in half by Partition, the west going to India, the east to Pakistan. Many miles of India separated East from West Pakistan, and no sooner were the flags raised than the troubles began. Bengalis were dominated and economically exploited by West Pakistan, where political power was concentrated. Finally, in 1971 the Bengalis revolted, aided by India, and succeeded in establishing the new state of Bangladesh.

His position fell somewhere between that of county chairman and ward boss; his influence cannot adequately be described by the duties of his elected office. It was he who represented local wants to higher authority. He was the man on the spot with access to power, the liaison between ordinary folk and the distant and mysterious government. That relationship had remained constant through two generations and three eras—British, Pakistani, Bangladeshi—and through many changes of government. Altaf was a force to be reckoned with.

He lost no time in letting me know how central his role in the riot had been:

So at ten o'clock in the night, the Hindus came to me. First came the Hindus, then came the Muslims. I told both parties to stop thinking about rioting; "I'll take whatever steps are necessary to prevent a riot." But I was afraid that there might be a riot, in spite of my warning, because I knew that Hindus were already out recruiting other Hindus. So I informed the police station about this development, and asked them to send some forces to come here.

The police staff came to my house an hour before dawn. Then I took them to that locality. . . . I saw many people gathering already. Communal feelings had been aroused. Neither Hindus nor Muslims could be stopped.

No question about Altaf's importance: both Hindus and Muslims called on him for help. Realizing, however, that he could not control the tempers of his people, he performed the prestigious task of calling in the police. They acknowledged his centrality by assembling first at his house and using him as their guide to the community. Altaf identified his role precisely: he was the connecting link between villagers and authorities.

He was also the only local player carrying a gun, a fact of symbolic significance in a number of later accounts, as well as his own:

I first went to the Hindus' house. I had a gun with me. I asked them to hand over the cow to me. In the meantime, I asked the police officer to stay with the Muslims, to prevent them from doing anything suddenly.

Wait a minute: First I asked the policeman to go to the Hindus' house while I stayed back with the Muslims. But the officer said, "No, I'll stay with the Muslims, you go to the Hindus."

It was not immediately clear to me why Altaf stopped himself to emphasize this seemingly trivial point. As he went on with his story, however, it seemed to me he was underscoring the courage he had needed to confront the rage of the opposing community. He was also suggesting once again that his position was that of nonpartisan leader of the entire community. Perhaps, too, he was letting me know that his presence at the Hindus' compound was innocent, lest I suspect his complicity in what soon followed:

It was early in the morning, but there were already four or five hundred Muslims gathered. So I went to the Hindus, and they gave me the cows.

I was taking the cows back, when all of a sudden I saw the Muslims attack the Hindus' house and set the haystack on fire. At that time, I was inside a Hindu house; I quickly left, afraid that they could harm me, too, because I am a Muslim.

I came to the Muslim side and yelled to the police officer, "Why couldn't you stop them?" It had been his choice to stay back with the Muslims. After that I took the Muslims back to their side. Because there was a fire in the haystack, the Hindus couldn't stay silent. They, too, started to come into the field with their weapons, *dhal katra* [weapons of war]. I was running from one side to the other. . . .

By ten o'clock in the morning, there were almost ten thousand people, altogether ten thousand on two sides. Now I no longer have enough courage to go to the Hindu side, because there are many unknown Hindus coming from other places. They won't recognize me, so they might strike me. My identity as a Muslim was quite visible. I wore this long *kurta* and *toupee* and beard. I was all along asking the Muslims to stop. But they wouldn't listen to me.

Who started the fire in the haystack was a point of some controversy among subsequent informants. Altaf's story placed responsibility on the Muslims' side, but his fiercest blame was for the police officer. He had chosen to stay with the Muslims and yet had failed to control them. It is not clear whether Altaf meant to suggest complicity, or simple incompetence. Certainly he was telling me that he himself was not responsible, since the police officer had directed him to the Hindus. In any case, once the Muslims moved, the Hindus, in his version, had no choice but to retaliate.

With the fire Altaf retreated to the side of his co-religionists: "I quickly left, afraid that they [the Hindus] could harm me, too, because I am a Muslim." Still, he continued to run from side to side, until the numbers grew so large he feared that his reputation could no longer protect him. Too many among the mob were strangers. All the symbols of his person—his beard, *kurta*, and cap—identified him as Muslim, not as chairman. His influence over the rioters was at an end.

What Altaf described here was a clear point of demarcation in the progress of the riot. Local authority had lost its meaning as the crowd grew to include people from other localities. No longer was the fight about particular issues; it had become engulfed in something else, something that drew on more universal passions. It had become a "communal riot."

The Namasudras

When we finally left Basantibala's house, we headed to the homestead of Sunil Mondal, a Namasudra farmer and a representative of the third force in the drama. Our boat left the river and took us through the paddy fields. Now and then it became entangled in lilies or beached on a rise. But the boatman, with considerable lament and heroic effort, literally pulled us through. At last we landed on a steep and muddy bank at a homestead. We were still in Panipur Union, at a village called Shirachi. We walked past outbuildings and through yards filled with jute—green, cut jute in piles; jute poles bunched teepee-style to dry; jute fiber in huge skeins. Everywhere women and men were working. The women wore *sarees*, short and wrapped around their breasts, with no blouses. In the parting of their hair was the vermilion mark. One young woman was arranging food in front of a statue of Lakshmi, the elegant Hindu goddess of wealth.

At the third or fourth courtyard we came upon an older man, short, muscular, wearing a *lungi* hiked to his knees; he moved with efficient energy to finish his task of arranging jute skeins in the sun, and then he ushered us into a tiny outer room off the yard. The room was bare except for two wooden chairs and a bench, a large clay pot containing paddy, and a basket filled with some sort of seed, probably jute. The floor was covered with the beautiful, curved patterns of mud generally used to keep village homes tidy. Balancing the tape recorder on my lap, I asked Sunil about his farm. He began by bemoaning the declining fertility of the land. In his childhood, he said:

Crops were abundant, and people were well off and there were fewer of them.° Food was plentiful. But now we don't get that much crop. We get a fourth of what we used to get. The land that used to produce one *maund* [in Panipur, a little over eighty pounds] now hardly yields ten *seers* [about twenty pounds]. The fertility has gone down that much.

Why has the fertility reduced so much?

Because of the silting of the river, we don't get the rich soil we used to in the floods.†

As we settled in to talk, people wandered in and sat down. Sunil told us he owned about fifteen acres of land, a fair-sized farm in these parts, and that his farm had changed over the years:‡

I had people working for me, three or four men; I paid them a salary. I worked along with them.

Have you ever had any sharecroppers or subtenants?

°According to government figures, Faridpur's population approximately doubled between 1931 and 1988 (Government of Bengal, *Bengal District Gazetteer, B. Volume, Faridpur District, Statistics, 1921–1922 to 1930–1931* [1933] *and* Bangladesh Bureau of Statistics, *Upazila Statistics of Bangladesh* [1988]). It is somewhat problematic to compare figures, because districts were reorganized in the mid-1980s. The 1988 figures for Faridpur district are actually the sum of five districts which more or less coincide with the localities comprising Faridpur district in 1931. In 1931, Rajoir *thana*, the police district in which Panipur lay, had a population of 102,000. Rajoir *upazila* in 1988 shows a population of 174,-000. A study in 1945–46 revealed that Faridpur had one of the highest population densities in Bengal, about 740 people per square mile (Partha Chatterjee, p. 163).

†Soil erosion in the mountains north of Bangladesh, combined with river-course changes produced by hydroelectric projects in India, has vastly increased the amount of nonnutritive silt carried by floodwaters. These factors may also be stimulating more frequent and dire flooding. In 1987 and 1988 large parts of the country were under water, far in excess of the usual annual flooding. When I first visited Panipur in the winter of 1988, a few months after the floodwaters had receded, I hiked through ankle-deep sand—an entirely new phenomenon, according to local accounts. Floodwaters, which had always enriched agricultural land, were now instead smothering it in silt.

‡Sunil had inherited seven acres from his father in (by my calculation) 1936. "The rest I bought myself, through hard work," he told me. Partha Chatterjee writes about this trend in the first half of the century, noting that "the process which brought into existence a new class of richer . . . peasantry in Bengal, accompanied by the corresponding spread of sharecropping, also resulted in substantial transfers of land from the hands of the poorer peasantry" (Partha Chatterjee, *Bengal 1920–1947*[1984], p. 142). Several post-Independence land reform attempts presumably presented Sunil with opportunities to acquire land from his richer neighbors as well.

No, not then. Now I have sharecroppers. Because now I can't get good, sincere workers. These workers don't want to work on a monthly basis, only on a daily basis. It's more expensive that way.

When you used to hire workers, were they Hindu or Muslim?

They were all Hindus. Hindus had Hindu workers, Muslims had Muslim workers. The hired workers, too, would only seek work from people of their own community.

Why did you hire only Hindus?

I searched for Hindu workers because the person I kept on a monthly basis lived with us as a member of my family, so he had to be Hindu.

On a daily basis, it doesn't matter whether they are Hindu or Muslim. They work for the day, then they go away. When the work was greatest, I would hire both Hindus and Muslims on a daily basis.

What kinds of problems would you have staying with Muslim laborers?

Eating, going to the kitchen, because the person who would work here would be a member of my family. He has to have access to each and every corner of my house. In the case of Muslims, there's a communal difference. For instance, we won't let him touch the altar of the goddess Lakshmi.

What's the problem with eating?

Muslims take onion and beef. But we don't eat those things. . . . We don't use the glasses or plates used by others. Also, we don't touch the leftover food of others. But they don't have those same prejudices, they don't care. We care, they don't care. There are some Muslims who mind, but nowadays not many have that attitude.

Sunil clearly expressed a religiously based sense of community, identifying himself as a Hindu in distinction to Muslims. But Sunil was a Namasudra, a person of low caste, and himself subject to discriminatory rules of precisely the same sort from Hindus above him in the caste system.

History of a Tribe

The history of Bangladesh, and especially of this western district bordering India, is a drama with three characters: the Muslims, the caste Hindus, and a variety of low- or outcaste peoples and tribes who stood in the wings socially but center stage dramatically.

In the days of the British Empire, the Faridpur district population consisted of unequal numbers of Hindus and Muslims, and most of the former were Namasudras. Cultivators and artisans, they shared more customs and traits with their Muslim neighbors than with the caste Hindus who were landlords and moneylenders to both.

The origins and fortunes of the Namasudra community are interwoven with the history of the land. It is impossible to understand the character of these people without an image of the territory they occupy. Faridpur defies intuitive concepts of a fixed landscape. Growing up on the American continent, I had always relied on geology to stay put. "The land" as an expression was to me a metaphor for solidity, agelessness, groundedness. To be sure, I understood theoretically that the land had a history, but I believed that it moved in geological time, which is to say, so slowly as to be irrelevant. Bangladesh reeducated me. Time after time, people would point to some solid-seeming expanse of land many miles from anything wet and say, "Only a few years ago we used to catch the ferry here." Rivers wander, villages disappear overnight, and new lands appear, fertilely beckoning to litigious farmers.

I had thought I understood about the rivers. Only slowly, though, as I learned the histories of the people settled here and as I traveled from one distinct geographic area to another only a few miles distant, did I come fully to comprehend what a living, changing thing this land is and how much its changes interacted with the histories of the peoples occupying it.

The Namasudras were historically fishermen and boatmen, occupying the swampy territories of the districts where even today most live and where six months of the year the land is under water. Adept at the amphibious existence their environment demanded, they were nonetheless scorned by their fellows, partly because of their work and partly because they were newcomers to Hinduism. They were originally a tribe:

[Their] Hinduisation possibly took place at a comparatively late period, when the caste system had taken its fully developed shape and outsiders were admitted reluctantly and only at the bottom of the structure. This explains, to a large extent, the social degradations [they] were subjected to. . . . Many branded them as the "lowest of mankind," . . . whose touch defiles the pure.[21]

But in the nineteenth century, life began to change for the Namasudras. First, the swamps receded, leaving behind many square miles of fertile new farmland. This alteration in the natural and economic terrain was accomplished by British engineers, who cut a series of roads and drainage canals through the region, a land-reclamation project of gigantic proportions.

Traveling about Faridpur district is a journey into the lives of the waterways. Boats ply them, carrying passengers, jute, fish, and every other essential of village life. Bridges over them wash away in frequent floods. People bathe in them. Women launder clothing and small boys fish in them. Rural development projects are built on their banks. In the days of Empire, the waterways of Faridpur were a favorite topic for letters home from British officials and their wives. In 1884 Lady Beveridge wrote to her children a long account of a journey by boat through the domain of her husband, a district magistrate:

When we first started we were in a narrow river and our way lay through fields of rice without many houses but afterwards we came into a wider river and there were many houses on the banks each standing in its own grove of fruit trees. The country is flat and only a little above the water so that it is easy to see how bad the great storm waves must be when they come up from the sea and run over the land. [22]

In 1920 Lt. Col. L. N. Bavin described his adventures in the same territory in terms a good deal less favorable:

[It] was a terrible spot. . . . I used to tour about that country in a primitive houseboat called a budgerow, braving these perilous waterways, creeping up narrow creeks that wound on for miles from one river to another, crossing huge seas where you could get out of sight of land, and calling in at villages that were untouched by the waves of world upheavals. [23]

One can always tell canals from natural waterways: the latter wander all over the place; the former travel straight on for mile after mile. It is difficult to imagine the countryside without the canals, and easy to imagine what a difference was made by their construction. Their banks act as dams and their courses drain the channeled waters, leaving behind relatively dry land. Between the end of the eighteenth century and the beginning of the twentieth, the area under cultivation rose from less than fifty percent of the total to almost eighty. [24]

To the lives of the Namasudras these canals made a profound

difference. They opened up the possibilities of cultivation, and that transformation promised not only economic betterment but also a path to higher social status. Peasants enjoyed considerably more respect than boatmen and fishermen like the Namasudras. But little of the new ownership actually devolved on Namasudras. In the 1891 census, only fifty-seven Namasudras in Faridpur were reported to occupy land they did not themselves till; they constituted 0.04 percent of the Namasudra population. Even twenty years later, in the 1911 census, fewer than 1 percent of all Namasudras in Bengal owned enough land to receive rents.[25] Namasudras farmed the land, but caste Hindus and some few Muslims owned it. What a given peasant farmed, moreover, was very little indeed, whether he was Namasudra or Muslim. By the end of the 1930s, 64 percent of Faridpur cultivators held less than two acres a family—a far greater level of economic deprivation than in many other parts of Bengal.[26]

Nonetheless, enough of the new lands reclaimed in the late nineteenth century were possessed by Namasudras to solidify a very small affluent class. But social uplift did not automatically devolve from economic improvement, so a campaign to upgrade the status of their community was launched by the newly well-off among them in 1872.[27] As Rajat Kanta Ray points out:

Hindu society in Bengal treated other untouchable castes . . . with equal contempt. But in the case of the Namasudras their low ritual status coincided with an unusual amount of spirit and independence which did not make for tame submission.[28]

The Namasudras' first attack was on social customs that made them vulnerable to contempt. Women, for instance, always markers of status and power, were prohibited from shopping in the *bazar*, for only low-class people allowed their women to appear in public. An attempt was also made to attack the economic basis of subordination; Namasudras were prohibited by their community from serving in the homes of caste Hindus or Muslims. The resulting economic hardship was, in theory at least, to be redressed by the community at large. Finally, ritual status markers were adopted. As Sunil suggested, food is primary among these, and Namasudras adopted ritual codes of purity paralleling those of the higher castes.

In time, these symbolic and economic efforts at uplift altered the political landscape of the province, bringing Namasudras and Muslims closer together. New political alliances emerged:

By the 1910's, the high-caste, well-to-do Hindus were sharply polarized from the Muslim-Namasudra masses. Henceforth the peasants, especially the enfranchised section, defied the *zamindars* and the Hindu *bhadralok* classes in different ways.[29]

When the demand for a separate Muslim state was raised in 1940, Bengal was one of the more problematic provinces, since its population was close to evenly divided between the communities. Hard negotiating was employed to determine its destiny: did it belong by rights to Hindu-majority India or to Muslim-majority Pakistan? Sentiments ran strong and violent on both sides. In Calcutta, the mammoth capital city to the southwest of Faridpur, Hindus and Muslims slaughtered each other, and violence seeped into some of the larger towns of East Bengal as well.

In this charged context it was extraordinarily significant for an entire Hindu community to opt for Pakistan. But that is just what the East Bengali Namasudras did, defining their interests on the basis of class, not religion, and confounding expectations that Hindus all over India were united in their desire for undivided nationhood. Their future, these Namasudras believed, would be brighter in a state devoid of high-caste landlords than in one ruled by people who shared their religion but nonetheless oppressed them. As I questioned Sunil about the changes in his community, he told me the history of the alliance between Namasudras and Muslims:

In 1947, when there was Independence, many Hindus wondered, "Will we be able to live in peace in Pakistan?" The caste Hindus left this land for India at the beginning. But our middle-class people and peasants didn't want to go. Our—what's his name?—Mandal, a very big man: Jogen Mandal [leader of an association of Scheduled Caste peoples]! Our Jogen Mandal made an alliance with Jinnah [the founding father of Pakistan]. Many of us believed then, "Let the caste Hindus go, but those of us who are peasants, whether Hindus or Muslims, can live together as brothers." . . .

The sense of a division that we felt earlier was gone, because of what that minister [Mandal] said. We gained confidence that truly we could live together as brothers.

Group Identities, Solid and Fluid

Sunil's language is revealing. When he referred to "us," he identified his community as peasants, not as Hindus or Muslims. Indeed,
he specifically excluded the religious identifier as being relevant:
"those of us who are peasants, whether Hindus or Muslims." But
those whom he would just as soon see leave the country he identified as "caste Hindus," not as landlords. "Peasants" opposed
"caste Hindus"; not once throughout his long interview did Sunil
use the name Namasudra. It was "middle-class people and peasants" who chose to stay in Bangladesh. When he did use religious-
community signifiers, he stood the more common relationship between group and subgroup on its head. Everyone else used the
name Hindu to mean something generic presumably organized
around the centrality of those of caste and then designated the
minority as Namasudra. Hindu meant the whole, Namasudra the
particular, those with noteworthy differences. Only Sunil used the
name Hindu generically and differentiated the subgroup "caste
Hindu."* As a consequence, he himself became undeniably
Hindu and presumably central. At the same time he described
community in terms of religious identifiers only in an appropriate
context—when explaining his choice of laborers, for instance, or
later when describing contending sides in the riot. In another context—when deciding whether to opt for India or Pakistan—he
labeled his group in economic terms, "middle-class" or *"krishak"*
(peasant), because that was the basis on which he made his choice.

Sunil's language suggests his ambitions. Not only was he stead-
fast in his quest for social status improvement, but he was also
intent on economic betterment. He was himself unusually prosper-
ous for a Namasudra farmer; indeed, he had grown wealthier since
the exodus of the caste Hindus, more than doubling his landholdings, and eventually renting to sharecroppers. He had sent his
children to the university and was deeply desirous of their upward
mobility, even though he himself continued to till the land with his

---

*Other Namasudra storytellers used a similar language structure. A teacher,
for instance, described his community as Hindu until the moment when he explained the alliances forged by Jogen Mandal, the Scheduled Caste leader. "The
Muslims were more angry at the Brahmins and the higher castes," he told me.
"We are Namasudras, and between us there was no enmity. It was restricted to
the caste Hindus."

own hands. When I asked him about his ambitions for his children, his point of reference was, interestingly, the community of caste Hindus. His answer well illustrated the long history of class ambitions among Faridpur Namasudras and the intermingling of individual and group status mobility. (Notice how he mixed religious and economic signifiers in the context of class ambition, too, contrasting "caste Hindus" and sometimes "those Hindus" with "peasants"):

Your children are all highly educated. What was it that made you so determined to educate your children?

There were lots of caste Hindus around our place. My grandfather used to go to their places. He saw their customs. The relationship between the peasants and the caste Hindus was different. The way the caste Hindus lived and the way the peasants lived, anybody with a little vision could see that we are working so hard and producing crops, food grains, but we can't enjoy the fruits of our labor. We pay the price with our health.

On the other hand, those Hindus are living well, with just a little education. My grandfather realized it. I don't remember my father because he died when I was three. But I knew that my father got a little education from the fact that when I grew a little older I found my father's books from class nine, ten.

Even though my grandfather was overwhelmed with grief because of the deaths of my father and uncle, still he was conscientious about our education. Unfortunately, when I was in class seven my grandfather died. We lost our guardian, so we couldn't continue our studies. But I was a very good student. I always stood first in my class. I was heartbroken that I couldn't study any more. I knew that without a guardian I couldn't study as much as I wanted. So I prayed to god, "If you send me any children, please give me the ability to make it possible for my children to have education." So I worked very hard so they could study and become capable of mixing with [upper-class] people.

. . . My son asked me, "*Baba* [father], why do you work so hard? It's so hard for you to afford my expenses at the university. It's hard for you, and it's hard for me."

I replied that I have a dream. "To satisfy it, let me work hard. As for you, please try to have some compassion for my desire."

[My sons] said, "You haven't passed matriculation. You could stop sending us to school after we matriculated. We could try to send our children to the next level of education. Maybe their children will then try for a university degree. Then their children can try for a master's."

Then I told them, "The plan you are proposing will take four generations. I'll take the trouble, you also take the trouble, and let's do it now.
Finish your education. I won't stop until you get your M.A. But I will
make you indebted to me."

Then they asked, "What is the debt?" And I said, "Being a poor
peasant, a simple tiller, I could make you an M.A. So you think about
what you want for your children. I want you to think that your poor father
got us through an M.A. degree, so you should have even higher ambitions
for your children."

Sunil projected his progeny's destinies in a straight line upward.
No land-tillers appeared in his idealized future, no followers in his
own footsteps. After Jinnah's death, Jogen Mandal was ousted
from national power. Sunil explained:

We were very disappointed, we local people. Still, we were not willing to
go to India. This is our motherland. We are tillers. Cultivation is our only
job. Our forefathers were *krishak* [tillers], we were *krishak*, we thought
our children after us would be *krishak*. We didn't want to leave the land.

Sunil constructed a conceptual tangle of identities. His ardent
wish was that his children and their children *not* be *krishak*. And
yet it was precisely on the basis of his cultivation of the land that
he proclaimed his rights to citizenship in a Muslim-ruled country.
In one sitting, he spoke eloquently of his ambitions for class tran-
scendence—and equally eloquently of his connections with the
land he tilled. From his articulate tongue flowed the dilemma of
the peasant, defensive of his work and rights, land-proud, yet
wishing nothing more than that his children take their clean hands
far away from that land, to the cities where alone his ambitions for
wealth and status could be satisfied.

Most individuals can identify with any number of groups. Sunil
is a *krishak* or peasant, and he is a landlord. He is both a Hindu and
a Namasudra. He is a Bangladeshi. At what moment he chooses to
see himself as part of one group or another is important, for it
suggests the dynamics of identity. When hiring workers, Sunil's
view of himself as a Hindu is of primary importance, dictating that
he hire only Hindus. But when his community faced a choice of
nationality, of opting for India or Pakistan, Sunil's interests as a
peasant took clear precedence over his identity as a Hindu. As long
as the Scheduled Caste alliance with the Muslims held firm, he and

other Namasudras wholeheartedly supported the Muslim League and Pakistan. "Jogen Mandal," he explained proudly, "was the leader in the Muslim League of the Scheduled Castes from before the Partition." Even when that alliance broke down, he defended his roots in Pakistan, and now in Bangladesh, because of his relationship to the land. Presumably that relationship was not solely sentimental; to sell land in Pakistan and buy in India was beyond the limited means of a small owner like Sunil. Because of this crosshatching of identities and allegiances, this mix of consciousness and economics, the Namasudra community is a fertile source of understanding about group identities and their roles in social conflict.

But when it came to the riot, Sunil's position was unconfused. I asked in general about conflicts in his village, and he promptly began to tell us about the riot. By this time, sensing unease on Sunil's part, I had cleared the room of spectators, and he now vented his anger at the local Muslim leadership:

It started when a cow ate the crops in a field. The Muslims made the cows eat the crops of the Hindus. This fight was a result of the protest by the Hindus.

We complained to the leaders, but the leaders, instead of solving the problem, rather they said, "What is it? The Hindus are trying to live as they did in the past. Why are they making such a fuss about it? It was only a little *kolai* [another variety of lentil]. The cows could have eaten much more." The leaders used these kinds of inciting words, and said, "Teach the Hindus a lesson. Call our community together." So they did, and there was this communal riot.

So we too organized our community, in order to save ourselves. In actuality, they couldn't beat us into submission. If we had the strength of mind, we could have overwhelmed them. But because we didn't have enough strength of mind, we only stopped them and protected ourselves.

The Muslims were entirely to blame. They "made" the cow eat the lentil. The Hindus did nothing but protest. They were forced to organize their community for defense. Sunil's riot devastated choice. For his people there were no decisions to be made. They were victims cast in poses of self-defense.

The set of decisions made between the first round of the Panipur fight and its explosion into mass action was clearly delineated by many of my storytellers. First came the space in which the communities considered what to do. Despite Sunil's demurrals, he and his fellow Hindus participated in that process, too:

[Sunil:] I stayed home, but I directed others to spread the word throughout the community. The first day there was no fighting. It was all news. The next day early people began to gather.

[Mr. Ghosh:] People were sitting and talking about the fighting the day before. So I stopped to hear what they were saying. . . . I thought, "It will not stop; there will be another fight." So I hurried to my house.

Both Sunil and Mr. Ghosh made personal decisions about how to behave (directing others to spread the word; hurrying home). But those decisions were deeply informed by agendas that transcended the personal, that were located instead in the community.

Chapter Two

The Decision

From Hot Words to Collective Deeds

Many cows had eaten many plants over the years. Village fights were common. To be a farmer in a poor Bengali village is to be ripe for a fight. Toil is constant, and so is fear of an uncertain future. There is little margin for tolerance and generosity toward a neighbor who messes with your crop or your cattle.

But a riot is something else. It does not just happen. Many people made many decisions that resulted in the riot: to spread the word, to ask for allies, to seize the cow, to go to the field armed. Some of these decisions were made in passion. But however ill-considered, even those choices involved thought, justification, and organization.

The Man with the Cow

The day after I interviewed Sunil and the people at the Majumdar house, I went back to the village, accompanied by an old-timer from the development project. He had lived at Panipur in the early days and was taking me to visit two charming old men who came to be a sort of raucous Greek (or Bangladeshi) chorus connecting the parts of the drama of Panipur. In addition, they led me to the man with the cow.

It hadn't rained that day, and so we risked traveling by motorcycle, a journey that took a fraction of the time it had by boat. But

48

when we arrived at our destination, the homestead of Mofizuddin Haludar, it was, typically, surrounded by water. The only access was across a thin bamboo bridge that tested my capacity for balance and courage and found them wanting. There were no village boats in evidence, so we went on to the organization's local office and sent somebody to bring Mofizuddin there. With him came his friend, Nayeb Ali.

Mofizuddin was a very old man and frail, his pointed beard completely white. He leaned perilously on a cane, but his dark eyes were strong, mischievous, and huge behind improbably thick lenses, the heavy black frames somehow bending outward from nosepiece to edges. He wore the Muslim elder's blowsy cap, a smudgy white *kurta*, and a *lungi*. For all his age and infirmity, he exuded enormous vigor. He spoke in a loud and animated voice, in a dialect I could barely understand. As he and his friend told their tale, Mofizuddin became more and more excited, more and more combative, his narrative laced with an engaging blend of high humor and good-natured bloodthirstiness.

Nayeb Ali was Mofizuddin's junior by several years. He was a very handsome man with a full head of dark hair and a short beard painted with two stripes of grey. His face was strong and thoughtful, suggesting a solid store of wisdom residing behind it. Around his eyes lines of humor crinkled merrily, but the eyes themselves promised serious dignity and an ingenuousness born of pride. He joined in the storytelling with élan:

It was only a four-penny conflict. It came from a tiny thing. It was unimportant.

Having declared his opinion of the fracas so authoritatively, Nayeb Ali was immediately taken to task by a Namasudra man who happened to be there:

They burned Kumar Tarkhania's house!

Tumbling from the lofty vantage of the wise observer, Nayeb Ali was ready to fight the good fight all over again:

Kumar Tarkhania hit Golam first, with a sickle. Only then the Muslims went and terrorized them.

But then, remembering sins on both sides, he returned to role:

The Mussalmans hit them and tore them up and burned their houses.
How could they sit and tolerate it?

Mofizuddin commented judiciously:

Both parties provoked each other, the Namasudras and the Mussalmans.
Their houses were almost together. They could hear each other's voices
from their houses. They could call back and forth . . . [they were] that
close. They could have prevented it if they both had tried.

But they didn't try. They pressed and prodded and called their folk
together to fight.

"What's become of the man with the cow?" I asked eventually.
"Why, his name is Golam Fakir, and he lives over there," Mofizuddin replied, nodding toward a vast, waterlogged expanse. Mofizuddin and Nayeb Ali regaled me with stories for some time after
that.* By the time we were ready to seek out Golam Fakir dusk had
fallen, and the route, impassable by any means but boat, was
declared by the available boatmen to be too long and arduous for
the hour.

Wishes, however (at least my wishes, it seemed), had a way of
inducing action in Panipur, and early the next day a young staff
member from the development project appeared at my quarters
with a lean, lined-faced man, tall and wiry and looking quite nervous. "Here is Golam Fakir," he said.

All plans for the day happily abandoned, I sat down to talk with
him. I had been hastily warned by my hosts not to startle our
quarry, who they anticipated would be reluctant to talk about his
role in the drama, so I began by beating about the bush. When at
last I cautiously mentioned the riot and asked what had happened,
Golam thought a moment and said:

There was trouble with cows.

This masterpiece of understatement initiated a spare description
of the incident:

We all lived together always, Muslims and Hindus. . . . I tied my cow and
went home. But the cow got loose and ate the *kolai* of their field.

*Their remarks were reflective and thoughtful, and their comments on events
will appear from time to time throughout the account that follows.

What time was that?
It was four in the afternoon. Then they took away the cow.
Who did that?
Kumar Tarkhania.

Day One: Quarreling and Sparring

I soon realized my caution was nonsense, neither reassuring nor respectful, let alone productive. Once I explained what I was interested in and why, Golam relaxed visibly. He told me he had figured out what I wanted to know, but not why. Now informed, he continued his tale with simple, understated, methodical thoroughness. I was so absorbed that only slowly did I realize I hadn't even offered the poor man a cup of tea, a lapse about which I felt even more guilty when I learned he'd come from home without any breakfast, and that it had taken an hour and a half for him to reach us.

Where were you when Kumar Tarkhania took the cow?
I was at home. It was my cow. When I went [to the field] to fetch the cow, it wasn't there. I asked; someone said the cow had been taken away. A Namasudra had taken away the cow.

I went and asked them to let my cow go. "It has eaten your *kolai*, you can take me to trial if you want. But for now give me my cow."

But they wouldn't give me my cow. They scolded me and said, "No, we won't give you the cow. We'll sell it."

The cow was kept in the *matabbar*'s house. I asked the *matabbar* and he said, "Without a trial, the cow cannot be released."

. . . So I was still asking them [Kumar and his brothers] to give me my cow. But they wouldn't. They were speaking angrily. So I got angry, too, and spoke angrily. And I set my cow free. There was no real fight, only quarreling and exchange of hot words. There was a lot of shouting and hot words.

Then I said, "I've said I'll go to trial, so why do you want to keep the cow? Do you want to eat it?" And that triggered their rage. So finally I freed the cow. The cow was strong and it ran away quickly.

What did the Hindus do?
They were furious, but I ran away with the cow.

How was the cow tied? Was it securely tied well inside the field? Or was it where it could reach the crops?

No, it was well tied. Those fields were side by side, but I tied it well inside my field. But the cow got loose.

. . . It was tied with a rope. But somehow the rope got torn and the cow got loose. And then it went into his plot and ate his plants.

When I returned home with the cow it was night. My father was away, so I told my father-in-law and my maternal uncle about the incident. I told them, "They would surely have beaten me, and so I ran away from them with the cow." They replied that I had done the right thing.

That evening you talked about this incident to your father-in-law and your maternal uncle. Did you talk to anybody else about it?

No, I didn't say anything to anybody. I didn't talk to my neighbors. Since we didn't come to blows, only an exchange of hot words, I didn't talk about it to anybody except a few very close neighbors. I didn't say anything to anybody in the evening, but I talked to a few of them at night.

So ended the first day. Unlike Mr. Ghosh, Altaf-uddin, Sunil, and almost everybody else among the fourteen people we had so far interviewed about the riot, Golam Fakir spoke with little passion. His voice never raised, his body resting quietly on the sofa, he presented us with the details of the incident as only he could know them.*

A couple of points immediately interested me. First, everyone else had collapsed the time during which the fight brewed. Universally, people had reported that the two men came to blows almost immediately. According to Golam, though, on the first day there were only "hot words." Golam himself had escalated the war of words: "Why do you want to keep the cow? Do you want to eat it?" Those are fighting words to a Hindu, perhaps even more so to a Namasudra who feels he must defend his ritual status. From that moment arguing was over, and all Golam could do was free the cow by force and run.

The other point of immediate interest was the involvement of people other than Golam and Kumar. The cow was kept by a *matabbar*. *Matabbar* is a sort of generic title, awarded by common consent to people who are respected in the village. Generally they are elders, although someone relatively young but very prominent

---

*I was unable to interview several key players. Kumar Tarkhania, the man whose crop was eaten, had migrated to India and died there. No one knew how to locate his family. Aside from Altaf, we could locate no officials involved in the riot—a reflection, perhaps, of the many changes of state and regime in the intervening years.

may be called *matabbar*. It later turned out that the *matabbar* in question was an older relative of Kumar's. His intervention was therefore both reasonably legalistic ("Without a trial, the cow cannot be released") and also provocative.

We asked Golam how, when he found his field cow-less, he knew where the animal had gone. Neighbors had alerted him, he said, people living in the surrounding houses, both Namasudras and Muslims.

When he went home, Golam sought approval from his family elders, and they praised him. He presented himself in a nonescalatory light: "No, I didn't say anything to anybody." Well, almost nobody: "I didn't talk about it to anybody except a few very close neighbors." I had literally asked whom he talked to that evening, and Golam's first answer was literally true: he didn't talk in the evening, but *at night* "I talked to a few of them."

In a village, nothing is ever strictly private. From the beginning this fight had public involvement. If the interventions of others were not overtly inflammatory at the start, neither were they conciliatory. People pointed the way and watched what happened. Formal organizing had not begun, but the word was certainly put out, to spread as it might. This distinction between informal and formal organizing is an important one. All sorts of protest and resistance can take place embedded, indeed often hidden, in the mundane structures of everyday life.[1] Young men stealing cows, or even groups of mature men talking in the *bazar*, are one thing. A formal meeting convened for the purpose of deciding a shared course of action is another. Out of a set of decisions already made (to put out a call, to come together), people created a new structure (a meeting; an early-morning gathering with arms) by means of which they would pursue consciously constructed conflict.

Day Two: Rising Ire, Choosing Battle

It was the next day when the line to formality was crossed, and the fight rolled on from personal grievance to community affront. Day two started with a mild act of provocation on Golam's part and a definitive escalation by the Namasudras:

Then, again, the next morning I tethered the cow at the same place, on my land. Then I went to do some other work. I finished and came back.

I had a large plot planted with *kolai,* and the crop was ripe. I saw that all my cows, all six of them, were tethered at different places in *my kolai* field. In the midst of *my kolai!* The cows were grazing in my own field. They were moving slowly and eating up my *kolai.*

The six cows belonging to you were tied in your own field?

I came and saw this state of things. Seeing that, my mind was filled with anger. It was catastrophic. Who did it? Who did it? I started cursing, saying, "Which *shalar po shala* [a profane curse] did this?" At this time, they were just to the south of the field. They heard me cursing and told me to stop. They asked me, "Why do you let your cow loose every day? Your cow got loose yesterday, and ate our *kolai.* You took the cow away from us by force. This time we won't let it go!" They repeated these words: "This time we won't let it go!"

Notice the fine art of retaliatory action. Golam could have chosen other fields in which to tether his cows, but he returned to the site of the conflict. The Namasudras chose an act that was beautiful in its provocative righteousness: they put Golam's cows (now somehow become plural) in his own field, set to eat their own master's crops. Golam's gesture that morning was slightly ambiguous; Kumar Tarkhania's was not. The Namasudras had thrown down the gauntlet. And they were prepared for the consequences:

There were two of them. There were some other people there, too. They had *kachi* [big sickles] in their hands. But my hands were empty. I had gone there to see to my cows. There was not even a stick in my hand. When they moved toward me with the sickles in their hands, I picked up a mallet that I had used to tether the cows, fearing that they might attack me with the sickles.

I was standing there with the mallet in my hand and chasing the cows out of the field—they were loose in the field. The people came rushing toward me. The cows were all loose. One of them went over into their field again. . . . They were [Kumar's] two brothers.

One of them had a shawl around his neck. He took it off, and with the shawl he tied my hands. Kumar and [his brother] said that they would take not only the cow, but me also.

At this point, a Hindu named Jogendra Pal forbade them to do it and urged them to let me go. . . . Jogendra Pal was a man of that locality, and he was nearly seventy years old. . . . So they untied my hands. Then I told them that they would pay the price for what they had done.

When I threatened them with consequences, they again came rushing toward me. They caught me again. Again they tied me and started dragging me, and one of them hacked me with the sickle. He cut me on my right arm. I shouted. Some Muslims were standing a little distance away. Hearing me shout, they came running toward me. When they arrived, they freed me.

Battle now was right and truly joined. Jogendra Pal, the Hindu elder, had tried to intervene, ordering the men of his own community to free the Muslim. But Golam could not keep silent; he then threatened them, and the proud Namasudras struck the first blow. The injury to Golam's arm, the drawing of first blood, was decisive. Muslims standing nearby, presumably aware of the fight but staying outside it until that moment, now moved forward, physically and metaphorically:

We then seized the Hindus' cows and took them to our houses. They [the Hindus] ran back home. Reaching their houses, they grabbed weapons, like *lathi, ram deo* [curved knife], *dhal* [shield].

Why did you take their cows?

We did it because the wound caused by the scythe had enraged us.

Didn't you think that the Hindus would come to your house armed to get back their cows, and there might be a serious fight?

Yes, we knew that. But we thought it was necessary to fight with them. It was no use letting them go unpunished. If they hadn't come to get back the cows, we would have sold them and taken the money.

From here on out, Golam spoke in the plural: "We did it . . . ," "We knew that. . . ." No longer was he an individual hothead. Other Muslims had entered the fray and Golam was now representative of a group. So, too, was the nature of the cause altered, at least in its subsequent articulation. No more was Golam thinking of defense. Now it was not about getting back his cow or protecting his plants. Now punishment was the objective, through battle either physical or economic. Contentious gestures correspondingly proliferated, and everyone in the village either joined in or became objects of attack:

By the time we returned to our houses, the Hindus came out into the field and caught hold of three cows belonging to Muslims. They went back home with the cows.

Were your cows among them?

No. Those cows belonged to other people. Some belonged to my father-in-law. When they took the cows away, we also came out with weapons like *ram deo* and scythes, and the fight began. It lasted for a long time. They attacked us with the *ram deo* and we fought off their attack with our *ram deo*. The fight lasted for two to three hours.

How many people were involved?

Not many. Nearly two thousand.

Two thousand! So many?

It was almost afternoon by then. There were about a thousand Mussalmans on our side, and nearly a thousand on their side.

How did so many people manage to gather so quickly?

The villages where people lived were very close by. So they could come very quickly.

But how did they come to know of it?

They could see it happening from their own houses. We also sent word about it to the people living in nearby villages. Our messengers ran to those villages and gave them the news. They also conveyed the news in the same way.

Spreading the Word

How the news spread is a matter of interest, because it helps to track a growing intent and resolve, as well as becoming an element in the move from informal to formal organizing. It would be inaccurate, however, to say that, a decision having been made, the two sides set out to organize their fellows. Instead, the two activities intermingled. The elders decided to fight, and the young men gathered the warriors:

While the *matabbars* were talking about fighting, the youths divided themselves into batches and went to different villages with loudspeakers.

Organizing grew out of discussions in ever-widening circles. Here is Sunil's account of hearing the news:

I was at home. Around one o'clock, some people came and said, "They have damaged our crop. Moreover, they are saying provocative things. They're preparing themselves to beat us. What are we to do now?" The guardian sort of people among us said, "Don't do anything in advance. But be prepared to protect yourselves."

Who exactly came to give you the news?

Those people whose crops were damaged came. They were the Tarkhania family. They were going from house to house to inform people. . . .
I stayed home, but I directed others to spread the word throughout the community.

Some people learned about the brewing melee by proximity, while others got the news more formally. In a group discussion, people told us how they'd heard:

[First villager:] People were running to invite others to go throughout the whole village, and in the six or seven villages nearby, everyone knew it was happening. In K_____, S_____, Hindus and Muslims went around spreading the news. They used horses to go around.

And how did you get the news? Did someone tell you?

[Second villager:] No, nobody told us. We heard the noise. People were shouting in the field. Nobody came to tell us.

Even by such informal means, the crowd grew rapidly. The morning of the day after the original hassle, there were nearly two thousand people by Golam's estimate, and the thing became more organized. The word *thousand* was clearly impressionistic. Throughout these accounts, storytellers gave very specific numbers when describing crowd sizes. Clearly, they were guessing, and the numbers they chose expressed impressions of quantity and also sometimes something else: the intensity of what was happening, for instance, or the importance of the massing of men.

These discussions of numbers brought out the differences between my sensibilities as listener and those of the teller. "Two thousand!" I exclaimed, and Golam looked surprised at my surprise. To him, the words meant "a lot," and a lot of people was not a hard thing to come by in the village. To me, a middle-class urban woman, organizing two thousand people to appear at an event was an impressive feat.

Leaders and Followers

The fight was growing serious, not deadly but threatening. Where were the village leaders now? What had become of attempts to intervene? Golam continued his tale:

Chasing and counter-chasing started at noon, and it continued for a long time. As a result, many people were injured . . . some were sent to hospital, but nobody was killed. Some went to the doctor's dispensary, where there was a policeman. After getting the information, a police party arrived at six o'clock in the evening.

Nobody from the villages tried to prevent you from fighting all that time you were chasing each other?

Yes, some people did. They tried but they failed.

Do you remember the names of the people who tried to stop you?

Yes, I do. [Lists names, both Hindu and Muslim]

Do you know somebody named Altaf-uddin?

Yes, I do.

Did he come?

Yes, he did.

When did he come?

He came in the afternoon. By then the police had come and stopped the fighting.

The second day had seen the fight move from words to blows, from families to neighbors. But it was still contained within the confines of the village. Only those close enough to hear it happening, or to be told by someone they knew, were involved. But during the second night decisions were made to riot—in contrast to the skirmishes that had so far occurred—and the role of the leaders grew more problematic. Altaf-uddin had been less of a presence in Golam's riot than in his own, not appearing at all until we mentioned his name, and then arriving only after the police had already intervened. Some *matabbars* had tried to intervene, but with little success, and as Golam went on I began to wonder if their ineffectiveness could be attributed to their ambivalence:

That evening, we Mussalmans held a meeting. We thought we could not go on living like this. They often threatened us, they threatened to beat us. . . .

Who called the meeting?

We gave the call. We sat down together and decided to hold a meeting. We sat with the *matabbars*. It was decided that all the people would assemble at the house of Haludar. . . .

Many people came together that night. It was decided that it would be unwise to waste any time, and we should start the fight the next morning.

What a conscious process this was! As Golam reported it, people sat together, their leaders present, and said, "Things can't continue as they have. Tomorrow we will fight." The discussion so far had all been among the informal and traditional leaders. There was some concern about securing approval from more formal authority:

Altaf-uddin was then the chairman of the Union Board, and we thought we could not start the fight without informing him. So we went to his house. There were about twenty-five of us. He said it was quite okay.

In Golam's riot Altaf did not appear on the field of battle until late in the drama, but he was an important figure behind the scenes, bestowing legitimacy on the decisions of the Muslims to riot. Golam has him playing a double role, one privately among the Muslims, the other publicly as leader of the entire community:

In the meantime the Namasudras also went to him with a proposal for a compromise. The proposal was written on a piece of paper. It contained the names of 116 people. Altaf put forward the proposal. . . .
    I was asked to invite those people to a meeting to be held at Panipur High School. They were to sit in that meeting at the high school the next afternoon and settle the dispute.

The formal meeting of conciliation was held, and the Muslim *matabbars* behaved as they knew they should. But immediately afterward, meeting among themselves, they recanted:

There were nearly forty or fifty *matabbars* among them. Our *matabbars* decided that there would be no *nishputi* [compromise]. They often made compromises, but then again there would be a fight. So there was no need to compromise. They spoke this way after the meeting, not in Altaf's presence.

Golam was upset over this double-dealing by his own community's leaders. At the eye of a storm he had precipitated but now feared and resisted, he appealed to the union chairman for help—and got none:

So I went back to Altaf-uddin, alone, to hear what he would say. I was very young, and I thought about it a lot, and worried about what would happen to me in the future. He told me there was no need for me to

worry. It was necessary to teach them a lesson. Otherwise they would not
stop. They would reap the paddy that grew on a *char* [literally, sand bar;
land exposed by the river as it shifted course] and use it to feed their cows.

This incident evoked memories of many past losses, and filled the
minds of the Muslim community with *atanka* [panic]. They thought that
some trouble with them was imminent. . . .

I was not wanting to fight. I thought it would be better to compromise. The thing is, the *matabbars* said, "We won't compromise. We will
fight."

What a many-layered statement Golam made of his transactions
with leadership! Both Altaf-uddin and the *matabbars* explicitly
take on responsibility for deciding to fight. No longer is the matter
a personal one for Golam. His wishes, whether to fight or to compromise, don't matter. The leaders of his world, both official and
traditional, take the burden off his shoulders.

At the same time, Golam was making a point of describing this
scene to us. What we were hearing, I suspected, was as much the
story of Golam's anxieties, of the dilemma in which his rash actions had landed him, as it was the story of the riot itself. His fear
then of consequences continued into the present—witness his reluctance to begin telling the tale to us at all. Golam had known
staff members of the development organization for many years,
yet he had never told his story. Now he found himself seated in
the heart of the quarters (the *very* heart: a rattan shed that
housed the television set). To be cautious about how he represented himself in this world made a great deal of sense. The
organization wielded all sorts of power: to distribute supplies
after natural disasters, to treat sick babies, to apportion brand-
new irrigation equipment, and on and on. I did not know Golam's
specific relationship to the staff, but I did know the project's role
in that area, and I could speculate that, even without formal and
concrete ties, Golam would not want to jeopardize his reputation
and possible future access to their help. Add to this the fact that
Golam was talking to a female European stranger, who asked
questions in questionable Bengali, and it is easy to suppose a desire on his part to present me with a powerful character—someone I myself had first invoked and therefore had legitimated on
some level—who had explicitly accepted responsibility for the decision to riot.

Who Leads Whom?

Golam suggests that the leaders decided and he, ordinary fellow that he was, followed. Is that an accurate representation of the relationship between leadership and masses?

Two types of leaders appear in the story from start to finish. First come the *matabbars* (*matabbar* means, literally, "headman"). Golam explained their status:

They were advanced in years. They were also intelligent, and they owned a lot of property, too. But there were some people who had less land, but they were wise and intelligent.

By all accounts, people turned to them for counsel. Had they wanted to stop the fight, their influence for peace would have been considerable. As the fight proceeded, they did act to limit damage, protecting people of both communities from attack. But from Golam's perspective, they also led the people into battle, morally if not physically. To exercise moral leadership was appropriate, for their power derived solely from informal acknowledgment of their moral authority.

Altaf represented the second type of leadership, and was very different. His authority derived, not from traditional marks of respect, but from electoral politics. The Union Boards were created by the British government in the 1930s, a time when nationalist movements were winning small concessions toward self-rule. The boards were elected bodies of village notables with limited powers to administer their constituents' affairs. Although they were presented as a concession to the nationalists, they immediately became controversial, for they were seen as a vehicle for tax collection rather than a true organ of self-rule. The Indian National Congress, mainstay of the nationalist movement, the party of Gandhi and Nehru, promptly organized against them. But the Congress was dominated by rich landlords, in Bengal the upper crust of society. Not incidental to these landlords' opposition to the boards was the fact that they opened up a vein of power to lesser landholders, known as *jotedars*. In East Bengal many *jotedars* were Muslims. The Muslim and Hindu upper-class communities had often been divided on questions of nationalism. Once again they ranged against each other on the issue of the Union Boards, Muslim *jotedars* defending them, Hindu *zamindar* Congress-*wallahs* [members of the Congress Party] opposing them. Many poor peasants were initially swayed by the latter, but gradually lined up in favor of the boards. The fact that Altaf, and his father before him, enjoyed power courtesy of the Union Board contained within it a thick set of social relations.[2]

Altaf appears in a leading role throughout the drama. By his own account, he was mediator and liaison with governmental authority, the formal role accorded him by his position. But nobody else read his part so simply. From the start, as we heard narratives of the riot, people had suggested a more duplicitous role for him, and to the Hindus that role was ominous. Mr. Ghosh, careful as he was to give no offense, had located Altaf as lurking on the outskirts of conspiracy. Describing the second morning, when he encountered Muslims talking war in the *bazar*, he said:

As I was walking, I saw the chairman near that group.

Was the chairman talking with them?

No, but he was walking nearby.

In terms of narrative structure this statement is intriguing. Mr. Ghosh won't go so far as to accuse Altaf, certainly not to an unknown foreigner who has solicited a story he had not chosen to tell. But by placing Altaf physically in the public space in which plotting was afoot, he implicates the chairman from a safe distance—his own distance as safe as Altaf's.

Bhupendranath, a Namasudra from the village, used a similar structure to describe Altaf at a different scene, with even stronger effect:

Altaf was the leader here, the union chairman. He led the first group of fighters to the field.

Altaf told me that he tried to make peace.

The chairman? No, no. When D.M. *sahib* [the district magistrate] came to try to make a conciliation, then he also was present.

Did you personally see Altaf leading the Muslims?

I witnessed the whole thing. I saw Altaf carrying a gun. I was standing beside the Shiv temple [temple to the god Shiva]. It was slightly foggy, early in the morning, and I saw them with guns.

The incident of the gun may have been less malevolent than it seemed at the time, clouded in mist beside the temple honoring the Hindu god of destruction. Altaf had explained to me that he was the only local person armed and that he carried his weapon to keep the peace. But to the Hindus, to this man and to others who refused to go on the record, Altaf's armed presence (or that of a mysterious "them") was perceived as hostile and threatening.

From Golam's account it seemed that both perceptions—Altaf's that he was a peacemaker, the Hindus' that he was warlike—might have some truth. Altaf's position shifted over time. In the very beginning, when the fight was a matter of two young men slugging it out over a cow and some plants, Altaf told them to stop. As the fight gathered force, he publicly advocated resolution of the dispute, even taking up the Hindu community's proposal for a meeting of reconciliation. But when Golam listed leaders who were present in the field, actively trying to intervene, Altaf's name was not among them: "He came in the afternoon. By then the police had come and stopped the fighting." When the elders of the Muslim community among themselves advocated aggression, Altaf privately agreed: "He told me there was no need for me to worry. It was necessary to teach them a lesson. Otherwise they would not stop." Altaf's position would not allow him to be openly aggressive toward the Hindus, who were, after all, also his constituents. But he privately refused to lean on the *matabbars* of his own community to make peace. He agreed with their reasoning and cleared the way for them to proceed.

There is some suggestion in Golam's tale that he hoped Altaf would intervene for his own protection against the Muslim *matabbars*. Golam was worried that in a grand melee he would be left to pay the price, since it was his cow that had started the whole affair. Altaf clearly could have altered the advance toward hostilities in the beginning. But he chose not to do so, and before long the decision was out of his hands:

Couldn't Altaf-uddin have stopped it?

[Nayeb Ali:] No, he couldn't. Who listens to whom? Nobody was listening even to the police, forget about Altaf-uddin.

Where the *matabbars* clothed the decision to riot in moral respectability, Altaf's position hints at a legal sanction. Closely identified with official authority as he was, he implicitly promised that no one would intervene to stop the riot until a certain moment. In a sense, he made good on that promise. In one view of the matter, the police did not arrive until the rioters were ready for the event to end. As we shall see, the role of the authorities was opportune for the villagers, negotiated perhaps through the person of Altaf.

Here is a sense in which leaders played an active role, yet were not all-decisive. The villagers were ready to fight, and what they got from their leaders, both political and traditional, was a green light. The *matabbars* expressed the new idea: compromise doesn't work; times have changed; now is the moment to assert our power. They may have stirred the contentious stew, but they didn't stock it. The leaders came to a dinner the people had cooked; they came to eat, but it was the villagers who had slain the goat.

Discourses of Trouble

Why were they so ready? As we grew more comfortable with each other, Golam described more and more vividly the heated atmosphere of that time:

We had been oppressed by the Hindus forever. Now we thought that we would either die or kill them. This was the common feeling, shared by all Mussalmans.

In the days before Partition, in the days of the British rulers, they did not treat us very well. We had to bow down before them. They caused a lot of trouble to us Mussalmans about our land and property. If our children went to catch fish in the nearby canal, they would beat them. Just the other day, they were still beating our children.

I wondered whether Golam were describing a general atmosphere built on hearsay or whether he spoke from his own experience:

Who beat the children?

They. Including Kumar. They beat our children and the boys from the neighboring houses.

They damaged our crops. They interfered when we wanted to go to a *mela* [fair] by boat. They would reap our paddy and use it to feed their cows. If we ran into them someplace, they spoke to us rudely. They'd tell us to go away. . . .

They took the crop we grew on the *char*. They stopped our boats and took the grass we had spent all day in the marshes cutting. They took the grass to feed their own cows. These things happened day after day.

Did the Hindus of your own village do these things?

It happened not only in our village but in all the surrounding villages.

Hearsay corroborated firsthand experience. Golam told us that town Muslims were passed over for good jobs: "The Muslims did not have any existence. The Hindus were all." Jobs in town had little to do with Golam himself. Indeed, they had little to do with anyone from the village; the Hindus who got those jobs were not people of Golam's class. But the general sense of disadvantage that Muslims suffered vis-à-vis Hindus combined with a long list of petty indignities at home to create a general sense of injustice and resentment:

The elderly Mussalmans had all suffered a lot of loss during the pre-Partition days. But they could not make any protest during British time. They suffered one loss after another. As a result, *akrosh* [desire for revenge] had gradually grown in their minds. It was the case with almost every Mussalman. We felt bitter, and we didn't care to compromise.

They could not protest during the days of British rule. The implication is clear: Hindus were protected by the British. But now that protection was gone: "We felt bitter, and we didn't care to compromise."

The ideological steps between cow-eats-plants and all-out war were plain to see on the Muslim side. They, both local Namasudras and caste Hindus, had oppressed us for years. We could not protest because they enjoyed protection from the state. Now the state is ours. It is our turn. Now we'll teach them a lesson. To translate power on a state level into power on a local level was the task of the day.

Namasudras, too, understood the agenda that way. They sensed the aggressive stance of the Muslims, sanctioned by their leaders, and they set about building a defense. Said Sunil:

This fight was a result of the protest by the Hindus. We complained to the *matabbar*s, but the leaders, instead of solving the problem, rather they said, "What is it? The Hindus are trying to live as they did in the past. Why are they making such a fuss about it? It was only a little *kolai*. The cows could have eaten much more." The leaders used these kinds of

inciting words and said, "Teach the Hindus a lesson. Call our community together." So they did, and there was this communal riot.
So we too organized our community, in order to save ourselves.

What were the signs alerting people to the change of times? They were aware of the new government, and some—Sunil, for instance—were aware of details of alliance on that level. But it is a giant step from "government up there" to bloodshed in the village. Both sides understood that there was some new license for the Muslims to assert themselves. Both sides had watched the process unfold elsewhere. A Namasudra schoolteacher said:

[In 1947] there was a riot. Not here, but in West Pakistan. Also in Barisal at Muladi and many other places.

You heard reports of those events? What did you think? Were you frightened it could happen here?

Yes! Badsha *chacha* [Badsha Mia, president of the Muslim League in Faridpur] later told me, "At that time, when riots were happening all over, we here used to keep watch at night." [They were worried; the leadership was mobilized to try to keep peace.]

The riots at Muladi, only some thirty-five miles away, were a powerful signifier. They had occurred in 1950, four years before the Panipur incident, and they were important because they were the first major communal riots outside the big cities of East Bengal. Muslims massacred an unknown number (possibly in the thousands) of Hindus on the basis of a rumor, subsequently proved false, that a Bengali Muslim leader's son-in-law had been killed by Hindus in India. The port town where it occurred was connected to Madaripur by a major river, and the event was by far the closest and the most unsettling to touch Panipur. For the first time, people in this area of Bengal understood that violence was a real option, and some, the well-respected Muslim leader Badsha for one, mobilized to prevent its spread.

Other people were more compelled by violence closer to home and more like their own:

Were you hearing about this kind of trouble happening elsewhere at the time of the kolai-eating incident? Anywhere nearby, like Gopalganj [a neighboring locality where we had heard reports of conflicts] or any other place?

Yes, there were some troubles we heard about. . . . We heard that there was trouble between Namasudras and Mussalmans. Somebody has taken away the cow of somebody from near the *bil* [marsh]. The cow has not been returned. They fight each other. There had been small incidents like this.

Had you ever heard of any big riots?

We did not hear of any big riot other than this one.

You didn't hear of something at Muladi in . . .

We heard that there was a riot at Muladi.

Did you hear that there was a riot at Gopalganj?

Yes, we heard that also. Our incident took place after these.

Previous knowledge of other overt conflicts helped to establish an atmosphere in which the riot could escalate. The message conveyed was, not that there wouldn't be official intervention, but that despite the presence of peace-making leaders and armed police, the moral climate had changed and now was the moment to effect a shift of power.

Quickly the circles widened from nearby villages to more distant ones. Sunil told me:

[People] came from outside. From Faridpur. From Gopalganj. From Sariatpur. From all over.

How did those people hear about it?

They used mikes and loudspeakers and horses, and went around telling people.

Who was it spreading the word?

The community gave the job of informing others to some people from among us.

Was there any party or organization involved?

No.

I asked a Namasudra man:

How did it happen you went to the field?

I heard it over a microphone.

By afternoon, the sides had gathered in force, as Mofizuddin reported:

There were not fewer than thirty thousand people, probably more.

Where did they come from?

They came from K——————, they came here to eat our stuff. They
came from the banks of the Padma, from the south. . . .
    Mustafa went on his horses and swept up the people. He went all the
way to Gopalganj, and up to the Padma.

Communication went two ways, as Golam explained. People
began reporting news from the outlying areas:

I went back home. We had some Muslims living among the Hindus of
Batalya [about eight miles away]. . . . They had gotten the news the night
before when people went around with loudspeakers, and then they heard
it from other people, also. . . .
    Seven or eight of these [Batalya] people came to us at night. They told
us that the Hindus were sending horsemen to the villages urging people
to come out. "They will attack you in the morning. So what are you going
to do?" . . .
    We told them that there was no need to worry. We too had sent our
people to the villages for the same purpose. We also were preparing.
Hearing this, they returned to Batalya. As they left they said, "All the
Mussalmans living in Batalya will be there to help."

As news spread, it also changed:

The incident was exaggerated by reports as it went from mouth to mouth
(*muke muke*). The incident continued for three days. The big fight happened on the third day. The small incident was exaggerated many times
over as it passed from mouth to mouth. When they heard that a Mussalman village was burned down, they rushed to our place.

From cows and plants, the symbolic battleground shifted to
rumored burning villages. From neighbors hearing the fray and
joining in, strangers from distant villages were fighting. From familiar acquaintances who recognized local authorities and might
respect them, the warriors were now outsiders intent on fighting
their own battle, a different battle. Yet not so different; if the fight
was now about communities, not cows and plants, still the underlying dynamic was consistent. Everyone had heard about disorders
elsewhere—in Calcutta, at Barisal, and especially at Muladi. Muslim opinion was strong: "The time has come. Let's teach them a
lesson." Now it was Pakistan, the rule of Muslims. It was a new
game, with new rules.

Namasudras, too, had heard about Muladi. On one level, they were taken unawares. Sunil told me:

I was very surprised. How can it be? I thought. They damaged our crops, and when we protest there is this reaction. It was totally counter to the social rules.

But on another level they had been forewarned. Muladi had taught them they must hold firm or lose enormously, even though nobody we interviewed actually feared a repetition of the Muladi massacre (although those who subsequently fled may have been those most fearful).

Community Memory

Namasudras and Muslims both understood the nature of the showdown, and they knew just what to do about it. It seemed to me that their understanding was deeply embedded in their lives. Over and over, my historians linked their actions to past affronts, personally experienced and vividly remembered.

Midway through my conversation with the two aged commentators, Nayeb Ali suddenly turned to me and asked challengingly, "Who are you? From what book did you learn about this riot? Why are you interested?" I was happy to have the opportunity to tell him, "Fights like this happen all over the world. If we don't understand them, we can't prevent them. You are the experts; you've done it.*

"The books say you were misled," I said, concluding my thumbnail sketch of popular academic theories of communalism. "Were you?" Mofizuddin answered thoughtfully:

These cows and plants are symbols. After Partition, the minority community didn't take it well. There was Hindu-Muslim tension. The Bengali year was 1360 when this happened. There was a big flood, even more than last year. There's a song, "Azad Pakistan," it says there is anger in

*This was a highly biased statement on my part. How my biases affected the interview methodology is important. I could not be "value-free" any more than Mofizuddin could, nor did I wish to be. I brought with me a well-schooled belief in the superiority of verbal and cooperative methods of conflict resolution. As the conversation went on, however, I understood that Mofizuddin and Nayeb Ali disagreed with me.

us, even if we don't express it. That's internal talk, not something you speak about openly. Educated people don't ever mention that anger.

In our *rastriya* ["nation"], now it's Bangladesh, we all have to stay like Bangladeshis. In the British time, we had to obey the British laws. In the Pakistani time, we had to abide by those laws. There was no point in being angry. We felt it, but we didn't express our anger. Why couldn't they now accept our rules?

Through this beautifully framed statement echo sounds of the worm turning. After so many years of obedience to the rule of one alien force after another, these people felt it was finally their turn. Their complaints were not, however, merely personal. It was the mirroring of an individual's encounter with indignity in the lives of others, the slow building of a shared memory of wrongs, that formed a basis for eventual protest. To have been humiliated because you touched another person's food might rankle: to be excluded from the inner living space of one's neighbor, to see one's children harassed because they fished in a nearby stream, all the myriad injuries from cultures in strained coexistence could leave on the spirit wounds that might suppurate later. But the basis for a social confrontation of the magnitude of this one was not a simple compounding of individual wrongs. Something more interactive was at work. In the telling of other people's tales of woe, the social complaining of a whole community, an atmosphere was created that made the fight possible.

What crystallized action from those vapors was history. People knew, however vaguely and inaccurately, that outside their village forces were at work which corresponded to their own experience. Pakistan was formed. Pakistan represented the culmination of other Muslims' grievances. They knew those wrongs had to do with a state unfavorable to their people. Precisely in what way it was unfavorable was only vaguely understood—it had something to do with job discrimination and exclusion from schools. All that part of the story took place in a class universe far distant from the villagers. But it harmonized with their own experience. They too felt excluded and oppressed. Their landlord and moneylenders, the economic powers in their world, were Hindu, and the erstwhile state was somehow felt to be a Hindu state, even though it was known to have been British. In any case, now the state was Muslim. Those Muslims so far away in town, so far away across India, speaking another tongue and wearing a different garb, those Muslims had risen and won a new state. Such monumental events struck chords of harmony with the desires of the villagers in Panipur. "We've endured long enough," they said. "No more!"

Between the winds of history and the storm in Panipur came some process of synthesis and decision. To ask who put the parts together is to return to questions of leadership. Local leaders certainly played active roles. Muslim *matabbars* declared, "No more compromise!" Hindu *matabbars* warned, "Defend yourselves!" Were the common folk of the village whipped into a fighting mood by their leaders? They all said no. Instead they described a dialogue between tillers and leaders. As the mood among the peasants grew more and more feisty they consulted their leaders, and the leaders, while sometimes intervening to limit the damage, nonetheless agreed. At some moments it seemed that a particular *matabbar* provided leadership by articulating what was in everybody's minds. Some people saw Altaf, the elected official, leading the troops with gun in hand. Others saw him as tacitly approving others' plans to riot. In front or behind, his agreement was certainly important, as was the blessing of the *matabbars*, which legitimized the desires of the people. But nowhere in the stories I heard did I detect a hint of unwilling peasants being convinced by leaders pursuing their own agendas. What was said by the leaders was effective because it expressed what people felt and remembered, many years of wrongs and fears accumulated as a community.

When the decision was at last made and the fight truly joined, the manner in which it was engaged was articulate in the extreme. No leaders, however skilled and highly organized, could possibly have orchestrated the scene that followed.

Chapter Three

The Riot

Language of the Unheard

[Golam:] The fight continued for three days. . . . The two sides were sitting facing each other for three days.

Were they literally fighting for three days?

No, they were just sitting for three days and nights.

Sitting for three days and nights! There wasn't fighting?

Now and then someone would chase someone else, a little jostling would happen.

So culture-bound was my picture of a riot—people running about, smashing things, looting things, beating each other up—that I literally didn't believe my ears.[1] People sat, faced off, for three days, a ritualized battle of stubborn sides, each waiting for the other to blink. These rioters spoke a language of gesture quite different from my own.*

Action and Meaning

Crowds offer an opportunity for common citizens to speak openly, at the very moment when their lives are most unsettled and their consciousness most in flux. Although scholars rarely formulate their intellectual interest in these terms, in fact what crowd studies do

---

*By *language* I mean a set of symbols that express ideas and describe objects and events within a given community of understanding. Words express ideas, and so do behaviors.

is to listen to public statements made by people who are ordinarily privatized, statements made in the language of collective actions. How people behave, the precise acts they choose and the spirit in which they commit them, are windows briefly opened to reveal what they think. In the apt phrase of Sandria Freitag, crowd actions are texts,[2] expressions of belief and experience more articulate than those we normally receive. Viewed in this light, gestures become a rich language.

The ways people express themselves are not open to endless choice. One learns to speak a particular language because of the accident of birth. However, language is not static; it changes for a given community over time, and it changes for a given individual over a lifetime. Language embodies old ideas, new ideas, and lived experience. In childhood we learn a framework, and throughout life new vocabulary and new concepts are added to that framework. Experience, too, influences how ideas are formulated and, consequently, how they are expressed. In turn, language determines to an important extent the concepts of which thought is composed, and consequently the content of thought itself. How we speak and what we think intimately interact to form the consciousness out of which we act, so that actions are both expressions of thought and also the materials out of which new ideas and new expressions are formed.

What sort of ear we tune to this language of collective action has everything to do with our underlying theories of human behavior. The granddaddy of crowd studies, Gustave Le Bon, took crowds to be villainous assemblages of irrationality, both sign and conveyor of the downfall of civilizations. "In consequence of the purely destructive nature of their power," he wrote in 1885, "crowds act like those microbes which hasten the dissolution of enfeebled or dead bodies."[3] Le Bon's views today seem extreme, but his inclination to fear and condemn people massed retains a familiar ring, especially in the forms carried forward by his disciple Sigmund Freud. Freud drew heavily on the work of Le Bon when he studied group psychology and wrote:

In a group the individual is brought under conditions which allow him to throw off the repressions of his unconscious instinctual impulses. The apparently new characteristics which he then displays are in fact the manifestations of this unconscious, in which all that is evil in the human mind is contained as a predisposition.[4]

If the crowds massed in Panipur operated instinctively, what orderly instincts they had!

More recent students of the crowd have found in the variety of gestures a chance to solve the problem of social history: how to write history from the point of view of people whose views so rarely appear in the public record.[5] "There is anger in us," Mofizuddin had told me thoughtfully, "even if we don't express it. That's internal talk, not something you speak about openly." The riot was a medium through which to take that "inside talk"—all the old resentments, all the new possibilities—outside. What people did in the field that day described their rebellion and suggested its sources. Once I began to hear the details, truly to listen to *how* people rioted in Panipur, the questions multiplied: Who was there and how many of them? What exactly happened? How were they armed? What was happening on the periphery of the crowd? What did they eat? Who served them?

George Rudé, a historian who pioneered detailed inquiry into the actions of crowds, is said to have "put mind back into history and restored the dignity of man."[6] From within that tradition, it seemed to me entirely right that the villagers of Panipur sat down. It was a gesture both dignified and mindfully appropriate. In a mobile and commodity-dominated society rioters run about and grab television sets; these peasant rioters occupied land, stubbornly asserting their rights and rules.

At the same time, the consistency of their action was contradicted by the language in which they described it. All the villagers used the English word *riot*. The event might be better described as a sit-down strike or an occupation maneuver. *Riot* was a label the British attached to civil melees of a variety of sorts, and the Bengalis had adopted that designation. When the British used the word, they meant to suggest strong disapproval. Riots were acts of illegality, the mindless acts of recalcitrant subjects. In accepting the label *riot*, the Bengali peasants seemed to have accepted the disapprobation as well. They seemed reluctant to confess to the deed, telling the story only when asked directly.

It was perhaps significant that they told the story to me, a thoroughgoing outsider, a foreigner, a woman, a "European." Although my "outsideness" was ameliorated in some ways (I spoke Bengali and was introduced and accompanied by people known to them and respected), nonetheless their decision to speak to me symbolized on a minor plane the major decisions involved in when to bring the "inside" talk out. I was reminded of James Scott's notion of public and hidden transcripts. The former are the stories told by the subordinate to the dominant, stories carefully crafted to please. In private, people tell a different tale, but only occasionally are these hidden transcripts made public, at moments of resistance and rebellion.[7] That the villagers talked to me thus reflected a very particular decision. It was, in other words, itself a meaningful gesture. All the more ironic, then, that they labeled their action *riot*, unaware that they were using a word from my language that connotes a censure they understood I did not feel, or so I infer from their act of speaking and of speaking without shame. Here was a prime example of language as a transaction between cultures; a dialogue of many meanings was contained in the use of a single word.

But while the word *riot* may have been loaded, the villagers were in fact describing events sharply distinguished from what had come before. One major difference between this event and the urban conflicts usually called riots is that the latter commonly involve strangers. When people in Panipur described the early phases of their "riot," they named names. Almost everyone was known to them, recognizable, placeable by community, kin, and class. It was only when strangers arrived that the riot* proper can be said to have begun. Altaf named the moment:

Now I no longer have enough courage to go to the Hindu side, because there are many unknown Hindus coming from other places. They won't recognize me, so they might strike me.

The Panipur drama fell neatly into five distinct phases: quarrel, decision, riot, intervention, resolution. The moment when personal recognition failed and community identity took over, when the

---

*For convenience, I will forsake the use of quotation marks around the word *riot*, leaving the reader to bear in mind the problem therein.

process of conflict moved beyond a quarrel over garden-variety village concerns, was when the riot proper began. With the arrival of outsiders, numbers swelled and personal familiarity waned, and the main act of the show was under way.

Day Three: Gathering Forces

Golam continued his story with the morning of the third day:

Then it was morning, and people of our community came with their scythes, *dhal*, and *bolum* [swords]. Many, many people came and assembled near our house. They came very early in the morning; it was still dark. They came armed with *ram deos*.
. . . By that time, nearly ten thousand people had gathered. They were all Mussalmans. But we couldn't see any Hindus on the other side. Altaf-uddin said, "There is no need to fight," not what he had said the evening before. He told us to release their cows. The *matabbars* also had changed their opinion. They said that it wouldn't be good to fight just then.

Why did the matabbars *change their opinion just at that point?*

The sight of such a big crowd frightened them. They thought of the consequences if there were a murder.

Hadn't the matabbars *thought of that the night before?*

Yes, they had. But they could not imagine that such a fearful thing [such a huge crowd] could happen. These *matabbars* were not educated people. They could not think that there would be such a big gathering.

As people gathered in the early hours, the leaders grew faint of heart. It was one thing to stir opinion to battle at night, in the lantern-lit glow of familiar rooms filled with lifelong acquaintances. It was quite another thing next day in the morning light to urge on tens of thousands of heavily armed men, many of them strangers. Nudging the juggernaut into motion had been easy; applying the brakes was not. Both sides turned to the authorities for help:

Ten thousand people gathered there. And the officer in charge of the police station came there in the morning. Both the Hindus and the Mussalmans went to the police station to give the information. . . . But the Mussalmans were still gathering there. The number of Mussalmans was gradually increasing. There were new arrivals and the size of the gathering went on increasing. . . .

The people had all gathered near our house. The Mussalmans were sitting on the northern side, but the Hindus could not be seen on the southern side.

The Muslim forces were now coalesced. Even though the Hindus could not be seen on their side of the village, the Muslims were certain they were there. Now the leaders—village headmen, Altaf, and outside officials—made a concerted effort to intervene:

In the meantime, the president [Altaf] and the O.C. [the police officer in charge] came here and forbade us. They said there was no need to make trouble. Then their *matabbars* were advised to free the cows, and our *matabbars* also were advised to free the cows. We freed all six cows we were holding. Trusting what our *matabbars* told us, we let the cows go. We let go all six cows. They [the Namasudras] had captured three cows. Sometime later, they also freed those cows.

Golam and other local players complied with the leaders' demands. But they were no more in control than the *matabbars* and Altaf were. Tempers had gone well beyond the question of cows. The time for conciliation was past:

The moment the Hindus freed the cows, the Mussalmans started running toward the Hindu *para* [neighborhood], with all their arms and weapons. They started running toward the south, toward the Namasudras.

Nobody could deter them, not even a threat of arms by the police officer. Young Golam tried to stop their rush:

Now we—I myself, the O.C., and Altaf-uddin also—were all trying to prevent them. But they paid no heed to what we said. They even came and tried to strike me with a weapon. They said they would murder me if I did not move out of their way. . . . The O.C. showed them his guns and told them to go back and made as if to shoot them [if they did not]. But the Mussalmans did not come back. They rushed toward Kumar . . . Tarkhania's house.

One of the more controversial acts of the day's drama now took place. All accounts agreed that the Muslim crowd were the initial aggressors. Golam, the focus of the Muslim cause, emphasized over and over not only that the Muslims were not provoked on the big day but that they couldn't even see the Hindu crowds. But between massing and fighting an event happened that ended once and for all any hope of nonviolence and reconciliation: a structure

on the Tarkhania homestead was set afire. Who set the fire and
what burned were matters for disagreement.

Arrived at the Tarkhanias' house, the Muslims found it abandoned:

I was also with them. We went to their house, but nobody was there. The
people had all gone away, even the women.

Their ardor somewhat deflated by the absence of an enemy, the
Muslim crowd allowed itself to be influenced by the authorities:

They wanted to loot the things inside the house. The O.C. and Altaf-
uddin were all present there. We prevented them from looting. So we
pushed all the people back to our place.
   We had gone a little way into the field. We looked back and saw a fire.
The Hindus had themselves done it.

Until this point, Golam's account had been surprisingly forthright. When his side struck a blow, he told it that way without
equivocation. But now suddenly he insisted that this decisive moment in the history of the riot was "their" fault, not "ours":

There was a big cow shed. The cow shed was bigger than this hut
[gestures to room in which we sit]. They also set fire to a haystack at
Kumar's homestead. The Hindus had themselves done it. We understood
later why they had set fire to their own cow shed and haystack. They
wanted to show the public that the Mussalmans were burning down their
house. "So all of you come here and save us": this was their aim. After
setting the fires, in a moment, ten thousand of them came out of hiding
and gathered in the field.

We pressed the point, wanting to know how he could be so sure it
was the Hindus who burned their own structures:

*How did you know that it was the Hindus who started the fire? It might
have been that someone among the Mussalmans remained there in hiding.*

No, no, that could not be. We had taken all of them back with us. How
would anyone remain behind there? Wouldn't he be afraid? He might be
killed.
   We came back and they started the fire with pieces of wood.

Did you actually see them doing it?

Yes, we saw them starting the fire. Seeing the fire, we became afraid, and
we withdrew some distance.

Did you see it with your own eyes that they started the fire or what?
Yes, I saw with my own eyes.

It was curious that Golam so insisted on this point. The Hindus, of course, were convinced Muslims had set the fire. Bhupendranath told us:

Muslims attacked the Hindus first, and we Hindus took refuge in the southern part of the Hindu areas. One Hindu house was set ablaze.

Even other Muslims we interviewed were sure their own side had done the deed. Altaf told us:

I was taking the cows back, when all of a sudden I saw the Muslims attack the Hindus' house and set the haystack on fire.

But Golam was not to be shaken. This was the crucial act of provocation, and it went beyond his capacity to accept responsibility. To him, it was a Machiavellian deed intended to rally the Namasudras to fight back.

Who exactly set the fire?
They were Kumar Tarkhania and Sidheshwar Tarkhania. Having started the fire, they gave a loud call to those who were nearby to rush to their aid. And in a moment about ten thousand people gathered and attacked us.

But the people on our side were greater in number; they were nearly fifteen thousand. They didn't budge from their position. They sat down in a line [across the field]. The Hindus advanced a little and then they, too, sat down in a line. There was an empty space. It was as if there were a canal, with two parties sitting on the two sides of it. A group sat on that side of the canal, a group sat on this side of the canal, and the space between them was empty.

Without organization, without command, these many thousands of men knew exactly what to do. They rushed each other, but did not attack. Instead, they sat, immovable, in tidy lines, as if there were a canal separating them. Not a river or a stream, but a canal. What distinguishes a canal from any other waterway is how straight it is. The lines were drawn with precision; thousands of heavily armed men, fighting mad, sitting in the field in serried ranks.

Meanwhile, more warriors continued to arrive. They came from greater and greater distances, from towns and villages in neighboring subdivisions. Everyone had contact with people from some distant place, especially from Gopalganj, an area some thirty miles away that had had its share of communal friction. Some came from reputedly peaceful regions, too, like Tariapur, about ten miles to the east. By now rumors were flying, and many of the newcomers thought an entire village had been burned down. Muslims were sure it was a Muslim village. Incensed as that news must have made them, they nonetheless joined the tacitly agreed-upon action—they sat:

So we sat in lines. Our *matabbars* told us to sit around our houses in such a way as to prevent them from being destroyed by the Hindus. Their *matabbars* also told them to sit round their houses in the same way, with the same aim.

The positions were overtly defensive, but they also had the character of an aggressive face-off. The main form of battle was sedentary. On the fringes, however, more active combat took place. According to Altaf:

There wasn't any big attack; only a few people chasing each other and throwing rocks at each other. On one side of the field, people were chasing each other, but in the larger part, both parties were sitting facing each other.

And Golam essentially concurred:

But on the western side, their people started chasing ours, and our people started chasing them. The fight had already started on the western side. The Hindus were sitting on the southern side, and the Mussalmans were sitting on the northern side. . . .
    The Mussalmans on the north were chasing the Namas who were on the south, and the Namas on the south were chasing the Mussalmans on the north.

Poor Golam was carried along, despite himself, on these waves of activity:

I had to go with them. They kept asking, "Where is the *shalar po shala* who started the whole thing? Keep that fellow by our side." So they kept me by their side, and I was with them. . . .
    My hands were empty. They were armed. I would go behind them, and return behind them. My arm was already wounded, and I was afraid that I might get hurt again. I had no intention of fighting. I had no interest in

fighting. I didn't have the strength. Still, I was with them. What else could I do?

Violence and Restraint

Every account we heard emphasized that the major activity was "chasing and counter-chasing," although occasionally men did come to blows:

Chasing and counter-chasing started at noon, and it continued for a long time. As a result, many people were injured. Many people were injured, some were sent to hospital, but nobody was killed. Some went to the doctor's dispensary.

The history-tellers tended to downplay actual bloodshed. Perhaps they felt some shame, or, more likely, worried that even now they might be held accountable. But even allowing for this tendency, it was strikingly clear that nobody died from any of this fighting.

All along, the leaders had in mind a particular kind of fight, one played out within constraints. Throughout, they used their authority to contain violence within acceptable boundaries. But they were not in complete control of events. As Golam told us:

At that time, I was standing there. The police officer called me. He asked me what I thought should be done.
"Cool it out and ease the tension."
The O.C. said, "We have no power to ease the tension."

When I asked whether Altaf-uddin couldn't have stopped the riot, Nayeb Ali promptly replied:

No, he couldn't. Who listens to whom? Nobody was listening even to the police, forget about Altaf-uddin.

The crowd was impressively armed; they carried knives and spears and swords and scythes. Yet all wounds we heard about and scars we saw were on the arms and legs. It is hard to believe that a crowd could have been sufficiently controlled by an unarmed leadership to prevent a single killing had the people themselves not been less than murderous.

The line between fisticuffs and murder is a distinct one. Rudé has classified riots that way:

Destruction of property . . . is a constant feature of the pre-industrial crowd, but not the destruction of human lives, which is more properly associated with the *jacqueries*, slave revolts, peasant rebellions, and millenarial outbursts of the past, as it is with the race riots and communal disturbances of more recent times. . . . The famous "blood-lust" of the crowd is a legend, based on a few carefully selected incidents.[8]

In fact, communal riots were sometimes bloody and sometimes not. Only eight years before the cow ate the lentils, the first major communal slaughter had blighted Calcutta, and bloody clashes had occurred in numbers of Bengali cities from then on. Such bloodshed was considered an urban phenomenon; rural riots usually involved greater numbers and lower mortality.[9] But, four years after the first slaughter in Calcutta, uncounted numbers of Hindus had been massacred about fifty miles from Panipur, in a rural town called Muladi. The Panipur riot, though, had all the earmarks of a "preindustrial" event rather than a true communal confrontation or a peasant rebellion.

We might note parenthetically that Rudé's characterization of race riots as murderous is not uniformly accurate either. The Kerner *Report*, for instance, commented in the late 1960s that the riots they studied "involved action . . . against symbols of white American society—authority and property—rather than against white persons."[10] Another counterexample is the very serious riots that happened in Brixton, England, in 1981. Sparked by a long series of confrontations between police and people from the black community, when the furies were finally loosed they burned hot. Fire bombs were thrown, property burned and looted, battles fought between youths and authorities. In the end, over 200 vehicles and 145 buildings were damaged or destroyed; there were 7,300 police on the scene and 354 arrests. Four hundred and fifty people were injured, many of them police. But there were no fatalities.[11] To be sure, other riots—communal riots in India and Bangladesh, racial riots in America and England—have been bloody. But a more refined theory is needed if we are to understand why these American, British, and Bengali riots were not, given that all were so passionate and in some respects so violent.

If the Panipur crowd was not murderous, still the weapons they used suggest some fairly serious intent, if not to damage, then

certainly to intimidate. Many people picked up whatever was close
to hand. Having at each other with functional farm implements
suggests spontaneity, a quarrel arising from the normal activities of
village life. Powers of invention were such that almost every imple-
ment of rural function—scythes, knives, fishing spears, *lathi*, mal-
lets—could be and was turned to violent use. "There was not even
a stick in my hand," Golam said about the first physical encounter
of the quarrel. "When they moved toward me with the sickles in
their hands, I picked up a mallet that I had used to tether the cows,
fearing that they might attack me with the sickles."

But not all weapons that appeared in the Panipur riot were farm
tools. Two other categories of weapons with particular significance
also appeared in people's accounts. First were the *ram deo*s, huge
curved knives used by Muslims during religious festivals, especially
Eid, when animals are sacrificed. Not only are these knives threatening in appearance, but they have historically been put to controversial use. Many Muslims told us how resentful their community
had been for many long years because the local Hindu *zamindar*
prohibited ritual cow slaughter in his territory. The killing of cows
was a symbolic act of resistance that was of a very high order of
significance, and the tool used for the sacrifice was this very *ram
deo*.[12]

Mr. Ghosh's list of weapons in fact concluded with the *ram deo*:

[They fought] with big swords and *katra*, *koch* [both fishing implements],
and *ram deo*.

*Ram deo*s borne by an angry Muslim crowd may have seemed
particularly threatening to the Hindus, although Golam made a
point of mentioning that Hindus, too, carried them:

We then seized the Hindus' cows and took them to our houses. They [the
Hindus] ran back home. Reaching their houses, they grabbed weapons,
like *lathi*, *ram deo*, *dhal*.

The fact is that most objects in Bengal, however laden with ceremonial significance, are also used for banal purposes. One is as
likely to use a *ram deo* to cut open a coconut as to slash the throat
of a cow or a goat in ritualistic bloodshed. This mix of sacred and
mundane meanings gives a sort of double-entendre effect to events
like riots. What at one moment is presented humorously is the next

moment ominous. Is one to hide in terror, or to root for the home team?

A second set of weapons with particular meaning were the swords and shields, implements with no function other than warfare. On the second day, according to Golam, the weapons were farm implements and *ram deos*:

When they took the cows away, we also came out with weapons like *ram deos* and scythes, and the fight began. It lasted for a long time. They attacked us with the *ram deo* and we fought off their attack with our *ram deo*. The fight lasted for two to three hours.

But the next morning, when the crowds had gathered in earnest, their seriousness was symbolized by the weapons they bore:

Then it was morning, and people of our community came with their scythes, *dhal*, and *bolum*. Many, many people came and assembled near our house. They came very early in the morning; it was still dark. They came armed with *ram deos*.

Bhupendranath, too, said, "They took *dhal bolum*." Were Golam and Bhupendranath using a figure of speech? Where would these villagers have come by true swords and shields, implements of war? People answered vaguely, shrugging off the question. Only later did I discover that most households did in fact have these weapons secreted in their thatched roofs. They were left over from the days when peasants served as reserve soldiers for the local *zamindar*, and they were still carefully maintained and ceremonially used. Each year, for instance, the locality sported a boat race. Teams from various villages rowed long, narrow vessels down the canal, amid much hullabaloo and merriment. Occasionally on these race days, teams came to blows over minor disagreements. Indeed, the sport is formulated in warlike symbolism. A drum at the stern marks the rhythm, and the biggest man available, usually heavily bearded and dressed in as threatening a manner as possible, stands fiercely in the bow. Hidden in the bottoms of the boats are these *dhal* and *bolum*, rarely used but kept at hand just in case.

The appearance of these weapons on the field of action suggests another transition of importance. On one level, they represented an escalation in the contest of power gestures. The number of men massed made a statement of power. So did such specific acts as burning the cow shed. To pull the *dhal bolum* from the rafters and bring them along said something about a willingness to fight, despite the care everyone took not to shed too much blood. As the confrontation progressed, to be armed as fully as possible made good sense, both as aggressive gesture and as self-defense.

But a second set of meanings was conveyed by the association of the *dhal bolum* with past uses. They were weapons used in fulfillment of the peasants' obligation to defend the *zamindar*. Because the peasants' rights to the land they tilled were complex and had long histories, they were simultaneously defending their own rights and the communities formed around land usage. In other words, these weapons, seldom used as actual tools of war and never in the lifetimes of the current generation, nonetheless were part and parcel of complex relationships to landlord, land, and community. When they reappeared from the rafters yearly during the boat races, those old times were reevoked and redeclared. But the boat races divorced their meaning from its class roots. The races were not about landlords and tenants and obligations and land rights. Rather, they were about the village community and a unity declared through and above competition. Everyone, of whatever religion or *para*, took part.

That significance both carried into the riot and did not. It did in that the *dhal bolum* still spoke of a shared past and a past agenda. But now there were two agendas, one for each side of the confrontation. The Muslims used the weapons to say, "Now it is our turn." But the Namasudras used them to say, "We have the right to defend ourselves." Weapons that in the past had conveyed a unity of community both with the *zamindar* and against the enemy from without who threatened the *zamindar*'s domain now were used to pursue internecine conflict. At the same time they lent to the proceeding the dignity and legitimacy of a public occasion, like warfare, like ceremonial boat races.

Tending to the Mundane

If *dhal bolum* clothed the proceedings with dignity, other objects on the field of conflict reminded the participants of more banal needs:

People were cooking, bringing food to the people sitting in the field. They brought tamarind. The Hindus brought Hindu food to the Hindus. The

Muslims most of the time used tamarind, so they wouldn't be thirsty, because most of the time they couldn't get water. The Muslims ate *chal*.

This description by a Hindu man suggests that, as everywhere in Indian life, food occupied an important position in the playing out of the riot. People ran to the field, taking with them their arms— and their provisions. Bhupendranath was a child at the time. What he remembered was the anger of the adults and what food they carried into battle:

They took *dhal bolum*; they also took *moori* [puffed rice], *chirra* [flattened rice], *tetul* [tamarind] to quench their thirst.

Every account contained details about the food. Nayeb Ali recalled:

In the morning I ate breakfast and went there. I came back just after the firing happened at four o'clock. In between I only ate rice.
Where did you get food? Did someone bring it from Panipur?
No, it wasn't cooked. We had raw rice.

Mr. Ghosh had said:

There was a big mat; everybody, all the Namasudras, were bringing food there. Those who were fighting would come and grab some food. . . .
    The Namasudras were greater in number, and they were more courageous. They had a lot of food. But the Muslims, they didn't have much— only some *chal*. They would eat a handful of *chal* and some water. Since the Namasudras had plenty of food, they had plenty of courage.

Was it a riot or a picnic? Here again, the combination of the banal and the extraordinary is very powerful. People were playing out an exceptional drama, but they were mindful of the ordinary, too. Not only was the body fed, but rules of social behavior were observed. Food defined the group. Even though Bengali food habits and methods of cooking are similar across community lines, there are distinct markers of difference. Everyone commented on what the two sides ate: uncooked rice and tamarind for the Muslims; processed rice cereal and water for the Hindus. In the midst of mayhem, the act of eating both evoked community identities and at the same time recommitted the sides to shared understandings of the conflict.

    In fact, all the acts of rioting served to intensify division, which in turn strengthened the rioters' determination to stand firm in their confrontation. Lines were drawn more and more deeply. We asked some men who had been children whether they had had friends from the other community before the riot, and they said they had. Hindus and Muslims sat together, talking with us, side by side on a bench outside a village house. They leaned on each other's shoulders, jostled playfully for space, interrupted and corrected each other with easy camaraderie:

Did Hindus and Muslims from this village go together [to the riot]?

No, the Hindus went from the Hindu*para* and the Muslims from the Muslim*para*. We went to one side of the field, they to the other. Now we are friends, but at that moment we were enemies. How could we go together?

Friends were enemies, the lines drawn by every action, including what food was served to whom.

Although they were swept along on the tide of the riot, people observed social proprieties even when their hearts were not in it. Golam, seriously worried by now about the consequences of the fight in his own life, nonetheless dutifully did the needful:

I was very young, and I thought about it a lot and worried about what would happen to me in the future. . . . There might be a case of murder, and I would have to bear all the cost connected with it. Nobody else would pay anything.

Yet, Golam noted, by the end of the day:

No rice was left in any house in our village. It had all been eaten up. The entire stock of rice and water was exhausted, since we had to give each Mussalman a handful of rice and a little water. We had to go without food that night.

He had also been noticing what the Hindus served:

The Hindus supplied people with *moori* and *chirra*. They spread out a big piece of cloth, brought food from all the houses, and kept them there. They ate those things and drank water and fought.

Women's Support and Resistance

Food presented an opportunity for children to participate. All the younger men we interviewed described themselves running back and forth with provisions. Women, however, whom I would have expected to be involved in food service, stayed away from the field. It was difficult to build a detailed picture of the role of women, for a number of reasons. For one thing, it was far harder to talk with them. The public world continues to be male in Bangladesh, even though some few women are active and well respected in organizations such as the one with which I was connected. I asked repeatedly to talk with women, but few interviews were arranged in advance with them. My interpreter was a young woman, selected for her gender precisely because I knew having a male coworker would foreclose any possibility of discussion with village women. Now and then we would turn an interview inward, from the front and public verandah to the women's inner world of the courtyard. These interviews tended to be brief; men would almost always intrude, not with bad intent, but with disbelief that we could be learning anything useful from the women. Hard as we might press for the space to hear women talk, it was an uphill battle. We developed a technique; Dilruba, my interpreter and assistant, would continue the public discussion while I turned aside with the tape recorder and quietly asked the women for their views.

What we learned was that, by their own telling, women unanimously resisted the riot. Men, too, always answered questions about what their womenfolk did (whenever they overcame their incredulity that we were interested) by saying that they had tried to restrain the men from going to the field.

It was not that women lacked animosity toward the opposite community. On the contrary, they often pursued banal village battles vigorously, seeding streams, for instance, with broken pottery to keep children of the other community from fishing in their waters. Often women described friendly feelings toward women across the community divide as well, although many were isolated within their own neighborhood. But women, too, were scrappers; we heard stories of women hurling insults at each other and staunchly defending the community honor.

But when it came to overt group action the women were unconfused. Both Namasudras and Muslims pleaded with their men to stay at home, to keep the peace. Food supplied to the warriors was uncooked—raw rice for the Muslims, along with raw tamarind to control thirst; processed cereals, puffed and flattened rice, for the Hindus—a suggestion that women refused to prepare food for the gathered men. The role of women in this and other social conflicts needs more research. Where have women contributed to the hostilities (as in Ireland, for instance), and where have they resisted?

The Bangladeshi men, predictably, saw their women as passively waiting outside the process. But women took an active role as storytellers, suggesting a more autonomous position for them. It was a woman, as I've said, who first broke the silence of the men and told me that the riot had happened. Women in general were more articulate about their fears and grievances (I'll say more about that later). When women kept silence and when they spoke was enlightening. I suspected that they told me what they had not told my local friends both because I was a woman and because, more important perhaps, I asked them the question. In the telling they implied criticism not only of the opposite community but also of their own menfolk. Laced through their decisions in the present to speak or not to speak, as well as what to speak, was resentment from the past about how the men escalated trouble and brought it home.

For the men did escalate the riot seriously. Foreshadowing what was to come, Golam combined his memories of the ordinary act of eating with the horror of police gunfire:

It was at two o'clock when the firing happened. They brought *moori* and *chirra* and poured them out on the sheet of cloth. The time was two o'clock; the firing took place then.

Golam placed the firing in time by linking it with the Hindus' food service. The portrait of a spirited rivalry over menus changed abruptly as the newcomers raised the numbers to critical mass. By two o'clock the action had become more dangerous:

At last the fight started. When the people came on horseback, those who were sitting there started the chase. They ran into the village. There they caught a Hindu man. The Mussalmans struck him ten times with their weapons. He was struck in the arms and legs. The Muslim *matabbars* then grabbed the man to prevent him from being hit in the belly and being murdered. One of the *matabbars* took him to a room and kept him shut up in it.

Chapter Four

Intervention and Punishment

Enter, the State

The riot voiced "inside talk" in the outside world. "Outside" is relative, though. At first the public forum remained within the village community. Next, people from extended communities arrived on the scene, strangers who were nonetheless involved because they were Namasudras or Muslims, members of the groups in conflict. With the arrival of the police and the authorities, however, "outside" took on new meaning.

To this point, the state had appeared as a category in people's recollections, a sort of abstract shadow of distant rules and laws cloaked in veils of inevitability. As Mofizuddin put it:

In the British time, we had to obey the British laws. In the Pakistani time, we had to abide by those laws. There was no point in being angry.

Golam was more explicit:

We were less strong because the state belonged to them. The Hindus outnumbered us. So we were afraid of them.

People had acted as if the state were not a party to the dispute. Its nature, whom it represented, to whom the state "belonged" had formed a highly relevant backdrop, but to all appearances what was occurring was a fight between Namasudras and Muslims. Now the state strode upon the stage of Panipur as a character of flesh and blood. The tide turned: no longer was the riot about making "inside" talk public; the outside world had moved corporally into

91

the village and the drama, apparently wearing the uniform of a peacemaker. In fact, as it played out its expected role, the state revealed itself as a character with more dimensions than were represented by the explicit lines it spoke.

The history of police repression of riots in general and communal riots in particular is very varied. How armed authority treats the crowd is a direct expression on the one hand of policy, and on the other of the allegiances and beliefs of policemen, officials, and soldiers. Most discussions of communal riots in India treat the police and the army as unpredictable variables:

Efforts to find a pattern in the handling of the riots and to codify the roles played by authorities, police, politicians and army were illuminating only in that they proved almost entirely futile.[1]

In some instances the police were strongly suspected of collusion. It was not uncommon for newspaper stories to complain of inaction, as does this one about a Hindu-Muslim fight in 1907: "Riots are taking place under the nose of police yet they are not doing anything to disperse the mob." In this case, the accusation was of partiality toward the Muslims. "The Hindus are holding out bravely. When Mohammedan mob went to loot Binaoti village, the villagers held up a strong fight."[2]

Years later, the same suspicions turned in the other direction. When Hindus gathered to attack Muslims at Rourkela in 1964, for instance, the inaction of the police and authorities contributed to rumors that the government had condoned mob action in retaliation against Muslim violence toward Hindus in Pakistan.[3]

Sometimes police policy seemed politically motivated. A few years later in Ahmedabad, for example, when riots were brewing, "the police acted promptly and brought the situation under control." Later, however, the authorities responded permissively as communal incidents escalated, and the town soon erupted in violence. Speculation was common that the government's lukewarm intervention was politically motivated: "If the Congress government had come down hard on the rioters . . . , the political cost might well have been a[n opposition] government in 1972."[4]

Since I had no access to government documents about the Panipur riot, we cannot directly know the official view of this and other disturbances of the period. If, some day, archives are available to scholars, we may learn more (although we may not; official records can obscure as well as enlighten.) Until then, however, we must read the language of official behavior somewhat as we do that of the villagers, with the serious limitation that we did not interview the individual policemen or authorities. What is beyond dispute is that in this case police and administrative authorities responded quickly and decisively and that their intervention did more than simply still unquiet waters. It codified a new set of relationships both between the two communities and between each of them and the state.

Police, State, and Community

How were the authorities alerted to the problem? We heard three stories. According to one, Altaf sent for them early on:

I was afraid that there might be a riot, in spite of my warning, because I knew that Hindus were already out recruiting other Hindus. So I informed the police station about this development and asked them to send some forces to come here. During that night I did it, informed the police.

In the second version, Hindus and Muslims alike sent word to the police. "Both the Hindus and the Mussalmans went to the police station to give the information," Golam had said. In the third variation, also supplied by Golam, the authorities came to the village simply because word got out, not as a result of decisions by a responsible leadership. As the injured made their way to the medical dispensary at Panipur *bazar*, the police could not help but know what was up:

Some [of the injured] went to the doctor's dispensary where there was a policeman. After getting the information, a police party arrived at six o'clock in the evening.

As soon as armed force entered the picture, people's stories reflected their partisanship. Who gave the order, who fired the shots, what they fired and toward whom, all appeared differently in different people's versions. But certain observations were consistent. Everyone reported that the top police official was a Muslim, Mr. Rahaman, and his second-in-command a Hindu, Raghu Nandan. This communal symmetry was noteworthy. So, too, was the fact that the rioters were not deeply impressed at first with the police presence. "We have no power to ease the tension," the police officer in charge told Golam. "What should we do?"

They went to President Altaf-uddin. He said, "If it's going to take firing to stop it, then fire on them."

The O.C.° said, "We have no orders to open fire."

It is curious that Golam's police officer solicited advice from members of the community. In Golam's version it was not the police who suggested firing on the crowd, but Altaf. We cannot know with accuracy what the discussions among leaders were, but it is suggestive that Golam, who was not present and was running on hearsay and imagination, places key responsibility at Altaf's door. In Golam's universe Altaf was the embodiment of power, the only person representing the state with whom he'd had firsthand contact before that day. Typically, state power is represented on a village level by the person of an official. Sometimes a bureaucrat or an officer of the law, in the case of Panipur it was Altaf, the elected representative. Golam made a clear association between Altaf the person and the power he embodied. To Golam, the police were not playing a new role in the drama; their lethal action was simply an escalation of Altaf's role, and Altaf had been a decisive player all along. It was he who had been public mediator, but when the Muslim elders determined to "teach the Hindus a lesson," Altaf had disappointed Golam by looking the other way. Now, again, Golam hoped the authorities, empowered by Altaf, would do the proper thing and bring the riot to a halt.

°A brief description of the administrative hierarchy and its representatives on the spot may be helpful here. At the time of the riot, Faridpur district contained 4 subdivisions and 24 *thanas* or police districts. The *thanas* were further divided into unions, of which there were 258 in Faridpur. From these various administrative units, an impressive array of officials arrived at the riot. The players our informants mentioned on the side of the civil authorities were the subdivisional officer (S.D.O., the head of one of four subdivisions of the district) and his superior, the deputy commissioner (D.C., the administrative head of the district). From the police came the officer in charge (O.C., the man in charge at Madaripur, the *thana* level), the superintendent of police (S.P., chief district level officer), and the D.I.G., probably a district inspector-general. In the mid-1980s a major Bangladeshi reorganization took place, breaking up the districts in an attempt to decentralize services and reconstitute local power configurations. The units I've named therefore do not correspond to contemporary administrative arrangements.

Altaf, however, told a very different story. This time he flatly refused responsibility. He may earlier have boasted about his power to elicit police intervention, but it was not *he* who ordered the shooting; it was the S.D.O., the top civil executive of the subdivision. In fact, by his own account Altaf did everything possible to prevent it. He even suggested that such dire measures were unnecessary or were provoked by the very presence of the big guns: "Before [the S.D.O.] came, there wasn't any big attack, only a few people chasing each other and throwing rocks at each other." Altaf welcomed armed authority, but he felt ambivalent about the civil higher-ups. Once the S.D.O. came on the scene, Altaf detached himself from complicity and aligned himself with his constituents:

The S.D.O. came. He asked me to stop this. Then I took the microphone and said, "The S.D.O. has come. He asks you to stop. So please, it is my ardent request that you stop."

It was around 10:30 or 11 A.M. when the S.D.O. arrived. Before he came, there wasn't any big attack, only a few people chasing each other and throwing rocks at each other. On one side of the field, people were chasing each other, but in the larger part, both parties were sitting facing each other. . . .

The S.D.O. said, "I'll give the order now to fire. So stop." But nobody listened to him. Even when the S.D.O. was writing the order, I ran forward and told people, "He is writing the order. Still there is time. Please go away."

Why was nobody listening? Was it because they didn't believe the police would shoot them, or because they were too caught up in the standoff to be willing to blink? If they assumed the threats were not serious, they were mistaken. For the police, carefully cloaking themselves in the chain of command, moved toward the use of deadly force. Said Mr. Ghosh:

The second [police] officer . . . went to Madaripur, riding a horse, to get the order to fire from the S.D.O. Instead of giving the order, the S.D.O. himself came here, and all the other big officers came, too. On that very day, they came.

Golam added detail to the same description:

They estimated the crowd at nearly fifty thousand people on each side fighting with weapons, and asked [their superiors] for instructions about what they should do. This letter [asking for orders] was written to the S.D.O. He gave that letter to a policeman, told him to go to the S.D.O. by cycle and come back in an hour. The S.D.O. did not send an order, but he came himself. The D.C. also came, and some other officers, and they gave the order to open fire.

The D.C., or deputy commissioner, was a celebrity, the highest civil authority anyone in the village could imagine. Above him stood abstract symbols of government in far-off Dhaka, the capital. That he came in person rather than sending written orders Golam found striking. Although nobody else placed so high an authority on the scene at that point (Altaf had the S.D.O. giving the order on the spot to fire and the D.C. arriving the following day to deal out punishment), Golam was at least impressionistically correct. The civil authorities were taking matters seriously enough to arrive in person and preempt local leadership.

Climax and Anticlimax

The single most highly charged point in the three days was clearly the moment when bullets began to rain on the crowd and men fell in the field, injured and dead. That every firsthand witness reported on the scene and that each reported different details was only to be expected. It was a time of considerable dust and disorder. Huge crowds (now, by Golam's count, grown to the zenith, about a hundred thousand) sat facing each other, but they did not exactly sit still. The very first thing about the riot Sunil told us was, "It was so noisy, I couldn't hear anything." Everyone mentioned the "chasing and counter-chasing," the pushing and shoving going on at the outskirts of the crowd. Men who were children at the time described circling the field, trying without success to catch a glimpse of their fathers.

In the chaos it is unlikely that anyone knew for sure how the police shooting came about, although each person spoke as if he did know. What we were getting, therefore, was a symbolic representation. People's memories combined what they saw, what they heard, and what they fantasized, all synthesized into an account they were convinced was factual. The story they told me was this concoction filtered further through their reading of my interest (and my interests).

Who actually pulled the trigger? Communal politics colored the versions:

The C.O., Mr. Rahaman [a Muslim], came. Our Madaripur people and our Rajoir people, two hundred police came from those two *thanas*. Raghu Nandan [a Hindu] was the second officer. He was a Shaha.* . . .
The Muslims fell a little back, and the Namasudras advanced. Then Raghu Nandan said to the S.D.O., Raghu*babu* said, "Sir, this is the time to give the order to fire. Otherwise, there will be a lot of bloodshed." So the S.D.O. said, "Inform both sides, if they don't stop, we'll fire." Then Raghu Nandan rode his horse and went to both sides and told them of the S.D.O.'s decision, and said, "I'll raise a flag, and as soon as I raise it, you all leave this place. Otherwise we will fire." As soon as the flag was raised, the Namasudras left. But the Muslims attacked. And the police fired. One or two—I'm not sure how many—were killed.

Mr. Ghosh, a caste Hindu, had Raghu*babu,* another caste Hindu, initiating the firing. When ordered, the Namasudras left the field, but the unruly Muslims surged forward, provoking police action.
Altaf's story was similar in some important respects. He, too, remembered the key moment when the Muslims refused to retreat, and he suggested a very important reason for that refusal:

The S.D.O. came. He asked me to stop this. Then I took the microphone and said, "The S.D.O. has come. He asks you to stop. So please, it is my ardent request that you stop." . . .
The S.D.O. said, "I'll give the order now to fire. So stop." . . . I ran forward and told people, "He is writing the order. Still there is time. Please go away."
After he gave permission, the police took up a position in a square formation, in the east side of the field. As soon as the whistle went—Raghunath and the O.C. of Madaripur were both there—they shot blanks.
But the Muslims understood that it was blank fire, and *they thought they wouldn't kill the Muslims,* so they kept on. [My italics]

Altaf had earlier identified the O.C. as a Muslim, so he had a representative from each side wielding a gun. That the Muslims believed blanks were to be fired is very significant. It confirms the

*Shaha is a subcaste closely associated with money-lending. Many peasants in the area hated Shahas for their usurious practices.

idea that they expected support from the authorities of what was now a Muslim-dominated state. That belief, however, was proved wrong:

Then the police fired on the people. Instantly, two people fell.

Sunil added a third confirmation that the Namasudras retreated when warned, while the Muslims stood their ground:

Then the officers arrived. They made a camp on one side of the field. They were asking people to stop, but nobody was listening. Finally, they gave the order to fire. Now I have to tell the real fact. They aimed at one side, and one side fled.

Which side left?

The Hindus left, because they could see the police were aiming at them. They vacated about three-fourths of the field, but a few Hindu people were left. The police aimed at those few people. The Hindus said, "Please don't fire on us. We're few people and we'll soon leave." Still they fired. Two men were killed on the spot.

They didn't fire at the Muslims?

No, not at first. But later they fired blanks at the Muslims.

Sunil read the way the police aimed their weapons as expressing intent and malevolence. His reading of the situation corresponds precisely with Altaf's interpretation of what the Muslims were thinking. Both sides believed the police were partisan, that they would fire on the Namasudras but not on the Muslims. Both sides understood that the state "belonged" to the Muslims, and they expected the state to point their guns in the direction that would reflect that fact.

Golam took exception; as usual, he had a more judicial view of the question:

Then the S.D.O. wrote down on a piece of paper the order to fire and showed it to the people. He said that he had already written down on paper the order to open fire. If they did not leave immediately, they would open fire. . . . He showed the paper and spoke loudly.

Then they started firing. When the Mussalmans heard "tss tss tss" [sounds of firing], they got up and ran away. They ran toward the village in the north. They fired in the other direction also. The Hindu officer in charge of Rajoir police station, named Raghunath Shaha, fired on the Muslims. A Mussalman policeman belonging to the same *thana* fired at the Hindus. His name was Shamsul Huq. One person died on each side.

Where Sunil saw outright injustice in the choice of target, Golam saw absolute fairness. Sunil saw the guns all pointed one way, whereas Golam's portrait was entirely symmetrical.

There were also some fascinating points of disagreement about *what* the police fired. According to Altaf, they shot twice, first with blanks, later with live ammunition. Others—Sunil, for one—saw the choice of blanks versus bullets as more malevolent. Golam, reasonable as always, claimed, "They used small bullets, not poisoned bullets." They killed people, in other words, but it was not as murderous as it might have been.

When we asked, "Who died?" we got a variety of answers. Golam thought "One person died on each side." Altaf said, "Four people died. Two Muslims, two Hindus. All of them were peasants." Nayeb Ali's version was, "Two or three [people died]. One of them was a *kopiruddin* [a Muslim village doctor], a guy with a beard. Another boy died, a handsome man wearing a shirt,* but I don't know who he was." The most amazing statement we heard came from Mr. Ghosh:

Two Muslims were killed, and one Hindu. Since two men were killed on the Muslim side, they had to kill one more on the Hindu side. Otherwise it would look like the police were partial. So the police later ran and killed a man on the Hindu side, to make it even.

What do these accounts tell us about the tellers and about the events? Reports of the initial quarrel had a similar quality; people unselfconsciously told the tale from their own points of view. When it came to accounts of the riot itself, however, the stories agreed more closely. To be sure, accounts tilted toward descriptions of one side or the other as being the more aggressive. But they concurred in important respects: seated armies, scuffles on the sidelines, the nature of the actual combat.

It was in the fighting stage of the riot that people were personally most active. That they knew more details, had to guess at fewer, were more balanced in their memories and in their telling may suggest the influence of activity. During the quarrel most were onlookers, with the exception of Golam, whose story was the most detailed and also the most balanced.

Now, however, initiative passed from the people to the police

---

*The shirt (in a western style) suggests that this boy was a Hindu, since Muslims ordinarily wear *kurtas*.

and authorities. A few individuals may have played some role in determining the intervention. Golam was consulted by the police; Altaf ran back and forth to alert the crowd to the imminence of firing. But for the most part the rioters were acted upon by those in power without prospect of response. They were hardly passive, however; more accurately, they were distracted by the fight and refused to believe in the reality of bullets. But there was a change in the dynamic of the riot. The people were no longer shaping their destinies. Greater powers were taking charge. That was how they experienced it, and their stories bent memories to reflect that very particular emotional experience.

At the same time there was a way the people were still active. Although estimates of the size of the crowd were impressionistic, ranging from twenty thousand to a hundred thousand, it is indisputable that the police were very seriously outnumbered. The crowd was well armed for hand-to-hand combat, and some had bows and arrows as well. Engaging the official forces in battle was not out of the question. A decision had to have been made, therefore, to accept the police intervention. It may have been informed more by fear and incredulity than by calculation, but at some level the rioters deliberately handed over power to the authorities.

The Hindus, though, felt an intense sense of victimization, formulated as the notion that the authorities were selectively punishing their community. The most clear-cut claim of discrimination was Sunil's. In his riot the Hindus were blatantly slaughtered, although they offered to clear the field. The Muslims were protected; even when they later tried to keep up appearances and fired on their fellows, the (presumably Muslim) police shot only blanks. It is interesting that Sunil, since he had no personal knowledge of the officials, never directly ascribes a community affiliation to them. Nor could he tell us who the victims were. He was at some distance when the shots were fired: "I saw the firing. I was on the eastern side of the village and I saw it." But he was not close enough or closely enough involved to identify the fallen men.

It is understandable that Sunil would nevertheless remember the shooting as biased, given the aftermath of the riot. Hindus did lose power in ways more or less subtle (which I shall discuss in the next chapter). Whether or not it was literally true that the police shot to kill Hindus but not Muslims, Sunil's vision of the scene

reflected an actual aspect of the relative positions of the two communities. There is a kernel of emotional truth in what may in every
detail be an inaccurate statement.

On the Muslims' side, people recalled the firing not as unfair but
as inevitable. Mofizuddin, for instance, a feisty man, adopted an
attitude of sympathy for the authorities:

> The police couldn't control it. Early in the morning, they just couldn't do
> it. . . . They worked from early morning until four o'clock. Then the
> magistrate and the D.I.G., who had come, they ordered firing. Two to
> four people died.

There is no moral outrage in this statement, no indignation that the
police ignored other methods of crowd control, no suggestion that
shooting to kill might have been excessively brutal. Many people
were morally indignant about actions by the opposing community.
But nobody complained about the fact that the police killed people.

So thoroughgoing was the lack of protest about this lethal event,
in fact, that I myself didn't note its absence until, back in the
United States, I found myself in a discussion about the Panipur riot
with a group of American students. A young African-American
man among them, hearing my report of the police firing, exploded.
"How could they do that!" he exclaimed. "Didn't they know the
police are supposed to do everything *but* shoot directly at people?"

What this student knew of riot control was confined to police
action in the United States during the sixties, and discussion of that
history tended to support his view. The Kerner *Report* reviewed a
list of interventions by such "control forces" as the police, national
guard, or army—tear gas, shooting of blanks, firing over the
crowd.[5] When authorities did fire on crowds, as in the notable case
of the national guard at Kent State, their action evoked popular
protest loud and ardent.[6]

But in the United States, too, censure of police violence tends to
be selective, reflecting lines of power and discrimination. A book
called *Riots, U.S.A.*, for instance, passes quickly over the subject of
armed action against rioters in Watts. The only reference to the use
of gunpower by the national guard is this: "Only when sniping
gunfire was returned and strict curfew imposed on the area for
three days did the insurrection cease." The author then gives figures on injuries (10 national guardsmen, 773 civilians), but he does

not mention what a previous chart reveals: that thirty-four people died.[7] How?

I don't believe the lack of indignation in Bengal is a reflection of that stereotypical eastern fatalism; Bengalis are among the most rebellious, least fate-accepting peoples I know. The riot itself is evidence of their penchant for activism. Why, then, did the erstwhile rioters not comment critically on the killings? What they reported instead was a mixture of sorrow and fear, mingled, perhaps, with some relief that the thing was over.

That sense of relief I detected led me to speculate that the villagers were demonstrating a very important point of theory. The villagers knew the police would arrive at some point; perhaps they factored that knowledge into their script of the confrontation. The police, in other words, played a role that was not antagonistic to the rioters' desires, and that may have been another reason no moral indignation was voiced. Faced off as they were, mass against mass possessing land they all knew they must at some point relinquish, the villagers had few options for how to bring the confrontation to an end. The two forces could come to serious blows until one side vanquished the other. In the process life would almost surely have been lost, and that was an outcome no one desired. Alternatively, one side could retreat in shame. But the stories had a tone of mutual respect, even when the tellers were most hostile to their opponents. It was hard to imagine that either side would retreat voluntarily or that either side would wish such social humiliation on the other. Yet food was running out and the ponds were drained of water. Something had to give. The arrival of the police was, in this regard, providential. Enter from the sidelines a third force, the state, empowered to enforce disengagement and prepared to act. That the rioters left the field so precipitously was no doubt due in each individual case to terror. It is no game to be fired upon. In the aggregate, however, a number of options could have been pursued and weren't. People could have decided to regroup elsewhere and begin again. Other types of hostilities could have been pursued, sub rosa: scattered attacks on individuals, damage to crops and cattle, and so on. The fact that no such actions occurred goes beyond the reach of simple fear into the realm of collective strategy. As Altaf saw it:

Then the police fired on people. Instantly, two people fell. There were many rounds fired, but only two Muslims fell on the ground. Then all the Muslims fled, and also the Hindus. The Hindus were already running, so those who fell were further away. After that, there was not a single man in the field.

There was no one to bring water to the wounded lying on the field. So I brought a little water for them. But they didn't survive.

Seen this way, the fact that the crowd retired as soon as the police fired, that the field cleared so quickly and so thoroughly, suggests a sort of deal between populace and police. We'll set the terms, the rioters seem to say, and you get us out of the stance.

What remained was the clearing up, negotiating more overtly the punishment and restoration of community (and family) relations. Said Golam:

Eleven people were injured on our side, and on their side thirteen were injured. . . . The police transported the injured people immediately to the hospitals at Dhaka and Barisal.

It was a big *chak* [field]. It became empty within half an hour once they heard the sound of gunfire. I started walking very slowly, taking one step after another, away from the police, fearing that they would arrest me now. . . .

Everyone had left the field [after the firing] except the policemen and officers. . . . No people were left. Only [the authorities] remained and those who were injured and couldn't run away. They were lying wherever they had been hit. Nobody went to help them, out of fear. The policemen brought all the injured to one place.

By night, by almost eight o'clock, we had all fled. I ran away to another village. I ran away to the village to the north of ours.

Golam, knowing he had been the cause of the melee, hid out, all the while calculating the enormous costs:

I came to the side of the pond, which covered an area of nearly three *bighas* [man present says that in that region one *bigha* equals 0.52 acres], and saw that there was no water in it. The entire water of the tank had been drunk up by those who were fighting. . . .

The *kolai* had been completely destroyed, trampled underfoot. Nothing of it remained. *Til* [linseed] had also been growing, up to the height of a man's throat. The *kolai* was ripe. Nobody could bring home even a handful of *kolai*. Even in those cheap days, *kolai* worth about one or two *lakhs* [100,000–200,000] of rupees was destroyed. A crop worth two *lakhs* of rupees was lost.

No rice was left in any house in our village. It had all been eaten up. The entire stock of rice and water was exhausted, since we had to give each Mussalman a handful of rice and a little water. We had to go without food that night. . . .

Our house was near that place, the policemen came to our house, took all the things out of one room and put them in another . . . so that they could stay in that room. . . . They cleared the biggest room in the house, the room in which we lived.

Were other people in your house at the time?

None, except my mother. By this time, she was almost mad, seeing all these things. One moment she was shouting, and the next crying. Nobody paid any attention to her.

Judgment and Punishment

The authorities gathered and the business of punishment and reconciliation began. But first the policemen established a camp. Golam continued his story:

They told the villagers to come there the next morning. The policemen grabbed hold of the few people left in the village and commanded them to bring provisions, rice and chickens, to boil the rice and kill the chickens. They did it that very night. The people did what they were told, and they fed them.

By this time, a police officer, perhaps a D.S.P., arrived and said that it was not possible to stay there. He said that he had to visit the toilet. He asked whether there was any *pukka* ["proper"] toilet in the village. But there was nothing like that in the village. He asked where there was a *pukka* toilet. There were *pukka* toilets at Panipur, where the Majumdars lived, half a mile away. He said, "In that case, we will go there." So, taking the policemen with them, they went to the doctor's dispensary at Panipur.

Moving in physically was an act both practical and symbolic. There was a history of British authorities establishing an armed presence in troubled regions during the days of Empire. Small contingents of soldiers asserted control through the use of ceremony and a public show of armed might. In the cities, governmental pomp was an accepted part of life. But in the villages, where formal authority is distant and mystified, the corporeal presence of the state is potent. The villagers were not so much intimidated as impressed. What the camp told them was, "You are making changes in your world, and we are a party to the negotiation." It also said, "We may be a new state, but we continue to work in the old ways. Don't expect easier treatment from us than you would have gotten from the colonial rulers."

[The police officer] then told the people to assemble there [at the dispensary]. The officer in charge also went there. The *matabbars* of the village grabbed me and took me there with them. They said, "The O.C. said you must go there, so go there you must." So we went to the medical dispensary at the Majumdars' house. The police inspector and other superior officers came and asked the O.C. why he had not recorded the case in the police diary.

When many thousand people have taken to the field without visible organization or leadership, it is a problem for those imposing justice to figure out on whom exactly to impose it. How that riddle was answered conveyed information to the people, and sometimes surprised them:

He then started writing the diary. He wrote down the names of the people who were injured by arrows. Then all the people who were wounded were charged. We thought that the greater the number of the wounded people, the stronger our case would be. This would prove we were beaten more badly. But we found that anybody and everybody wounded was charged.

On their side also, many people were charged in the same way. Three hundred seven or eight people were charged on each side.

He fitted the wireless apparatus there at the dispensary and talked with people at Dhaka and Khulna.

There were few ways to confirm who had actually taken part in the fighting. Wounds gave the show away. The people saw injury as proof of victimization. The state viewed injury as proof of participation. For them there were no innocents in Panipur. Everyone involved was, in their view, guilty.

How they ultimately constructed punishment was not whimsical. That the local authorities consulted their superiors at Dhaka, the capital of East Bengal, indicates that the punishment accorded with official policy:

The officers surveyed our villages for some time, and then they held a big meeting at the Rajoir police station. It was attended by the D.M. [district magistrate], Judge *sahib* who was the head of the district of Faridpur, the D.I.G., and the big officers. They took a statement from me. All the *matabbars* from the villages, including Altaf, attended. The *zamindar* was not there; he was away, in Calcutta. People went there from our village, from R_____, K_____, and F_____. The district magistrate of Faridpur took a statement from me about the cause of the trouble. He took a statement from Kumar [Tarkhania], also. The *matabbars* told us, "Don't falsely implicate anybody. Tell the truth, and the truth only." They told us to state only those things which had actually happened. "Don't tell any lie to implicate anybody!" . . .

Judge *sahib*, the D.M., told the S.D.O. of Madaripur to inquire into the case and to settle it. A lot of my money was spent. The police and the military personnel that came had to be fed by us for eighteen days, by both sides. There was a Union Board at Panipur. The S.D.O. came there from Madaripur four times to hold court. He heard our statements and decided the case. He punished all of us—three hundred people from each side, six hundred in all—by telling us to remain standing for one hour with our eyes fixed on the sun.

Were both Hindus and Mussalmans standing together?

Yes, we the Mussalmans and the Hindus stood in lines together to do it. We stood there for one hour by the clock. He was looking at his watch. That was our punishment.

Then a written agreement was made. It was stated that if any trouble broke out between Hindus and Mussalmans in that area within seven years, everyone would be fined two thousand rupees. The fine would be collected from each one of the people who was charged.

The process of judgment was finely tuned. Justice came to the village, to the nearest embodiment of the state, the Union Board offices at the *bazar* headquarters. It was interesting to me that Golam repeated the *matabbars'* injunction to him and to Kumar to tell the truth, which implies that the judicial process could have been used as an opportunity to continue the fight. The warning "Don't falsely implicate anybody" conveys a decision to accept the outcome of the struggle to that point. It would be illuminating to know whether leaders from both communities took the same position, or whether the Hindus, whose power was declining, played the judicial process more politically than the Muslims, whose power was ascending.

Punishment took four forms. First was a de facto tax imposed on the community to feed and quarter the police and civil authorities. Such taxes were a common tool of the British, now passed into the hands of their Pakistani successors. The second form of punishment was corporeal. Six hundred people, Hindus and Muslims side by side, were made to stare at the sun. This gesture was dramatic. The winter sun in Panipur tends to be muted by haze, but it is nonetheless a serious matter to expose one's eyes to it for an hour. Six hundred people were chosen (one wonders how) as proxy for their communities to endure this most personal humiliation and pain.

The third form of punishment assigned explicit community responsibility. A paper was signed, threatening action against representatives of the community if anyone acted badly in future. The policy of collective responsibility had been used by the British in Bengal beginning in the 1920s. "Let the respectable leaders of both communities know that we expect them actively to assist in controlling their co-religionists," the governor had written to his minions, "and shall be extremely displeased with them if they don't." To guard against displeasure, he imposed taxes on both communities, even in cases where one had clearly been the aggressor.[8] More than personal punishment, like the sadistic act of making people stare at the sun, this assignment of blame in anticipation was a technique used when those in power meant what they said: No more fighting.

A second statement was contained in the act of collective punishment, one that had evolved in an earlier history elsewhere in India. To hold communities rather than individuals responsible is to establish a relationship between those communities and the state.[9] The communities of Panipur had taken to themselves the project of establishing primacy and subordination within their own boundaries. Now the state reabrogated that authority. You may dominate at our behest alone, they said to the local Muslims. It may now be a Muslim state, but it is first and foremost a state. We may support you, but it is we who rule, and we insist on certain laws of civic behavior.

The people of Panipur did not seriously contest that description of power. By accepting responsibility and discharging their penalties, the villagers, both ordinary folk like Golam and leaders like the *matabbars* and Altaf, tacitly declared their intention to rebel no further. The process of punishment and reconciliation, in other words, constituted a new agreement between people and rulers, a renewed acceptance of the terms of subordination within the altered framework of village relations between the communities. The fact that a Muslim government was "neutral" tacitly condoned that new imbalance of power. Neutrality in the face of unequal power favors those on top. The authorities may have verbally promised to protect Hindus' rights, but by deed they conveyed a different message: the two communities were punished equally, suggesting that the state would intervene, but not so as to prevent the Muslim community from seizing the upper hand. Because the Muslim community felt victorious and the Namasudras resigned, a bargain was struck among all three to sign on to the new arrangements.

There was one other arena in which state and people cooperated in establishing policy, and that was the promulgation of news outside the village. We were seriously surprised that so few people besides those directly concerned knew about the riot, a fact suggesting at the very least censorship of the press. To be certain, we checked back files of all papers published at that time and found no reference to the disturbance in any of them. That outsiders knew nothing carries a significance beyond the overt act of the government, and I shall return to a discussion of its implications in the next chapter. But the decision of the government to ban reportage was a conscious act designed to contain "contagion," and in it the villagers fully cooperated.

The final punishment was the imposition of large personal fines. Golam's ordeal was not over:

Did you and Kumar talk to each other afterward?
No, he left the village.
Did he go immediately afterward?
No, one year after.
You didn't talk with him ever during that year?
Yes, I did. We had a talk before he left. He realized that we had made a mistake. He said, "It was neither your fault nor mine. Other people caused . . . " It cost a lot of money. At that time, the price of paddy was six to eight rupees a *maund*. I had to pay nearly forty thousand rupees. I sold off my house and my cattle.

Did you personally pay forty thousand rupees?
Yes, I did. They also had to pay forty thousand rupees.
Did you and your family pay the entire amount? Or did others in your community contribute?
No, I alone paid it. Nobody paid any subscription. They [the Namasu-dras] did it with the help of subscriptions, but the Mussalmans did not pay any subscriptions. I told them, "I myself will bear the cost as long as I have any money. You can begin to pay when my money is exhausted. . . . I had some cash. A relative died, leaving me four thousand rupees. I spent that amount. I sold off my cattle and [part of my homestead]. Altaf-uddin advised me not to sell my land or [house]. Then [the relatives of] those who were murdered wanted money from me [from time to time].

Golam felt it was a matter of principle to pay his fine personally, although Kumar's penalty was paid by his community. I thought the difference might have been explained by Kumar's migration soon after the event as much as by the moral rectitude Golam claimed for himself—and no doubt deserved. The families of victims, too, claimed recompense. Both state and community turned to Golam and Kumar as those personally responsible, at the same time that both state and community understood the riot to be a collective event.

Altaf, as usual, had a story different from Golam's, one in which judgment was far less severe, thanks largely to his intervention on behalf of his constituents:

It was already 4 P.M. [after the firing]. I realized that there would be some aftereffects. I hadn't eaten anything, so I went to a house and begged some food. I considered myself neither Hindu nor Muslim, and I knew I had to beware. Otherwise, there could be a big conflict as an aftereffect. I am the president of this area; it was in that capacity that I was present.

By that time the S.P. arrived with the police force from Faridpur. I described the whole incident to him, and I had to stay there for that night. All the people escaped. The whole night I talked about the incident with the S.P. We ate together, along with his forces.

The next day the S.D.O. and the D.C. came, and in the description that the S.P. gave to them he highlighted my role. At my request there were no arrests made, and all those accused in both communities were released on bail.

The trial was held at my place [*amar ekhane*]. It was a very nominal trial. After that there were some meetings concerning this incident. Big leaders of the Hindu community came here, and from the Muslim side I was there.

Even the M.P.s [members of Parliament] came here. An M.P., after hearing my speech, said, "Altaf is neither a Hindu nor a Muslim. He is the president of this area. We are not needed here. He can handle it."

Then I called for a meeting of the Hindus and Muslims and made a reconciliation between the two communities. Whatever happened, happened from a very personal cause. It wasn't anything worthy of so much trouble.

If actions speak, what did the stories of repression tell us? First, that the rioters were controllable. Other riots were not so easily squelched. Deaths and injuries notwithstanding, the countryside had a wide experience of communal strife that flared up over and over again, even after such bloody intervention. Were these villagers more readily intimidated than others? Or had they basically finished what they were about by the time the police arrived?

Second, the stories map presumptions about power. That Muslims acted as though they anticipated favored treatment and Hindus as though they anticipated persecution accords well with my informants' verbal statements of their thinking at the time. Both communities assumed that Muslim rights were on the rise. Despite evidence suggesting an equal and nonsectarian intervention, people persisted in seeing the police action as biased. What they grasped accurately, however inaccurate their reading of specific events, was that the new government favored Muslim fortunes over Hindu.

Chapter Five

Reconciliation and Thereafter

An Uneasy Peace

[Sunil:] After the firing, the whole field was empty. . . . After that, the officers from the government were there. They questioned both sides and tried to make a reconciliation, tried to make us join hands.

Was it a true reconciliation?

We were forced to reconcile. But in our hearts we have never reconciled. We still have the apprehension that it could happen again in future.

For Altaf the whole event may have arisen from personal causes, not worthy of so much trouble. But to Sunil, who was personally involved in only tangential ways, what the riot wrought was very important indeed:

That incident expressed what was in the minds of the Muslims. They thought, "Even if we harm them, they have no right to protest."

Altaf dismissed the process of reconciliation with a wave of his hand: "Then I called for a meeting of the Hindus and Muslims and made a reconciliation between the two communities." But for Sunil the "reconciliation" was in actuality a restructuring of rights and power. "It is a Muslim country," Sunil said. Now, when conflicts arise:

we keep silent, in fear that it might lead to a repeat of the riot. If something like that were to happen now, we couldn't defend ourselves. We wouldn't have any avenue of escape.

Cows had eaten crops and villagers had fought about it for as long as memory stretches. But this particular wayward cow left behind

111

barren fields, dry ponds, slain villagers, and an altered social landscape.

On the surface, Altaf was right; the village had seemed to return to normal. Little tangible was different. No land or weapons or wealth changed hands. Despite some tall tales of police injustice, the physical consequences of the riot were evenly distributed. The death toll was equal; both sides were fined, held responsible, and personally penalized. Yet relations between Hindus and Muslims had been thrust into permanent imbalance. How exactly were those new relations reflected in the life of the village?

The first and most evident consequence was that many Hindus left for India. There are several ways to assess the new community relations in Panipur: overt descriptions, stories of subsequent social conflicts, and the history of migration across the Indian border. I start with the last, because migration is an especially articulate action, expressing sentiments so strongly felt and so clearly articulated that one is willing to abandon the familiar for the unknown. Who left, when, and for what reasons—once again, the language of behaviors—tells us a great deal about the aftermath of the riot.

Migration

Prominent among those who left Panipur for India was Kumar Tarkhania, the Namasudra whose crop had been eaten. When we tried to locate him to get his side of the story, we learned from relatives that he had crossed the border soon after the riot and had died recently in India. As Bhupendranath explained, many other Hindus left as well:

The Hindus were generally upset. Everybody was upset about what was happening in the area. We thought about leaving.

Why didn't you?

Things gradually were reconciled. But some people were more sensitive to these things afterward, and they left.

How many families left?

Since that time about one-fourth of the families in each village left.

Were there formal discussions within the community about whether to leave or not?

After the conflict, the D.C. *sahib* came to the spot with the military, and he discussed the matter with leaders from both communities. They had to sign a contract that it wouldn't happen again. . . .

D.C. *sahib* consoled the Hindu community and warned the Muslim community that next time they would not hesitate to arrest the responsible people.

Some people were reassured by these warnings from on high. To hold selected individuals in a community responsible for the actions of their fellows is effective where a reasonable amount of local-level social control exists. The fact that (as far as we could find out) no repetition of the riot occurred suggests that such control existed in Panipur. Hindus could be reassured by the district commissioner's admonition to the Muslim community, because they understood how much the riot had been a community endeavor to begin with. Had the *matabbars* and the elected leadership not condoned the fight, the Hindus believed, it would probably not have happened.

Perhaps another reason, even more compelling, why no repetition occurred was that this one riot had done its job. It marked and formalized on a local level a shift in rights and power that had already been accomplished on the state level and was being reenacted in other localities by other means. There was, in other words, a change in power relations going on throughout the area, a new climate blowing in, and the riot was only one of many object lessons in the new order, one tool for its construction.

Altaf disagreed that the riot itself had convinced many people to leave the village:

The 1954 riot had no big effect on Panipur. With my hands joined, I begged people not to leave, to forget it. There was some migration, but from 1947. It had nothing to do with the '54 riot.

His own authority was at stake, and his view of the migration was colored accordingly. He is probably right, in the sense that people had been considering leaving even before the riot. Until the mid-fifties, the migration had consisted mostly of caste Hindus. Namasudras and other Hindu cultivators were waiting to see how they might fare in this new land free of high-caste landlords. Sunil had told us it was shortly before the riot that the alliance between Namasudra and Muslim leadership broke apart. In fact, a new constitution instituted two years later still assured protection for Scheduled Caste peoples.[1] But Sunil's impressionistic memory described a growing sense of foreboding, the onset of disbelief among Namasudras that they would be welcomed to power by the Muslim majority.

Economically, too, Namasudras had had a chance to see the country recoup from the misfortunes of Independence and to test the direction from which new winds would blow. By 1954 many were convinced that continuing hardship was to be their lot. It was true that new land had become available for redistribution. But the quantities were small, and resources for its cultivation by an impoverished peasantry, Namasudra or Muslim, continued to be lacking. For many, the riot was not the sole reason to leave, but only the last in a chain of disappointments.

At the same time, we should not underrate the drama of the event itself. It was the first experience any of the villagers had ever had of force on that scale. Never before had a facing-down lasted three days, and never had it drawn such huge crowds. Never had such an array of policemen and officials appeared in the village, and never had guns been fired and people slain. Every oral historian of the riot emphasized those points. The lesson was there to be learned; the dialogue of action had taken on a new and, for many, a daunting seriousness. What exactly it meant to those who left in its aftermath we do not know from accounts so far. Everyone I spoke to had chosen to stay. Many people had been shaky in that decision, but their point of view was still that of those who remained behind. It would be illustrative to interview people from Panipur in India, an endeavor of some difficulty given problems of locating expatriates from a particular locality, but still worth doing.

How many people actually left Panipur in the aftermath of the riot is difficult to determine. Statistics are sketchy at best. Nonetheless, some crude reflection of shifting populations can be seen from the following table showing the percentage of the population that was Muslim:[2]

	Faridpur district (old)	Madaripur subdiv./Zila	Rajoir thana
1901	62	60	n.a.
1931	64	71	50
1961	74	85	58
1981	81	84	61

The proportion of Hindus in the *thana* (a police district, the smallest administrative unit for which statistics are reported) went from 50 percent in 1931 to 42 percent in 1961. It continued to fall thereafter, reaching 39 percent in 1981. The Bangladeshi gazetteer neatly accounts for the rising percentage of Muslims in Faridpur district by citing higher Muslim population growth and migration into the district in 1947.[3] It is, understandably, in the government's interest to downplay the departure of disgruntled Hindus and cite instead a flow of people into the country. Anecdotal data contradicts that explanation, however. Everybody we interviewed commented on the departure of local Hindus for India, and nobody mentioned a noticeable arrival of Indian Muslims. In the thirty-year period spanning Partition the Hindu rate of population growth was absolutely flat in Rajoir *thana*, but the Muslim population increased 36 percent. It is hard to believe that Muslim numbers would have increased sharply and Hindus not at all had there not been a selective migration. So unlikely is a drop in birth rates sufficient to account for a zero population growth that the only other plausible explanation would be extraordinarily high death rates among Hindus, and one would certainly expect an event so dire to appear in anecdotal evidence.

Nobody was quite sure of the current ratio of Hindus to Muslims in Panipur itself. For one thing, definitions are foggy. If you ask, "How many Muslims and Hindus are there here?" people give different answers depending on their conception of "here." Sunil supposed the numbers were about even in Panipur. But whatever the actual figures, they were less relevant than impressions; he and the Muslims knew full well that overall Hindus were a minority. To silence the Hindus, nothing more was needed than the anticipation that Muslims would invoke their majority in a confrontation. "It is a Muslim country," said Sunil. If the other community attacked, "we couldn't defend ourselves. We wouldn't have any avenue of escape."

Then and Now: Peace and Fear

While some Namasudras left the community, others accepted the new conditions and stayed. Some people told us nothing had changed, but everyone who made that claim was either a caste Hindu or was speaking when Muslims were present. "Present conditions are quite good," said Mr. Ghosh, sitting side by side with Altaf. "If things go on this way, we'll have no problem."

But few cultivators, either Namasudra or Muslim, told us that relations between the communities remained the same after the riot. "In our hearts we have never reconciled," Sunil said. "We still have the apprehension that it could happen again in the future." We asked what had happened since the riot to keep that fear alive:

Now and then there's scattered trouble. . . . In P_____ they damaged our crops. . . . Cows eat our crops. They [the Muslims] cut our paddy. If we try to protest, they attack us, the minority community, and speak aggressively. They often beat us if we speak up. And if we again protest, because we are not altogether a minority right here, then they call other Muslims from other places where they are a majority, and they gather here. So at that point we have to go to them and beg their forgiveness.

Day-to-day transactions between communities, now as then, are mediated by relations of power. I would venture that Mr. Ghosh was more vulnerable than he admitted at that moment and that Sunil was less endangered than he thought. Educated caste Hindus told me frequently of subtle ways in which they felt disadvantaged in present-day Bangladesh. Some defended their own disadvantage, advocating affirmative action to help Muslims make up for their severe oppression before. An elderly Hindu schoolteacher in a nearby town, for instance, told the story of how he was passed over for promotion to a headmastership in favor of a less qualified Muslim. Thoughtfully, he commented, "He deserved the position. I knew more, could do a better job, but how else would it ever change?"

On the other side, Sunil had prospered since Independence. He complained about hardships, many of them natural (at least in his view), not political. The soil had lost its fertility; population density had increased ungovernably. But within the parameters of a destitute nation, he had done relatively well. His children were highly educated, his prosperity far greater than that of his forefathers.

Yet Sunil's sense of danger cannot be discounted. It was based on intangibles, but its reality was corroborated by many others. In mixed company, the theme of Hindus' fear was muted but nonetheless apparent. Our conversation with Altaf and Mr. Ghosh, for instance, read like a dramatization of quiet tensions and underground conflicts. Mr. Ghosh ricocheted between protestations of camaraderie with his Muslim neighbors and defensive-sounding proclamations of his rights:

This is our land also. We have as much right as the Muslims have to this land. . . . This is our birth-land, so we should stay here with the Muslims. If they do anything to us, we can reply [stand up for our rights].

From across the room a quiet voice cut in:

At night we can't sleep.

The speaker was a visitor from another district, a little man who had been lounging on one of the two huge beds in the room. From time to time I had noticed him listening attentively, but his face was in shadow, and I had not registered his responses.

Now his comment galvanized the room. Several voices hurried to correct any negative impression the man's comment might have given me. He was speaking of bandits, not communal friction, they insisted.

Embarrassed, the visitor agreed:

The fear is not so much about communalism, but of looting. . . . Most Muslims don't make trouble for us. Some good Muslims want to protect us from harm. But there are some outsiders, not those from our neighborhood, but people from outside, some *mastans* [criminals] who do these things.

All of which was well and good, but he could carry appeasement only so far:

Although most people don't harm us, even so they often oppress us in little ways. For instance, they take the fruit from our trees, fish from our ponds. That of course is a kind of oppression: we can't eat our own fruit and fish.

Altaf quickly disassociated himself and his folk from such behavior:

No one would dare to steal other people's fruit in my area!

The pendulum that was the caste Hindu, Mr. Ghosh, facing a choice between abandoning another Hindu and crossing Altaf, an influential Muslim, hovered uneasily in the middle:

Maybe there are ten Muslim houses and one Hindu house. Then the children may go to that house and eat coconuts. That might happen. You may chase them off, and they may talk fresh. But that's not saying anything about society. . . .

In our Panipur Union . . . nothing of that sort happens. We don't have problems like that here . . . . If we have any trouble in our Hindu*para*, Muslims help us. . . . The Muslims are always sympathetic to us.

Perhaps what Mr. Ghosh said was as much wish as description, a sort of hopeful injunction to Altaf to be sympathetic. In a certain sense, of course, it was true: there was no trouble between the communities most of the time. But when alone, Hindus revealed a different reality, a hidden transcript of genuine and abiding anxiety. Almost universally Hindus, both in Panipur and elsewhere in Bangladesh, privately told us that they felt threatened. As peaceful as relations normally were, they said, they had no confidence that they would continue to be so if some event crystallized contention. Many expressed a desire to leave, to resettle in India. The more disadvantaged they were, in general the more strongly they wished to leave.

Reflecting a relative sense of powerlessness, women often gave us a more negative assessment of the situation than men. While Altaf, Mr. Ghosh, and the visitor from another district went on with their conversation, I turned aside to Basantibala. "How do *you* feel about staying in Bangladesh?" I asked. She said under her breath, "My son is here, he has a job. It wouldn't be good to go."

"If he could get a job there . . . ?" I asked. She thought; her eyes shifted toward Altaf-uddin; she scowled and said with her chin tucked down, "This is our country. We're here. My desire is to stay."

In the boat going home, our guide explained that Basantibala's son had no college degree. He worked in the local high school, a well-reputed institution founded by an ancestor. As a descendant of the founder, he was guaranteed a job—"has rights" was the expression the guide used. But if he went to India, he would have no privileges and would be thoroughly unemployable.

This sense of the economic boundaries to their options was common in women's statements. After I talked with the school-teacher who was so generous and understanding about his loss of a headmaster's post, I interviewed his wife. Her point of view was a little different:

Do you like it here?
I have no choice but to like it. My children are here. I'm reconciled to being here. My two daughters are in India. They are married in Calcutta. I used to go often, but now I can't go. My sons, one is in N_____, one in K_____, and the other Dhaka. My youngest daughter, too, is in Dhaka. . . . We've now bought this house.

My eldest son and the middle one often say among themselves that this is a Muslim country and they don't want to stay here. But the youngest one, he is very friendly with Muslims. The eldest wants very much to go to India.

How's the situation here?
Not so bad, but sometimes it gets a little hot. For example, now we are hearing the story of Ram Mundir in Ayodhya.° There's a little tension among Muslims here over that issue. Seeing these feelings among Muslims, we are a little distressed. . . .

People talk about it. If the temple is built there, there is bound to be a reaction here. . . . An advocate came . . . and said, "*Mashima* [Aunt], there is a conflict going on around the issue of Ram Mundir and Babir

° Ayodhya is a town in India where Hindus and Muslims were contesting a holy site. Babir Mosque was built in the sixteenth century on a spot that some Hindus claim was the birthplace of the god Rama. A major campaign was launched by a Hindu fundamentalist political party to destroy the mosque and build a temple, Ram Mundir, in its place. In 1990, governments were toppled and hundreds killed as a result of the Ayodhya movement. Hostilities spilled over to neighboring Bangladesh, where Muslims retaliated against Hindu aggression aimed at their co-religionists in India. Although Bangladeshi disturbances were relatively mild, they were already arousing anxiety among Hindus in Panipur when I was there.

Mosque. Things are getting a little tense. We're feeling a reaction among the Muslims." Although nothing has happened so far, people will try to do something. Especially since the Muslims of M_____ [her town] are touchy about these issues.

What will you do if there's trouble?

What can we do? We have to live here, whether we live or die. We do want to go, but my younger son won't leave, so we stay. He is in K_____, and he's left us here to see to the house. We are ailing, we might die any time.

For this elderly woman, there is little alternative to staying. Her preferences are clear, but her choices are dictated by circumstances outside herself—the plight of women in much of the world. Dependent on husband and children, she remains where she must.

Women spoke so much more freely than men about their dissatisfactions, it seemed to me, because they *were* truly more dissatisfied. Upper-caste or -class women (Basantibala represents the former, the teacher's wife the latter) felt more vulnerable, less certain of protection than did their more powerful men. Men operate in public arenas, where they interact with people of the other community and where rules of behavior offer some controls. But women inhabit a private sphere, which is both more protected and, paradoxically, less predictable. Confined more to their own households, they did not socialize with Muslims and could not draw on memories of personal friendliness. As public symbols, women are frequent markers in the struggle between communities; people sometimes illustrated tales of conflict with complaints about how their women were mistreated—girls sexually harassed, women spoken to harshly in public places, and so on. The women, too, seemed to experience themselves as targets of inter-community hostility. Standing as chips in a battle in which they could take little direct action (remember Golam's mother: "She was almost mad. . . . Nobody paid any attention to her"), women expressed their sense of powerlessness, their inability either to ward off impending danger or to remove themselves from harm's way. Moreover, many of these Hindu women saw their menfolk as unable to protect them, a perception that reflects the generalized sense of weakness in the community as a whole.

Were the Hindus paranoid, imagining ill will that was unreal?

No Muslim said anything to us that approached an overt communal threat. But it was not hard to pick up a fighting spirit and a keen sense of community among them. People referred frequently to the past, remembering old mistreatment, and they were clearly now endowed with a militant sense of their rights to redress. Occasionally that resentment reappeared in action. Soon after these interviews, in the town where we had interviewed the schoolteacher's wife who had been nervous about Ayodhya, Muslims rioted— exactly as she had feared.

We asked Mofizuddin and Nayeb Ali whether there had been other conflicts in Panipur since the big riot. They told us of one incident in the *bazar*. It happened in the early sixties, escalating from an incident so trivial that even Mofizuddin was embarrassed:

It was about buying an ordinary jackfruit. I'm ashamed to admit it. [Laughs.] It was Madhan Thakur, and someone from a house on the other side of the river who came to sell milk. He wanted to buy the same jackfruit. . . . Madhan Thakur, from the Namasudra area, at that time he was fifteen or sixteen years old, he fought with two Muslim brothers.

Nayeb Ali joined in:

I was there, I took part. When we heard about it, I went to the fight. I have evidence [raises his sleeve and shows a long scar]. I was very much involved. Still today, if someone said, "Come and fight!" I would go.

How old are you now?

Eighty-five. If we could eat like you, we could still go on fighting.

Why did you want to fight?

. . . It was a sense of community. When I heard that they hurt my people, I wanted to beat them up. They'd feel the same way if their people were hurt.

If it had been a fight between two Muslims, maybe from different villages, would you have gotten involved?

No, if it had been between two Muslims, I'd have tried to get a compromise first. But the majority of the sellers in the *bazar* were Hindus; we were the majority of the buyers. It was my cousin who was hurt by the Hindus; maybe they'd think we were soft and couldn't fight back. So

Part Two

Making Sense

Chapter Six

Lessons of Panipur

And so there was some trouble with cows in Panipur. A riot happened and ended and became a story, and life returned to normal. But it was a new normal, not totally unlike the old one, but different in important respects. For the villagers, the story became a morality tale, told with more or less humor, more or less regret, more or less bravado, more or less wonder, depending on the teller, the hearer, the purpose, and the moment. "How can it be?" asked Sunil. "They damage our crops, and when we protest there is this reaction. It was totally counter to the social rules."

I, too, wondered what had happened just then to cause such a change in the "social rules." Why had personal enmity suddenly burst into flames of collective conflict? How had neighbors come to see each other as enemies and to act on that idea? These two communities had lived peacefully for most of time. "The fact is," Mofizuddin told me, "we Hindus and Muslims cultivate our lands in the same place. We share common borders." Neither Sunil nor Golam seemed to me fanatically wedded to a religious viewpoint. Day-to-day life in the village revealed some predictable pigheadedness but little communal prejudice. People knew each other too well for that, knew their neighbors' personal stories, who married whom and how he treated her, whose fortunes prospered and whose failed, whose crop was well tended and whose was neglected.

Indeed, it was just this sense of easy familiarity between communities, crossed with a certain tension ordinarily unspoken yet intuitively perceptible, that gave rise to the central questions of my research. It seemed clear that there existed a potential for hostility between members of the two communities, but there equally existed its opposite. Why conflict erupted when and as it did was not obvious. The huge explosions of communalism that had accompanied independence from Britain and the formation of Pakistan were seven years in the past. The region surrounding this village had never been heavily involved and was generally peaceful at the moment. What transpired to tip the balance?

I wanted to explore the steps from neighborliness to warfare, because it seemed likely that if we could understand how these Bengali villagers conceived their riot and their contending communities, we might learn more about how people generally "think conflict." That is not a new inquiry. There are numbers of literatures focused on the question of why people rebel against authority, for instance.[1] But most of these involve scenarios of dominance and submission. The question they consider is when and why people reach limits of endurance for unequal power relations. In Panipur, however, the conflict was between peers, a situation not at all uncommon. When Americans of different races clash, or ethnic minorities in Eastern Europe, or blacks in South Africa, similar challenges are presented to analytic frameworks for understanding social conflict.[2]

Theories of Communalism

Discussions of communalism divide more or less according to three tenets of human behavior:

People are beasts driven by innate aggressive instincts.
People are misled into betraying their own true interests.
People act out a drama that is meaningful within the frame of their own lives.

The first explanation parallels the viewpoint of Le Bon and Freud and rests on assumptions about unconscious antisocial forces within the human psyche. It characterizes an imperialist view of communalism: tension between Hindus and Muslims is inbred, and so ancient as to constitute unchangeable character. A British official looking back after Independence summed up this viewpoint neatly:

During the long period of inter-communal tension we were directed to form Conciliation Committees of leading Hindus and Muslims wherever the situation seemed to require it. I formed one, and there learned what our statesmen failed wholly to understand[:] that, after all the arguments have been rehearsed and considered, there remains a residue of pure prejudice, pigheadedness, fanaticism—call it what you will—which makes any solution of inter-communal disputes on rational grounds impossible and necessitates a forceful decision by an outside party. This is as true of music before mosques as it is of Kashmir, but it is a principle which neither the British Government of 1947 nor U.N.O. [United Nations Organization] assimilated. The former, starting from the assumption that we, the British, had no right to be in India[,] were thus led up the garden path to a point where the atavistic impulses of the masses took charge and wrecked the work of centuries.[3]

At its kindest, British belief had it that these smoldering conflicts must be benevolently contained.[4] At its worst, the English colonists saw such strains as an opportunity:

If we destroy or desecrate Mussalman Mosques or Brahmin temples we do exactly what is wanting to band the two antagonist races against ourselves. . . . As we must rule 150 million of people by a handful (more or less small) of Englishmen, let us do it in the manner best calculated to leave them divided (as in religion and national feeling they already are) and to inspire them with the greatest possible awe of our power and with the least possible suspicion of our motives.[5]

"Atavistic impulses" powerfully justify a policy of divide-and-rule, especially since the people are already divided "in religion and national feeling." The theoretical underpinnings are clear: people (at least *these* people) are beset by base instinct that must be tamed—or utilized—by "civilized" outside powers.

On the flip side of this self-serving British coin was a predictable nationalist response. Instead of communalist instincts justifying British rule, in this second view it was precisely British rule that created communalism. The phenomenon was wholly provoked by divide-and-rule policies.[6] Indians, both Muslims and Hindus, were victims of a conscious policy imposed upon a population that had hitherto lived in harmony.

This view is very similar to a Marxist version that saw the masses acted upon by indigenous people seeking power: "Communalism was the false consciousness of the historical process of the last 150 years because, objectively, no real conflict between the interests of Hindus and Muslims existed," wrote Bipan Chandra:

> Communalism involved "either conscious deception or unconscious self-deception"; the communalist was either deceiving others or, more likely, he was deceiving himself as well . . . because the interests he claimed to represent did not exist in real life and the demands he undertook to fulfil were incapable of being fulfilled.[7]

By implication, communalism was a mistake. It was promulgated by self-interested blackguards (the British, or communalists with particular agendas) and accepted by unconscious peoples who allowed themselves to be deceived into acting against their own true interests. To accept this explanation is to make unnecessary any inquiry into substantive reasons for clashes between communities, since it assumes there are no such reasons. But it raises the very important question of why people allow themselves to be duped.

Another variation on the same theme is an updated version that blames nationalist politicians rather than the British:

> The division of India . . . took place due to power-mongers like Nehru and Jinnah, who were willing to risk communal riots [to further their own ends]. . . . They put forward the idea that Hindus and Muslims could not live together, then [solved the "problem"] by dividing the country. They were happy because they succeeded in achieving their goal of ruling as heads of state.[8]

From a vantage point almost half a century post-Partition, the British seem less likely villains than do the politicians who have so badly failed, in the view of this correspondent, to solve the pressing problems of nationhood.

But the underlying theory is the same: people are somehow duped into acting against their own interests. There is something about humankind, according to the implicit assumption, that creates a vulnerability to deception. Unwilling to ascribe such passivity to the common man, some post-Independence scholars constructed a third position that challenged the very idea that inter-community conflict was a problem. They reframed the discussion, removing normative assessments and painting communalism as a constructive process. Ethnic conflict was simply another way to negotiate demands and power, wrote N. C. Saxena:

Communal movements, especially of minority groups, can be seen as a form of social movements which are "organised attempts of a group to bring about change in the face of resistance from other groups or the government through collective mobilisation based on an ideology." Such movements can foster self-esteem and pride within a group which subsequently hasten economic growth and all-round development of that group.[9]

Saxena's theory mirrored an American sociological argument of the 1950s, in which some writers cast conflict as a positive event and contesters as contributing to the social process.[10] To see community conflicts as social movements is a positive contribution, because it allows us to ask a set of questions that are irrelevant if people are either beasts or dupes: What is the goal of a given confrontation? Why is it happening now? Why in this form?

The problem with Saxena's theory, however, is that, while it dignifies human beings, it fails to emphasize the unequal power arrangements within which they live out their lives. Saxena is thereby led to eclipse some very important differences between "other groups" and government. That rebellious peasants may be massacred by government bullets diminishes the esteem-generating benefits of protest. Ruling elites, meanwhile, remain protected, not only from physical force but also from the political imperatives of a disenfranchised people. Indeed, it is within this paradigm of powerlessness that phenomena such as communalism emerge as means to negotiate power. Exactly how and why that happens is the concern at hand. Although his description of communalism as social movement helpfully challenges conventional wisdom codified behind walls of value judgment, Saxena leaves himself no way to address that central question.

What Saxena does do is to lead us to questions of agency. To see communal conflict as a meaningful process of working out issues genuinely relevant to the lives of those involved is to see the actors as central to their own drama. The questions we are considering become very fundamental ones, not just about how two groups of peasants came to blows, but about how people engage their own historic fates.

Ideas about where the individual fits into the process of making history have been hotly debated by historians and activists for a very long time.[11] Broadly stated, there are two opposite theories: that history is a series of momentous deeds by great leaders, or that abstract material dynamics are the force driving social change. Marx and his followers argued the latter position, because they opposed the idea that progress was the property of elite men. That power was controlled by small numbers of upper-class rulers was a phenomenon of particular periods of history, they contended, but not an inevitable fact of life. Ordinary working people could take power, indeed *would* take power as dynamics produced by economics and technology necessitated that change.[12] Their viewpoint opened a space for revolutionary activism, but it also gave rise to several theoretical problems. If history is the inevitable outcome of abstract forces, where is the motivation or place for willed action by living humans? If ordinary folk can take power, why have they not? It was to answer this latter question that theories of false consciousness (such as Bipan Chandra's) were proposed, but they in turn implied a passive naiveté among the masses that did not ring true to many activists and thinkers.

Some Indian historians gathered in a school of thought called Subaltern Studies have recently confronted this dilemma by objecting, as does Saxena, to views of common people as either dupes or beasts. But they go beyond Saxena in rejecting his neutrality and positing a world polarized by power inequities and injustices. Colonized nations suffered a three-tiered power structure. On top were the imperialists; in India, these were the British. Next came the local elites, who also formed the core of the nationalist revolt. Below were the subaltern masses—peasants, workers, laborers. Rewriting history from the perspective of the bottom gives new meanings to events like communalism:

By making the security of the state into the central problematic of peasant insurgency, [colonial historiography] assimilated the latter as merely an element in the career of colonialism. In other words, the peasant was denied recognition as a subject of history in his own right even for a project that was all his own. . . . Even when a writer was apparently under no obligation to think like a bureaucrat affected by the trauma of a recent jacquerie, he was conditioned to write the history of a peasant revolt as if it were some other history—that of the Raj, or of Indian nationalism, or of socialism, depending on his particular ideological bent. The result . . . has been to exclude the insurgent as the subject of his own history.[13]

Subalternists draw deeply on the work of the Italian revolutionary Antonio Gramsci. Gramsci sought to reconcile the paradox of human agency in a history driven by material forces; he did so by exploring the role of ideas, which he placed in the realm of social relations of power.[14] Culture, he claimed, is controlled by those in power and produces a hegemonic, or dominating, philosophy; indeed, it dictates the range of consciousness within which debate and inquiry can take place. Dominant classes thus rule, not by the gun, but by the power of ideas. Gramsci was much influenced by Marx's formulation, "The ideas of the ruling class are in every epoch the ruling ideas."[15]

Anthropologists like Clifford Geertz took the investigation of culture and ideas further, looking at the socially generated nature of cultural institutions, including that most natural-seeming set of ideas called common sense, which Gramsci had made problematic.[16] Geertz also studied religion as culture, a discussion to which I'll return below.[17] Diminished in the anthropological approach, however, were the questions of power that most interested Gramsci. Geertz gave us a nuanced and more encompassing understanding of the institutions Gramsci identified as hegemonic, but he himself delved little into the manner in which they in fact exercised hegemony over the willingness of individuals to comply with power or to protest.

Many Subalternists use sophisticated tools of cultural analysis in their effort to engage the debate, although they tend to shy away from explorations of the terrain of individual consciousness and community dialogue. Culture is for them a coin used in transactions of power. But the nature of the transaction as perceived by the insurgent herself remains mysterious. Since they tend to view matters from a perspective other than that of the actors, what they can say about the nature of the subaltern masses as subjects is limited.

Clearly, those who do not wield state power are severely constrained by oppressive institutions, an observation at the heart of notions of false consciousness. Yet they are also capable of exercising will and creativity in shaping their world, as both Saxena and the Subalternists recognize. How are we to resolve that contradiction? It is my attempt in this work to explore the ways people who are relatively powerless take power, or, more accurately, negotiate it, within the limitations of institutional arrangements they cannot effectively challenge. We can define a fourth position in the debate about communalism, an elaboration of Saxena's view: People act out a particular drama, attempting to renegotiate rights and powers in forms limited and distorted by oppression. The particular frame in which they engage in meaningful struggles, that is to say, is constituted by unequal power relations that constrain the spaces within which they can move toward well-being.

The riot in Panipur was an upheaval, not a revolution. It did not question fundamental social structures such as property relations, because those relations as such were not up for negotiation. But within those structures it did rearrange power. Once we view it as a renegotiation of rights and privileges, we can begin to address the question of why it took a communal form on a more subtle level, the level of the consciousness and interests of players who were very much its subjects. The inquiry now moves into a territory between the poles of the Subalternist analysis—structure and culture—placing the individuals who compose those collectivities at the center of the study.

A Matter of Method

The Panipur riot has several characteristics that make it especially useful for this project. One reason studies of the internal landscape of social conflict are few and far between has to do with the problem of method, well described by Sandria Freitag: "Crowd behavior . . . is a problematic historical topic, for we cannot know the thoughts of the individuals who make up a crowd."[18] When people produce no written records (and, historically, writing has been a luxury of elites), the only way to know their thoughts is to ask the individuals concerned, an enterprise made impossible beyond a limited stretch of time and hard enough in any case. The drama in Panipur was recent enough to allow oral accounts by participants to be readily available, yet it was far enough in the past for its causes and consequences to be digested and defined. It was a finite event, arising at one identifiable moment and ending at another. I could therefore study it in satisfying detail.

Even more, the riot provided a focal point upon which different stories coalesced. From studying the differences among accounts we can learn much about the processes of formulation. Because it was an unusual event in the history of Panipur—nobody there had ever rioted before—memories were sharp and dramatic, symbolic grains around which ideological conclusions had crystallized.

Indeed, village riots as a category were rare in East Bengal. As I have noted before, overt communal warfare was believed to be an urban phenomenon. Some rural incidents had occurred before the mid-1950s, but they tended to be relatively minor.[19] In the cities, however, personal passions had collided with diverse political agendas, creating explosions of violence in which many thousands died; by the mid-1950s a large section of the urban Bengali population had been personally touched by violence between the communities. The massive slaughters of the late 1940s were city-based. Villagers had heard stories of that violence; many interviewees told me of a relative or friend injured in Calcutta, or of someone caught in a distant city when all hell had broken loose. But their own villages had not been visited with such mayhem. The Panipur riot thus has the virtues of virginity; the villagers may have been touched by stories from elsewhere, but they themselves had no tradition of rioting on this scale. The experience of conflict alters forever how people feel about each other, as well as how they experience themselves as Muslim or Hindu or whatever, and how they calculate their options to act. In Panipur, people were having that experience for the first time.

Much of the urban history of community conflict was intertwined with traditions of political organizing. Mass campaigns to recruit people to a point of view, to join a nationalist campaign or support a day of advocacy for the formation of Pakistan, for instance, were frequent. But the infamous "outside organizer," that mythic culprit blamed so regularly when "innocent masses" rebel all over the world, was absent from Panipur. It was not that organizers had never worked the area. Indeed, Faridpur district is known as a familiar arena for communist organizing, as well as being the home of well-established *dacoits*, or bandits, perhaps the most organized groups of all.* But in no account did anyone ever contend that a stranger stirred up tempers or engineered action,

---

*An often-quoted jingle describes Faridpur: "*Chur chotta khajuria ghur | A niya Faridpur.*" (Thieves, cheats, date molasses, | These things are Faridpur.)

and that is unusual in histories of contentious activity. To trace through stories of outside agitators would be a very useful exercise, but that they did not figure in accounts of the Panipur riot lends its study a simplicity that allows us to focus on the local people themselves.

There is yet another sense in which the Panipur riot represents a "pure" example of the genre. Not only in its enactment but also in its recollection it was isolated from outside influence to an uncommon degree. Nowhere was the story of Panipur publicized. When in our over-reported world do we have an opportunity to build a mental picture uninfluenced by the media? I found myself in the very unusual circumstance of constructing a history exclusively from the accounts of participants. Not only was my mental movie of the riot free of anything I had read or heard about it outside the village, but the Panipur people's own recollection was similarly insulated. What we "know" of something like a public gathering is usually compounded of our own experience and the stories told by others about that experience. Some of those stories are "official," either actually so—the reconstructions of police and courts and administrators—or made official in spirit through the power of the electronic or printed word. Few Bengali villagers are literate, but written material nonetheless finds its way into community consciousness through transactions with literate others. For instance, had the riot been known to the development workers of the area, educated people who today represent a major link between village and city, the people of Panipur would have had reflected back to them other views of their own history. Newcomers would have asked questions about it, and those questions would have suggested judgments and opinions. The organization's programs might even have been influenced, however subtly, by anxiety about a possible repetition of the event. In many ways, overt and unstated, the experience of the villagers would have engaged the reactions of the outsiders and would have been altered in the process.

I was hearing stories composed of direct sensation and firsthand discussion, an ideal circumstance for studying the thought processes and interactions of the people involved. To be sure, the riot was well digested within the village community. Nobody's recollection was exactly pristine. Everybody had heard others' accounts and had recited their own often enough to have transformed raw experience into a good tale. But the layers of consciousness created by nonimmediate sources, by written reports and electronic depictions and the responses of outsiders, were missing from my introduction to the Panipur story. Consequently, I could listen with more simplicity to the processes of formulation of the conflict by those involved. I could also track more cleanly the lines of storytelling to subsequent generations, the ways the tale of the wayward cow and its consequences helped to shape community relations after the event. [20]

Lessons of Panipur

What can we learn about the concoction of the Panipur riot from the stories I was told? Long before I reached Panipur, I had formed a number of opinions. I believed that people were not uncivilized beasts whose base instincts erupted as soon as society's control weakened. Although I could see that disinformation existed, both in the form of generalizations about the intentions of one group or another and also as rumors, I was not prepared to accept that the villagers had been duped. It seemed clear to me that the process of two groups coming to blows involved a good deal of interaction among people in communities they defined for themselves, and that those communities included influential leaders, but I suspected the process was more complex than a simple dynamic of leaders dictating actions to obedient followers. While I knew that religion figured into the story, at the very least as the formal basis for sorting out communities, it was hard for me to believe these fights were in fact religious conflicts.

What seemed to me to need explaining was why the communities became defined as they did, why conflict occurred when and as it did, and why the individuals composing the communities did or did not join in. As I studied the interviews, three conclusions emerged:

1. The villagers chose to riot. They were not swept mindlessly away on tides of passion, nor were they forced by circumstances to behave in ways destructive to their interests, although both passion and circumstance figured into their decisions.

2. Decision-making was a process located in communities that themselves were chosen and reconstituted for the purposes of action. In the heat of conflict, why the villagers looked to associations defined by religious identity rather than any of the several other groupings available to them is not obvious and must be explained by examining both cultural and historically specific meanings attached to the communities.

3. The decision to riot was deeply informed by an awareness of history understood in terms of lived experience. The act of rioting integrated the village into a moment of national transformation which until then had been abstract and distant. In so doing, the rioters brought change home to the village and thus took their place in the making of their own history.

Let us look at each of these contentions in more detail.

Chapter Seven

Self and Decision

1. The villagers chose to riot. They were not swept mindlessly away on tides of passion, nor were they forced by circumstances to behave in ways destructive to their interests, although both passion and circumstance figured into their decisions.

We sat down together and decided to hold a meeting. . . . It was decided that all the people would assemble. . . .

It was decided that it would be unwise to waste any time, and we should start the fight the next morning.

Our *matabbars* decided that there would be no *nishputi* [compromise]. They often made compromises, but then again there would be a fight. So there was no need to compromise.

In each of these statements, Golam reports a decision a group of people made to act in public in a certain way. That the villagers chose to riot is obvious; that they did so by some process over which they exercised control, that they were not swept away on waves of passion or compelled against their wills by circumstance, is moot. Nayeb Ali expressed his sense of outrage quite passionately:

When I heard that they hurt my people, I wanted to beat them up. They'd feel the same way if their people were hurt.

Emotions—anger, fear, surprise, resentment, hurt—figured formidably in the villagers' accounts. But at the same time it was clear that those very emotions were familiar to the rioters; they had often felt them and yet not rioted. Again and again, Muslims told me how long-suffering they felt, and how long they had remained quiet. At the moment when they took action, something more than out-of-control emotionality was afoot, and what that was must be explained. In my view, emotion, far from being separate from or antagonistic to reasoned choice, is an integral part of that process. Decisions, particularly those we are considering here—decisions to act contentiously in a public sphere—are a process of collating information of a variety of sorts. Emotions are one form of information.[1]

Agency, Irrationality, and the Unconscious

To claim that the villagers acted reasonably is to engage the question of agency on another, more individual level. It is the premise of much psychological theory that people are bounded by their personal histories, that their options for action are limited by what they have experienced before:

Adults unconsciously look to recreate, and are often unable to avoid recreating, aspects of their early relationships, especially to the extent that these relationships were unresolved, ambivalent, and repressed.[2]

If the fundamental premise of psychology is that behavior is dictated by dynamics established in childhood or by biologically given drives and instincts, then the room for choice is severely limited. Not history-writ-large, not oppressive institutions or dominant classes, not social structure, that is, but psychic structure determines the boundaries within which individuals can construct their worlds. Freud himself considered human aggression a dismal given:

Men are not gentle creatures who . . . defend themselves if they are attacked; they are, on the contrary, creatures among whose instinctual endowments is to be reckoned a powerful share of aggressiveness. As a result, their neighbour is for them not only a potential helper or sexual object, but also someone who tempts them to satisfy their aggressiveness on him, to exploit his capacity for work without compensation, to use him sexually without his consent, to seize his possessions, to humiliate him, to cause him pain, to torture and to kill him. . . . In circumstances that are favourable to it, when the mental counter-forces which ordinarily inhibit it are out of action, . . . it . . . manifests itself spontaneously and reveals man as a savage beast to whom consideration towards his own kind is something alien.[3]

"If we could eat like you," said Nayeb Ali at age eighty-five, showing his scars and pithily underscoring Freud's dark eloquence, "we could still go on fighting."

Theories of irrationality attempt to explain what seem to the observer to be irreconcilable contradictions in behavior.[4] Those serried ranks of peasants faced off in the field behaved in a way difficult to explain. "People . . . are animals," observed Altaf-uddin, in seeming agreement with Freud. But to rest content with so simple a view leaves us ill equipped to understand why and how people came together in the particular groupings they did, what the nature of their discourse was, or why they acted as they did at that particular moment. Nayeb Ali wanted to "beat them up" when he heard "they hurt my people." How did he come to define "my people" and "them" as he did? And why did he elect to indulge his feelings when and as he did, not earlier, not later, not in the marketplace or at the polls?

Students of social conflict have tended to work around such primary questions of psychology.[5] In fact, the conceptual language of psychology is ill equipped to address them, couched as it generally is in ahistorical and asocial terms like *instinct* and *drive*. Social psychology needs more culture- and history-specific concepts if it is to develop adequate theories about groups in conflict.[6]

In the discussion that follows I want to suggest a framework for understanding the behavior of community combatants, to aid an analysis of the construction of communities and the ways people translate historic change into personal facts. First I will look at work by Nancy Chodorow on the formation of gender identity, because it suggests a model for integrating analyses of self and society. I will suggest, however, that Chodorow's model omits an important link in the chain from psychological development to behavior in the world, that is, it lacks a vehicle for translating personal experience into ideology and action. I will sketch some possibilities for filling the gap.[7]

Identities and Ideologies

Nayeb Ali's statement "When I heard that they hurt my people, I wanted to beat them up" demonstrated his sense of identity as a part of a Muslim community. Identity is socially based (without a group, identity has no meaning; its function is precisely to locate "me" in "us"), and it is also deeply formative of a sense of self. Identity is crafted from a set of ideas about similarities and differences, loyalties and obligations. It is highly emotional, plucking heartstrings, raising hackles, stirring fears and hopes. At the same time, identity is strongly grounded in institutional arrangements. To belong to one group or another might be of only passing interest (a fact of cultural enrichment, perhaps), were it not true that such identities correspond to highly entrenched lines of power and inequality.

Consider gender identities in this light. Chodorow's work on the subject is revelatory because she challenges some of our most tender assumptions, especially the notion that mothering is innately a female activity:

Women's role as we know it is an historical product. The development of industrial capitalism in the West entailed that women's role in the family become increasingly concerned with personal relations and psychological stability. Mothering is most eminently a psychologically based role.[8]

She goes on to argue that the gendered structure of the family (women mother, men don't) reproduces gender in the children reared there, and in turn gendered ways of being in the world reproduce the unequal relations that constitute patriarchy in its modern form. Her analysis rests on an asymmetry introduced into the developmental process for young girls and boys by the fact that mothering is so exclusively women's business. Infants of both sexes experience their primary care-giver, their mother, as self. When the time comes to define themselves as gendered beings, boys must break away from that earlier global identification with the woman who has mothered them, whereas girls do not. As a result, girls grow up with an unbroken capacity for relationship, while boys lose their sense of relatedness as they shift identity from mother to father.

Of all the reasons why women continue to mother, most prominent are the emotional consequences of the fact that they do. Mothering is preeminently "concerned with personal relationships," those very same relationships for which boys are so ill suited because of the gendered structure of the family. But connectedness comes easily to women, adult versions of the girls whose gender identity remains attuned throughout time to a female mother. What more "natural," therefore, than that women should continue to mother—and thereby continue the process of gender formation that dooms men's participation.

At the same time, a certain set of power relations is also reproduced. Men continue in possession of the well-respected public domain where material power is brokered, and women are consigned to a demeaned domestic arena where the only power to be gained is indirect, through the public actions of husbands and sons. Thus, social structure (specifically, the socially structured family) produces and reproduces psychological characteristics (in this case, gender) which in turn have central significance for the nature of social reality (in this case, patriarchy).

Chodorow's analysis accords well with the insight that institutional arrangements come to be represented in individual psychologies which in turn contribute to the perpetuation of social relations. But it also contains some problems. First of all, it is based on certain assumptions about the family. Not all families consist of two parents, one of each sex. Many families are extended, consisting of many adults under one roof, especially in agricultural societies like South Asia. Even in the industrial West, families take a variety of forms, often including one adult (usually a woman) and several children, and sometimes two adults of the same sex. Chodorow's family is a very particular one—nuclear, isolated, heterosexual. Research has failed to prove that children reared in single-parent families or families with two or more parents of the same sex display significantly altered senses of gender. Effects of culture are profound, as any parent can attest who is trying to steer boys away from guns and girls from dolls.

There are other problems with Chodorow's view as well. Her work has been criticized for its failure to account for change. Sexism, she says, which is linked to the low value assigned to domestic labor—especially mothering—performed by women, can change only when mothering is shared by men. Only then will society view "women's work" as worthy. Yet in the face of Chodorow's paradigm it is difficult to generate any optimism that men will—indeed, that they *can*—mother. How are men, whose capacity to relate is so damaged in childhood, supposed to learn those many relational skills of which modern motherhood consists? Chodorow's analysis may be an argument for long years on a psychoanalytic couch, but it is not an inspiration for political action.

More to the point from a theoretical point of view, it takes a position in the debate about who makes history. Based though it is on an intimate account of subjects within their most personal lives, Chodorow's analysis removes the individual from agency as effectively as does a primitive materialist view that sees history as the product of abstract forces. She is removed this time, not by the dominance of overpowering class force, but through the incorporation of that coercive force in the psyche of the young child where it remains throughout adult life, setting limits to the possibility of men's relationships and therefore to women's choices.

That Chodorow, an ardent advocate of change, ends up facing this dilemma is, I believe, related to the abstractness of the concept of psychic structure. To talk about structure is to say little about the concrete ways in which boys and girls experience and incorporate family relationships and become gendered men and women. How do boys translate the shift in identity from woman to man into feelings and behavior? Psycho-structural theories do not tell us, that is, about how those relationships are *represented* in the minds of living people. To say that a small girl identifies with her mother is to gloss over the complex of thoughts and emotions of which that identity consists. If we do not know exactly how children integrate their experience of their parents' genders into their own self-constructs, then we cannot know how those constructs change.

Let us posit that there is a thick set of ideas and emotions associated with the translation of family and social structure into individual psychology. We need, then, a theory of thought and emotion rather than one of early childhood development. We can look to cognitive psychology for "a theory of personality which maintains that how one thinks largely determines how one feels and behaves."[9] Cognition is often equated with thinking, but in fact it involves a process broader than thought. To George Mandler, a pioneer in the field, "Representation in the widest sense of the term is the central issue in cognitive psychology." [10] By *representation* he means a set of constructs that give rise to actions. Those constructs consist of both thought and feeling. Language is important, because it is the symbolic medium for representation, although it is not the only medium.

In this conception, emotion, which otherwise seems an act of nature, becomes susceptible to analysis as a cognitive process. [11] When Golam's cow ate Kumar's plant, Kumar may or may not have responded with anger. Had the cow belonged to Kumar's father-in-law, his anger would have been a very different emotion, perhaps fastened on the cow rather than its owner. Had there been no other bad blood between the neighbors, Kumar might have retethered the cow in the field and, mildly irritated, delivered a polite remonstrance to Golam. That Kumar became angry enough to retaliate was based on a list of grievances, a computation of a complex sort, drawing ultimately, as we shall see, on his knowledge of a change of state and his consequent reformulation of principles of justice. His action, in other words, resulted from a compendium of thought and feeling, of belief and impulse, interrelated in a very particular way.

Social Bases of Cognition

This example suggests another dimension of choice that is very significant for understanding social conflict: choice occurs in a social context and is made up of shared ideas. In recent years a new field of microsociology has arisen to study this link between society and psyche. Calling themselves sociologists of emotion, such thinkers as Arlie Hochschild argue for a view of emotions as socially influenced and having social function. [12] In her pioneering study of flight attendants, Hochschild writes:

What we think of as intrinsic to feeling or emotion may have always been shaped to social form and put to civic use. Consider what happens when young men roused to anger go willingly to war, or when followers rally enthusiastically around their king, or mullah, or football team. [13]

Hochschild details ways that workers' personalities are deeply altered by the adoption of "feeling rules" required by their work. Having accepted the idea that they must be cheerful and even-tempered, flight attendants learned to disassociate their "real" feelings from their work-based ones, giving rise to troubling questions about their concepts of self:

These emotional dues can be costly to the self. Institutional rules run deep but so does the self that struggles with and against them. To manage feeling is to actively try to change a preexisting emotional state. [14]

By implication, very basic structures of psyche are evolving all through life in response to material and cultural encounters. In turn these ever-changing individuals influence the realities that shape their lives. The contribution of such sociological investigations of emotion is that they lead us to a different and more concrete bridge between individual and society. The link between social forces and private feelings is ideas, which themselves are products of a social factory, constructed in the process of interaction with institutions encountered (and themselves in flux) throughout life.

I began this discussion by arguing that the rioters' choices were reasoned and not irrational. Now, having brought feeling, thinking, and social structure into a single paragraph, I want to qualify that statement. For while their decisions were reasoned and were in one sense reasonable, in another sense they were not. Some part of the Muslims' wrath was well directed toward their Namasudra neighbors, but some part was not. To the extent that their agenda was to redress wrongs visited on them by upper-class caste Hindus, it was futile to punish their low-caste peers. The Namasudras had no more power than they to discipline many of the people both groups held guilty. Was the tendency to lump Namasudras and caste Hindus together in one category not irrational, especially since more justice might have been won by a joint protest of all the tillers? Might the notion of false consciousness contain a kernel of truth after all?

The problem with such simple categorizations as *reasonable* and *irrational* is that they cannot describe the layered ways reason works. What is rational in one context is irrational in another, and contexts often change at rates different from thought. When formulating action, people use ideas and conceptions some of which were constructed in another time and context and therefore ill fit the current moment. They may think reasonably, but not linearly.

The minds of humans are living repositories of history; old ways of thinking commingle with new information, ancient fears and rages with clear-sighted awareness of new opportunities. The mix is often not well homogenized. But it does tend toward a point of reason. Let us now explore more fully the ways and means by which old ideas, new information, and changing social structures interrelate in the consciousness of individuals. In the next chapter we will then apply that understanding to the construction of community identities in Panipur. In the discussion that follows I mean to address the contradiction that gives rise to Chodorow's theory: that old and oppressive institutions endure within and through the medium of the human psyche. But I also mean to propose other ways of thinking about that phenomenon that draw on an underlying premise of rationality.

Ideology as Psychology

We think on many different levels at every moment of life. It's a beautiful day. The sky is cloudy. I have the following eighteen chores to do this morning. Simone is coming for dinner; I'd better clean house more thoroughly than usual. Simone is better organized, has a more beautiful house than I. I am getting older, looking wan, getting fat. How can I get through everything I need to do when I'm so weak? I'd better hurry up, work harder, do more, ignore my sadness, ignore my worries.

In this mix of ideas and thoughts, some are more emotionally persuasive than others. That the day is beautiful may be more or less moving. That I rake myself with doubt and contempt is very persuasive indeed. Each statement is linked to the one before, and together they add up to a certain ideological position.

Notice the value assumptions: That beauty and its enjoyment are less important than accomplishing chores. That there is a hierarchy of aesthetics and competency. That aging is not a good thing, and neither is deviation from a body ideal of thinness. That deviation from the ideal suggests weakness. That overcoming weakness is a higher value than experiencing beauty or sadness.

Without stretching my little example too far, we can relate those values to a certain social structure. Notice how alone the voice is. If there is too much to do one must work harder, not call for help.

Spurring my make-believe thinker on is the competitive structure
of her thinking: if I am less good at cleaning a house (itself a highly
ideological statement), then I am less good in an absolute sense.
My worth as a person is contingent on how well I stack up against
my fellows, on what I do rather than who I am. If I try to imagine
this internal dialogue in the mind of a Panipur villager, I fail. Yet
it is very familiar when set in the consciousness of an urban American woman.

Inner dialogues like this one have been described theoretically
as internalized oppression.[15] My imaginary woman has internalized highly prejudicial notions of women. She carries within her
own consciousness a sexist ideology that intersects and supports an
oppressive set of power relations. That housework, body size, age,
appearance define a woman's worth are all ideas consistent with
women's social assignment historically: to the domestic sphere, as
partners to men in the world, being chosen and valued because of
a superiority over other women in terms of external characteristics.

Similar dynamics exist for virtually every social being. I've constructed my example in the mind of a woman of a particular type
(most probably urban, western, heterosexual, a person with
enough material advantage to be able to engage in domestic competition), but comparable (and very different) tapes run in the
minds of men. For example, western industrial forms of sexism are
commonly internalized by men as injunctions to be strong, virile,
aggressive, unemotional. Notice that the gender-associated examples I've chosen parallel Chodorow's description of men's and
women's characters, but they are posed in terms of ideas people
think rather than psychic structure.

The most psychologically persuasive ideas are often also the
most emotional, and the most emotionally potent ideas are often
those least susceptible to examination. Some ideas, once learned,
disappear from view into a foggy domain of "truths." Both Geertz
and Gramsci, as I've said, talk about common sense as socially
constructed.[16] What I am suggesting is the mechanism by which
that construction happens. Ideas are learned, and then we forget
that they were learned, in large part because they conform to social
arrangements that so dominate our organization of experience that
they appear to be inevitable. We take both institutions and the

ideas to which they give rise for granted, seeing them as self-evident and beyond critical appraisal. [17]

What I am suggesting is a process reminiscent of role learning but different in important respects. Theories of roles suggest that social ways of being are learned through imitation. Internalization of ideas involves, not simple imitation, but complex processes of interpolation and deduction. How we are treated conveys messages, and often those messages are more compelling than verbal ones and also less available to critical reexamination. That parents in western nuclear families treat boy children differently from girl children, for instance, is meaningful. Researchers have observed that fathers tend to handle boy babies more roughly than girls, to toss them around, tickle and tumble and wrestle with them. In the process a number of ideas are conveyed to the child: that he is sturdy, that connection comes from physicality, that pain and fear should be overcome. Men more commonly handle girl babies delicately, as if they are fragile, tender, and, perhaps, sexually potent. Girls learn the message, sometimes developing fears about the physical world or rebelling against the implied lessons by becoming physically bold and "ungirl-like." [18] Similarly, Phyllis Chesler argues that mothers hold and nurse boy infants more frequently than girls. [19] Many women in western society grow up feeling deprived of nurturing, with a variety of consequences. They may believe, for instance, that they must nurture others and expect little themselves, or—paradoxically—that the way to win nurturing is to give it ever more self-sacrificially to others. Note that the problem of nurturance deprivation is highly associated with nuclear families, in which energy for caretaking is limited. Even if two parents are actively involved, which they commonly are not, they are unlikely to have enough strength left over from their difficult economic and emotional lives to lavish affection and sweetness on children.

The messages derived from these experiences are learned in a certain form that facilitates and is compounded by their internalization. They are generalizations (the general idea "I am weak" derived from the specific experience of being held gingerly) and abstractions ("The world is dangerous" rather than "The edge of that cliff is dangerous"). They convey injunctions about how to be in the world ("Be strong") and attributions about the individual who fails ("You are weak"). It is because they take forms so general and abstract, and yet convey instructions so specific and so destructive to self-confidence, that they have such power to direct behavior.

Taken all in all, these ideas recast social ideologies in psychological forms. Does that mean we are "brainwashed"? Is this a process of inculcation into a system of belief that is against our interests, one that is wholly oppressive? Is it, in short, false consciousness? Why, for instance, would boys willingly accept injunctions to be unfeeling or girls to be weak? To believe these ideas is to reconcile people to disadvantages they might otherwise protest, but their acceptance also reflects certain realities and is therefore self-interested. To reach such conclusions is often to make the best of a bad bargain. For boys, the alternative to thinking they must be stoic is to be excluded from a rewarding social web. Psychologically, boys who continue to cry beyond a certain age suffer severe disapprobation. To internalize an injunction of unemotionality is self-protective. It is also dangerous, in that its acceptance involves real sacrifices. Stifling emotion, as Hochschild so ably demonstrates in the realm of the workplace, requires fundamental psychic changes. Indeed, those changes are often physical; not to cry when sad takes an effort of control in the body, a tightening of the jaw, a stilling of the lower lip. Once learned, such physical measures become habitual and hard to reverse. They, in turn, require other body changes, a process overall described by Wilhelm Reich as "armoring."[20]

What begins as a functional accommodation to social realities becomes rigidified in the body and psyche. These injunctions and changes are carried forward in time, into other settings and possibilities where they may be truly dysfunctional. In this sense they are pieces of history carried in the body and hearts of individual humans into confrontations with new structures and circumstances. Because they are the embodiment of ideologies, their tenacity has political resonance and consequence, conflicting with an impulse to protest or to fight for constructive change.

The villagers in Panipur accepted ill-treatment, believing that it was in the nature of the world for it to happen. Mofizuddin told us:

In our nation [*rastriya*], now it's Bangladesh, we all have to stay like Bangladeshis. In the British time, we had to obey the British laws. In the Pakistani time, we had to abide by those laws. There was no point in being angry. We felt it, but we didn't express our anger. Why couldn't they now accept our rules?

Their worldview contained an attitude, that of acceptance, which indicated certain rules of behavior. Those who did not accept the inevitable were characterized: "People here, both Hindus and Muslims, are animals," said Altaf-uddin. "The main reason for the riots," countered a caste Hindu with daring prejudice, "was that the Muslims wanted to loot the houses of caste Hindus." These types of ideas—generalities about the world, moral injunctions or rules of behavior, attributions or social characterizations—combine powerfully to direct social behavior. They also reflect an established power order in the world and, by evoking emotions—shame and pride, for example—enforce it.[21]

Ideology is normally thought of as an internally consistent body of ideas. But I am proposing an expanded conception that embodies contradiction, and that is important because it makes possible a clearer understanding of certain types of ideology formation that are often overlooked and without which we cannot truly fathom social conflicts such as communalism. As I use the concept here, *ideology* embraces two distinct modes of thinking which intertwine to compose a highly convincing view of the world. The first mode is explicitly political. It is a system of ideas to which people are deeply committed and which contains an implicit goal: the attainment of power or the accomplishment of certain (usually economic) agendas. In this familiar conception, group identities may defend and support ideologies, but ideology is also a sense of identity. People are conservatives or environmentalists or what-have-you in a way that blends beliefs and sense of self, and because of that duality such ideologies are stubbornly enduring and often decisively defining.

This latter quality bleeds into the second and less familiar conception I've been describing: a body of ideas internalized early in life such that they form a set of assumptions about the nature of the world and one's responsibilities and capabilities in it. By "internalized," again, I mean they are ideas that are learned and then forgotten as ideas; they appear instead in the form of emotions and "truths," a sort of common-sense understanding of the world so ingrained as to be beyond question and, much of the time, outside consciousness. If the first set of ideas is explicitly ideological, we can call this second variety *implicit ideology*, a broader concept than the term *internalized oppression* and one that allows for explanations of more far-reaching experiences. It is ideological in the sense that it is about power. The world that is introjected is a politicized world, one in which people must accept a place in a hierarchy of rights and powers, and the existence of these ideas is itself a factor in maintaining that order. Implicit ideology is durable because it defines a deeply assumed picture of the world. But that is not to say that it is not influenced when it interacts with new events—changes of state, for example, which suggest new arrangements of power between communities. Because implicit ideologies are verbal, new understandings of the world do result from new experience. But traditional viewpoints deeply inform the ways people organize their responses to change, in communal or ethnic or racial forms, for example, and the new relations that result from their consequent social behaviors are shaped accordingly. Implicit ideology may be outside consciousness much of the time, but it is not unconscious in the Freudian sense, because it exists in the form of ideas and is thus accessible to verbalization. Nor is it false consciousness exactly, because it is at some moments and in some contexts functional for the individual. Given what resources seem available at the time, we make reasonable compromises with certain oppressive realities, a process very different from the wholesale acceptance of false and self-defeating ideologies.

The villagers of Panipur chose to riot; they were not swept mindlessly away, but the terms in which they formulated their reasoned decisions were a compendium of different types of thinking, including implicit ideology. As I've said, such systems of belief may run counter to agendas for social change. People in Panipur confronted a problem that deserved a solution, but the tools at hand included old ways of thinking about their communities as well as new conceptions introduced by the historic changes through which they were living. [22] I have proposed the idea that communalism is a means of renegotiating social relations within limitations imposed by oppression. What I am arguing in this chapter is that those limitations are represented in the grammar of consciousness. Just as dominant power is reflected in hegemonic functions of cultural institutions, so too the forms in which individuals think about their world embody hegemonic strictures on their capacity to rethink fundamental power relations. Yet people struggle against powerlessness, pushing against the boundaries to create pockets of relative autonomy.

One way to highlight this process is to consider differences in the positions of men and women, for we can learn something useful by focusing on this place where gender and community identity intersect. Women experienced the riot very differently from men. The men said, in essence, "We had to do it." For the Muslims that was because the moment had come for no more compromises. The Namasudras were equally convinced that they had to defend their community. Women of both communities, however, thought the riot was a mistake. They blamed the men—of both communities— for doing it. Women share with men a highly evolved sense of identity with others of their religiously defined grouping. Yet their conclusions about how to act were very different. Why?

As I explore the nature of community identities and of the villagers' understandings of the historic moment—both crucial themes in their decision to behave as they did—I shall return to the contrast between men and women to illuminate the dynamics of enemy-making.

Before moving on to that task, I want to place my discussion of the formulation of community conflict in a structural context. It is important to remember that conflicts like those in Panipur are not arbitrary creations of overactive imaginations. They are grounded in realities that exist outside the mind, in very concrete and coercive institutional arrangements. But if a theory of social conflict is to be useful, it must weave together the many levels of reality on which life is lived: individuals pursuing livelihoods in particular ways, thinking and feeling in response to their experiences and deciding at specific moments to protest or accept injustices; groups bound together by shifting ties of common interest and by culturally constructed, shared identities that help to legitimate their public behaviors; and institutional arrangements that are ideologically defined and broker the uses of political power.

Real disputes about material spoils are formulated in a variety of ways to produce certain actions in the world, and those actions give rise to new disputes and new ways to formulate them. That cycle operates on many levels: that of the individual, who formulates his world in terms of certain thoughts and feelings and decides how and when to act; that of the group, which defines certain interests and complaints shared by those who identify with each other and then endows with legitimacy the decisions of its members to act; and that of institutions, especially those that structure political and economic life, couched in ideologies of power enforced through programs of state. All of these processes are represented in particular languages and cultural conceptions. Ideas do not exist either in a vacuum or simply within the heads of individuals. They are social facts, interacting with institutional forces; they are not simply expressions of some abstracted human will. Too often social psychologies lean heavily in the direction of that which occurs (often unprovably) inside the heads and guts of individuals. My attempt here is to suggest a social psychology of conflict the very terms of which are symbols of institutional realities.

Chapter Eight

Community and Identity

2. *Decision-making was a process located in communities that themselves were chosen and reconstituted for the purposes of action. In the heat of conflict, why the villagers looked to associations defined by religious identity rather than any of the several other groupings available to them is not obvious and must be explained by examining both cultural and historically specific meanings attached to the communities.*

It needs no arguing that the decision to riot was made in community. "That evening, we Mussalmans held a meeting," said Golam.

We thought we could not go on living like this.

Did you meet together with the Hindus?

No, only the Mussalmans met. . . . We sat down together and decided to hold a meeting. . . . Many people came together that night. It was decided that it would be unwise to waste any time, and we should start the fight the next morning.

"We" was a very clearly defined concept: "the Mussalmans." It is tempting to assume that Muslims would seek other Muslims and Hindus other Hindus at a moment of anger. That assumption, indeed, could serve as a definition of the word *community*: those to whom one turns in moments of trouble. In fact, though, *community* is an elusive concept, sometimes used vaguely to denote geographic units (as in a neighborhood community), sometimes metaphorically to suggest commonalities among geographically, ideologically, and personally disparate individuals (for instance, the black community). In the first case, people are included because of the fact of residency, even though many may never have met each other, and in the second because of a racial designation even though given individuals may live very different lives. Sometimes the point of contact may be ideas (the Left community, for example) or an accident of birth (the Italian-American community). To be sure, each of these definitions is likely to have some truth to it. People living in the same neighborhood do frequently have something in common, since neighborhoods usually reflect socioeconomic characteristics and, in America, often racial ones as well. Still, in each of these cases community has more or less actuality for different members, and that actuality may exist more as potential than as reality at different times. Whether or not members of the community in fact call upon those linkages has much to do with the context and therefore with the function of an alliance. One would be less likely to turn to other Italian-Americans for help sand-bagging in a hurricane, for instance, than to neighbors, although after the fact one might seek financial help to rebuild from an ethnic community institution. *Community* is defined in practice, that is to say, in part by existential characteristics, but also very much by function.

In South Asia the concept evolved over time. Early in the British presence *community* meant the village.[1] By the end of the nineteenth century, however, the word had been assigned another, more ideological meaning. Communities came to be religiously reconstructed, a change with vast political consequences. As nationalists negotiated expanding arenas for self-rule, power was distributed to religiously defined constituencies in the form of legislative seats reserved for the minority "community." In turn, people forged new organizational forms to take advantage of those spoils or to resist their definition, shaping and reshaping these politicized associations.

At the same time, community continued to be formed on the level of daily life. As Sandria Freitag commented, "From . . . common experiences have emerged perceptions, definitions, and constructions of shared community."[2] In Panipur, for instance, people of like religion worshipped together some of the time. They gathered together for marriages and funerals and other rites of passage. They shared certain habits of eating and dressing, the construction of houses, the definition of domestic space.

But they also shared some of those qualities with people of other religions. Golam's house differed little from Kumar's. Language, a fact of major cultural significance, was also common to them. The Muslims of Panipur and the Namasudras may originally have been the same, or very similar, stock. One group converted to Islam while the other pursued tribal uplift, eventually attaining the status of a caste. Indeed, even religious rituals were commonly shared with those adhering to other religions. Villagers attended each other's weddings and funerals, although some particular rite might be barred to outsiders. Festivals were occasions for everyone to celebrate, and stories abounded of wild times had by Muslims during the Hindu festival of Holi, or Hindus bearing gifts to well-liked Muslim neighbors at the time of Eid.

During the colonial period, these definitions and commingling of communities in the course of daily life overlapped and interacted with emerging definitions in the realm of politics. Many shared experiences occurred in response to the imperial definitions themselves: contesting elections, the forging of alliances between Namasudra peasants and Muslims, and so on. "The sense of a division that we felt earlier was gone," said Sunil, describing the consequences of the alliance forged by the Namasudra leader Jogen Mandal. "We gained confidence that truly we could live together as brothers." The riot, an outgrowth of the most banal of daily events, a cow eating a crop—an act not at all connected to electoral politics in the village—nonetheless redrew political boundaries and reconstructed the sense of community all along the line.

As we question the concept of community, we should not assume even that community was the institution to which Golam and Kumar Tarkhania most naturally turned for help when the cow ate the plant and their fight began. Indeed, each went first to family. Along the way onlookers urged them to make peace, to come to their senses, and those interactions took place both within and between communities. Many of these same people later joined the battle, taking their places loyally in line behind their co-religionists, but that was a second, not a first, impulse.

Occasionally before, Muslims had coalesced to fight Hindus. Village quarrels, as I've said, were common. But never before had a riot happened. This time when the confrontation passed a certain point, communities—new and particular communities—combined with a new force of cohesiveness. Muslims from other villages, people unknown by sight or connection to the folk of Panipur, were invited to join in. That is a very significant fact. In the early stages of the dispute, familiar neighbors came to the assistance of the young men involved. They plowed in with a becoming mixture of humor, fire, and conciliation. But once messengers had been sent on horseback to arouse the surrounding countryside, a very different community was invoked and, indeed, formed through that action and its consequences.

Thought and Emotion in Forging Identity

Let us look more closely at the various community loyalties that became the foundation on which the riot was built. Said Sunil, the Namasudra defender:

The responsibility I felt was that they attacked us as a community. So my idea was that I must protect my community.

Nayeb Ali said the same thing more aggressively:

It was a sense of community. When I heard that they hurt my people, I wanted to beat them up.

Loyalty is something we "sense" or feel, not think. But Nayeb Ali overlooked the many times when a Muslim was hurt and he did not want to beat someone up. What thinking went into the feeling of community loyalty? "My idea was," said Sunil, "that I must protect my community." When the Namasudra leadership opted for an alliance with Jinnah and his Muslim League, they adopted a loyalty born of calculation. However they felt in their hearts about their Muslim neighbors, they figured their chances of life improvement were greater if they ranged themselves against the caste Hindus who exploited them all equally. Their intellectual identity, and in this moment their political identity, was with peasants, whatever their hearts might have dictated. In the intimate recesses of his own home Sunil felt discomfort with Muslim workers, but he was committed to an alliance with them as "Pakistanis" against the high-caste "Indians."

But, as Hochschild has demonstrated, to "think" a certain position (in this case, friendliness and joined fortunes) is in some manner to internalize it emotionally. Sunil was genuinely shocked when his Muslim neighbors and allies took the young men's quarrel to the point of battle. "It was totally counter to the social rules," he said. He could not anticipate what happened, because he was not harboring a sense of fear or distrust. That very distrust was precisely what he learned from the riot. Ironically, in the aftermath of the riot, it was the Muslims who greeted news of Hindu fearfulness with incredulity, so thoroughly had they digested the terms of peace and so invisible to them was the notion that for the Hindus it was a frightened peace born of defeat.

These ways that thought and emotion produced each other were central to the forming and reforming of community identities. It was precisely the fluidity of that relationship that made possible the contingent character of the identities, and at the same time their durability. Rational choice intermingled freely with language and culture in their construction, which is another way of saying that identity was both changeable and static.

On the static side of the equation were the many ways group identities defined an individual's sense of self. Those definitions took the form of shared cultural activities—rituals, habits, dress, and food—and of a shared morality. But in Bengal every time one names a practice that defines difference, there immediately springs to mind its opposite: a way some similar cultural act is associative instead.

Take language, for example. One's mother tongue is among one's most durable acquired characteristics. Most Bengalis have never spoken (many have not ever heard) another language, and never will. The Bengali language is the sixth most spoken language in the world,[3] and all Bengalis, Hindu and Muslim, actively identify on its basis and feel pride in the culture that derives from it. But Bengali speakers span an international border, living both in India and in Bangladesh. In the definition of nationhood, language figured large for Bangladeshis; indeed, the word means "land of Bengali." Language was an important bone of contention with the Urdu-speaking Westerners who dominated East Bengal under the flag of Pakistan. Yet educated Muslim Bangladeshis look to Calcutta, the heart of Indian Bengal, as their cultural touchstone.

Bangladeshis revere and quote Muslim poets, but Rabindranath Tagore, that preeminent Indian poet, a Hindu intimately identified with Calcutta, is considered an important founder of modern culture in Bangladesh as he is in India.

One evening in a northern district town, we were invited to dinner at the home of a modern Muslim family. After the meal, the daughter and father seated themselves on the living room floor with their musical instruments and sang for us. Not only was the image of a Muslim girl performing in public new, but it was noteworthy to other Muslims in the party that her father so willingly accompanied her on the tablas. Such musical soirees are associated with highly educated Hindu families, not Muslims; one expects to encounter them in upper-class Calcutta homes, not in provincial Bangladeshi ones. Prominent among the music this daughter and father performed, moreover, were songs written by Tagore, another cultural anomaly on which there was much remark. Culture distinguishes communities, but not in a simple way. Because education was the monopoly of Hindus, newly educated Muslims use elite cultural forms associated with Hindus. They themselves might contest the notion that they are borrowing Hindu cultural forms, for the culture is Bengali and, even though they note the fact that they are singing songs written by a Hindu, they also claim for their own all that is finest in Bengali culture. Here is an example of an evolving culture calling forth more complex identities among communities.

There are other ways that language both identifies and complicates identities. Bengali is spoken differently from one place to another; it is a national sport on both sides of the border to guess a Bengali's birthplace from her accent. East Bengalis use the Hindi word *pani* for water, while Westerners say *jal*, a word with probable Sanskrit origins. *Pani* suggests the influence of Urdu, a language used by the Moghuls while headquartered in western India. Although East Bengalis resented and resisted the dominance of western Urdu-speaking Muslims after Partition, they continue to use this piece of linguistic distinction. To complicate the coincidence of language and community further, even in the same localities different communities use different expressions and vocabularies. Within the East, now Bangladesh, Hindus and Muslims use different expressions for hello and goodbye.

I pointed out how important ritual and culture are in constructing identity when I described how Sunil's Namasudra community self-consciously adopted rituals that would proclaim their identity as Hindus and how Muslims seeking separate identities forsook one form of loincloth for another. Nonconformism to rules of dress can reveal the dynamics involved in these traditions, conscious and assumed. Consider the example of Sona Miah, an old man I interviewed in a district town. A government officer with a sparkling mind, Sona Miah was trained at the university at a time when Muslim boys were cruelly unwelcome. "I look like a Hindu," he told me, as indeed he did, dressed in pants and shirt, clean-shaven and bareheaded:

Many Hindus say, "You are a Muslim, but you look like a Hindu. Very nice. Very nice." If I wear this dress, no Englishman would recognize me [take him to be English]. But a Hindu, because I am adopting their culture, would give me a good certificate.

Sona regarded his ability to "pass" with ambivalence. On the one hand, he resented Hindus' congratulations; on the other, at the time he adopted this dress he experienced his appearance as protective:

And I felt rather elated. We were so helpless. In the classroom we were fifty students, a hundred students, only five or six were Muslims. All were Hindus. We were s-o-o-o-o helpless. Many Hindu teachers would say something insulting: "What have you eaten today? Beef?!" We were very helpless.

That Sona had long ago chosen to pass in public did not contradict the militancy of his private support for a Muslim homeland:

Yes, we wanted Pakistan, we had worked for Pakistan, and since they [the Hindus] left, we got it. It was a Muslim land, we visualized a Muslim land, politically this is a Muslim land. Pakistan means "Muslim land."

Yet he went on in this new Muslim land dressing like a Hindu who dressed like an Englishman.

Identity was a highly charged issue to this man, as was symbolized by the clothing he wore. His ambivalence about his costume embodied a set of social relations (how others felt about his attire, what it said both to Hindus and to other Muslims, what protection it afforded him in the world of the dominant Hindu elite). It also suggested a set of values, a moral code that dictated personal behavior. Morality is a central aspect of implicit ideology; it is a set of ideas taken so to heart that it is deeply assumed to be "right." To violate it is to *feel* inadequate or disloyal or frightened or dislocated. Hindus in Bangladesh suggest that their Muslim neighbors are more quarrelsome than they. Domestic spats are a normal way of life for Muslims, Hindus say. When Nayeb Ali declared militantly, "If we could eat like you, we could still go on fighting," I thought a look of censure crossed the face of Bhupendranath, a Namasudra villager. Nayeb Ali's bravado tapped a vein of stereotype that Bhupendranath, a sophisticated and well-educated man, nonetheless tended to believe. To many Hindus, it is a negative attribute to be warlike. Civility, forbearance, respect for formal ways of addressing conflict such as recourse to elders are all behaviors that Hindu morality values. Individual Hindus, of course, may value them more in the breach than in the observance. The Tarkhania brothers were provocative, unruly, violent, and unrepentant. Between belief and action lies a familiar gap, but belief nonetheless helps to define categories. "We Hindus compromise and work things out," people suggested. "We Muslims won't compromise, we fight things through," implied the other side, although individual Muslims are acknowledged to be among the gentlest and most conciliatory people in the larger community. These generalizations about ways of being in the world, about the very nature of right and wrong, define worldviews which in turn form powerful bonds among those who share them. Learned and assumed in a myriad of lessons verbal and behavioral, they constitute the heart of implicit ideologies that help to direct allegiances, but not necessarily actions, in a moment of crisis.

To some extent, therefore, both Hindus and Muslims felt unthinking censure of the other community's behavior and loyalty to "their own" at the same time that they thought very strategically about their actions. However tempting it is to assume that Hindus will line up with Hindus in a fight and Muslims with Muslims, given how high the emotional charge on such group identities can be, still it is not a foregone conclusion. Over and over people demonstrated how they also *chose* their loyalties; they were not predetermined or unconsciously ordained, as is borne out by Sunil's elaborate web of possibilities.

Why Religious Identity?

But in the end, Sunil, too, lined up on the basis of religion. We must, then, explain why identities based on religion were in fact the ones chosen in the moment of rioting. Religion has a characteristically compelling quality to peoples all over the world, although how and to what extent it compels varies enough to challenge notions of inherence. In a rural society where group arrangements hold true over long periods of time, religion is a very powerful source of definition. There are few arenas in which personal and public life are both addressed. Religion informs people in Bangladesh of the most detailed rules of living, from diets to hygiene to the organization of time. How people practice religious ritual helps to shape the nature of social bonds. Hindu worship dwells largely at home; each household nurtures its own altars, like Sunil's Lakshmi-shrine, dedicated to whatever goddess is special to the family. People usually "make *puja*" once a day, and worship moves into public temples only during special festivals honoring a particular deity. Muslims, by contrast, worship five times a day, often at the mosque if they are men. To gather a congregation so frequently in a central place of worship is a distinguishing feature of Islamic practice, and many devout Muslim men interrupt whatever daily agendas occupy them to comply faithfully. Hindu worship emphasizes kinship ties within a domestic sphere, whereas the Muslim concentration of people in a public place must affect consciousness of a wider community.

Religion thus links people to a politic and a community association which are crucial to existence in so stratified a society. Nothing else is as emotionally compelling and also as socially protective as religious affiliation. Moreover, stepping outside one's religious identity is likely to bring down censure. Sona Miah met stern disapproval from his Muslim elders because of his cross-appearance. Hindu young people who study abroad often lose their caste and are pressured to attend purification ceremonies when they return home. Very worldly and well-respected Muslim friends of mine, people of high spiritual as well as worldly standing, are nagged continually by family elders because they do not attend the mosque regularly. Religion is both a form of intense social control and a source of psychological organization, at the same time that it offers opportunities for community succor not often found in other associations.

Religion is a fundamental factor in the Panipur drama, and yet it appears nowhere in the events themselves. The fight was between "Hindus" and "Muslims," but Hinduism and Islam had nothing obvious to do with it. Instead, those designations referred to communities, or, in the more precise sense of that word for which I am striving here, to groupings of people that were overweeningly significant in the moment of battle. "There was a riot between Hindus and Muslims in Panipur," said a farmer in a nearby village, echoing every other informant's definition of the sides. In what sense exactly were people "Hindu" or "Muslim"?

Religion serves many functions.[4] It makes sense of the inexplicable or holds out promise that sense exists, however elusive it may be. It offers an ethical guide to life. It teaches people how to endure suffering. It provides a set of rituals that order time and reinforce commitment. These are obvious functions of religious belief and practice, but we might consider others: the more metaphysical and personal aspects of religious conviction, a sense of universality or timelessness; or the manner in which religions enable certain economic behaviors (as Max Weber explicated in his classic study *The Protestant Ethic and the Spirit of Capitalism*).

What was most important in the Panipur riot was the social role of religion, the way it forged group alliances and created adversarial teams:

A man who says he is a parakeet is, if he says it in normal conversation, saying that, as myth and ritual demonstrate, he is shot through with parakeetness and that this religious fact has some crucial social implications—we parakeets must stick together, not marry one another, not eat mundane parakeets, and so on, for to do otherwise is to act against the grain of the whole universe. It is this placing of proximate acts in ultimate contexts that makes religion, frequently at least, socially so powerful.[5]

Qualities of "Muslimness" or "Hinduness" formed the basis on which the sides were drawn. The fact that a given group could claim coherence as Muslim or Hindu gave it authenticity, and people frequently invoked those signifiers in that sense: "We Muslims suffered injustices," or "We Hindus were attacked." Geertz suggests an authenticity deeper than association with a social group, however. What he evokes is a thick system of ideas about the order of the universe that is sufficiently internalized as to appear natural or assumed. Against that set of assumptions, a given mundane act appears discordant and therefore wrong. Without the background of these powerful rules and definitions of the nature of the sacred, the villagers might not have felt righteous enough or empowered enough to have acted against each other. How exactly they might have acted instead we can only speculate. Perhaps they would have continued to accept certain injustices and frictions among themselves. Perhaps they might have remained united as a larger village community and have fought together for other changes that benefited them all—perhaps a true application of land reform or a system of justice that protected all peasants against those with more economic power.

We skate here on the edge of hypothesis, with too little direct data to make judgments. In Panipur it was not completely clear that this identification of mundane agendas—cows and crops, perhaps land and power—with sacred ones supported the righteousness of acts of hostility. It surprised me that people showed so little defensiveness about their actions. Often they seemed more mischievous than righteous, a quality I imagine to have amplified over the distance of time. To justify their violence they cited old grievances, without connecting them explicitly to a code of ethics specific to their particular religions. It is easy and tempting to believe such codes underlay their thinking, but we must treat that question as a hypothesis for further inquiry. I suspect that if each religion gives rise to a particular ethical foundation, so too does the shared life of the villagers, whether Hindu or Muslim, create a common set of beliefs and values that served to justify both sides in the dispute. That is to say, what Golam and Kumar had in common as Bengali peasants in a water-bound village gave rise to shared ideas about right and wrong that each called upon separately to justify his own acts. For Golam the sanctity of cattle ownership, and for Kumar the supreme importance of protecting a food crop, justified his wrath. On the next level, Sunil did have a greater tolerance for ritually constructed hierarchy than did Golam, and that tolerance was a direct outgrowth of a particular religious principle. But the Muslims' call to arms grew out of a greater adherence to the concept that the capacity to enforce one's rights indicated the righteousness of doing so—might makes right—and on some level the Hindus, too, accepted that very worldly principle. I did not take my conversations to a level that would give us straightforward data here, and consequently I cannot test the connections Geertz suggests. But I suggest that justifications for actions like the rioters' are compounded from many sources, of which the sacred is only one.

If we cannot prove that religiously founded concepts of justice played more than a subliminal role in forging alliances, we can still delineate other, more situational reasons for the abundant power of religion as an organizing force. Geertz again gives helpful direction:

For an anthropologist, the importance of religion lies in its capacity to serve, for an individual or for a group, as a source of general, yet distinctive, conceptions of the world, the self, and the relations between them, on the one hand . . . and of rooted, no less distinctive "mental" dispositions . . . on the other. From these cultural functions flow, in turn, its social and psychological ones.[6]

In a colonialized land, conceptual regions of such distinctiveness and connection are not easily found. Freitag argues that the intrusion of the imperial state into most arenas of public life made of religion an especially valued preserve for the expression of public agendas.[7] After Independence and the departure of the British, that equation shifted. For Bengali Pakistanis, religion now defined the official public arena. Yet new intrusions appeared, new agendas arose, and forums for their expression were still problematic. The young state was preoccupied with establishing a stasis both between peasants and landowners and between Muslims and those Hindus who chose to remain. Overt processes of renegotiating social rights in the villages were not high on their priority list. Alternative organizations that might help were also lacking. The area surrounding Panipur had old traditions of revolutionary organizing which at the moment of the riot were peculiarly undermined. Having won little credibility in the construction of the new states, the left was a submerged presence, little capable organizationally of giving shape to the project of redressing old grievances and ill suited ideologically for promoting a newly awakened peasant lust for land.

Religiously defined communities appeared all the more attractive as forces for change because other possible structures were lacking, and because they had just provided such effective definitions for pursuing the national project of state-making. What had worked for elites was worth the masses' trying. After Partition, however, these communities functioned differently for Namasudra and Muslim villagers. For the latter, for Nayeb Ali or Altaf-uddin, to identity oneself as Muslim was to claim association with the powers that be, the new government. No longer did religion define an arena exempt from state power; now it defined the nature of state power.

But the Namasudras continued to be cut off from state power. Lacking connections founded in religious commonality in Pakistan, they were also estranged from caste-Hindu power in India. At the moment of Partition they had cast their lot with their fellow peasants, but now, as those "fellows" turned against them, they had no power-rich associations on which to draw. The Muslim villagers now had a public arena in which to present themselves, and the Namasudras did not. For Sunil and his peers, religion still represented a protected space, but for Nayeb Ali religion was now not protection but association. What both were subsequently to learn, however, was that the difference was not after all so great. The new state looked little more favorably on their shared class interests than had the British. Nayeb Ali's new confidence proved unwarranted on this level.

Despite that error, the Muslims' actions were effective. By joining a cognitive definition of group in terms of religious categories with an emotional sense of self as part of that group—a sharing of outrage at grievances suffered by others, an acceptance of personal danger in defense of the group, a sharing of ambitions and rights even when the benefits seemed more likely to accrue to others in the group—a powerful impetus to unity was created at the moment of conflict. What the villagers derived from that process was instruction not so much about how to act as with whom to act. It located them in a group for purposes of action.

So emotionally clear was that location that even little children

knew precisely where they stood in the field of battle. We talked
with a man who had been a child at the time of the riot:

Was there a rift among the children?
Yes, we were on one side, the Hindu children were on the other side of
the field.
But did you feel anger at each other?
We were too far away. We couldn't see each other.

When tensions arose, Hindus consulted Hindus about what to do,
and Muslims talked to Muslims. It was interesting to me that this
Muslim man dodged my question about anger. By establishing
physical distance he managed to maintain a certain emotional distance, too. In the present, he sat on a bench side by side with those
same Hindus who as children had been too far away to be seen.
Now they were very close indeed. Too close to hate, I imagined.
Another man on that bench expressed the same idea more ab-
stractly:

The Hindus went from the Hindu*para* and the Muslims from the Muslim-
para. We went to one side of the field, they to the other. Now we are
friends, but at that moment we were enemies. How could we go together?

"We were enemies." Those are strong and defining words, set
paradoxically against their time-specific opposite: "Now we are
friends." Friend and enemy are categories as distinct and absolute
as Hindu and Muslim. That the former labels were attached to the
latter when and as they were was an exercise in abstracted definitions of complex realities. Those boys were clearly not "enemies"
to each other. They played together daily before the riot, and they
resumed their friendship afterward. They had done each other no
harm, offered no threat, represented in their persons no moral
failing. They were, however, associated with groups the adult
members of which, in and for that moment, defined each other as
enemies, and the children followed loyally along. That they did so
demonstrates the tenacity of implicit ideology: they never doubted
the overriding power of the labels, never tested them against their
own lives as children playing together and liking each other. The
abstracted definitions overwhelmed lived experience.

Women's Communities

These boys allowed their responses to be formulated by the shared drama of the moment. Interestingly, their mothers did not react in that way. I noted throughout my interviewing in Panipur the differences between men's and women's accounts. Women, as I've said, were harder for me to reach, but more willing to speak once I got to them. Men showed little remorse or shame about the riot. Occasionally, Namasudras were critical of Muslims' actions, but both sides tended to speak with little outrage or righteousness. Women were far more censorious. On both sides, however, they condemned the men of both communities. Where the children remained loyal, the women may have acted loyally (no one seems to have crossed over to try to make peace or breach the battle lines, actions which in any case would have been dangerous as well as unlikely in village society). But they reacted less as Muslims and Hindus than as women, angry at the men, all men, for risking so huge and frightening an event. Men assured me it would not happen again, either because as Hindus they believed they were not strong enough or as Muslims because they believed all was harmonious between the communities and therefore there was no need for such a confrontation. Women felt less sanguine about the future, especially Hindu women, who universally wished they could migrate to India, a desire not shared by many of their menfolk.

Both men and women shared community identities, yet their relationships to the riot were very different. Why? We cannot assume that something about being a woman predisposed them to pacifism. Women in other parts of the world—indeed, in other places and times South Asian women—have been militantly hostile to other peoples. Irish women, Israeli women, Chilean women are not loath to express their strong feelings in the streets. These Bangladeshi women were less ideologically driven by ideas about peace and violence than they were pessimistic that any good could come of the confrontation. Again and again they suggested, not that the grievances of the men were unfounded, but that rioting would not help. Skepticism combined with fears for their family members to dispose them toward opposition. Aggressive contention was clearly not a comfortable mode of action for them, not one

they had themselves experienced as successful. Remember that
women were accused of seeding streams with broken pots to keep
children of the opposite community from fishing in them. Such
gestures of resistance, couched in the banality of everyday life,
indirect rather than face to face, hostile but not too dangerous,
were more comfortable to them.

In a larger sense, though, women's reactions to the riot, their
reluctance to participate even in their own idiom—preparing food,
encouraging the men, and so on—suggests another reality, and that
is that women's communities are quite different from men's. It was
not that Basantibala and her friends did not share their menfolk's
stereotypes about Muslims. For instance, another young Hindu
woman told me with great indignation about the noise emanating
from her newly arrived and much resented Muslim neighbors. But
women have fewer encounters in public spaces. When they do
meet each other, it is privately, because they live nearby or because they respect each other's festivals. Women will come visiting
neighbors, for instance, to celebrate major holidays. Births and
marriages, illnesses and deaths also occasion personal contact. Men
meet more in public spaces, in marketplaces and fields, for instance, where sources of competition and conflict are common.
Women meet more on domestic and ritual grounds where they
have voluntarily sought each other out and therefore approach
with a more assured sense of friendliness.

I do not mean to suggest that women experience themselves less
as Hindu or Muslim, but simply that the nature of those self-
definitions is subtly different from men's, and that those differences
altered women's relationship to the riot. Having turned their backs
on the fight, in its aftermath they felt both more powerless and also
less polarized. Their major criticisms were along gender lines,
against men who rioted rather than against Muslims or Hindus
who rioted. For that reason, they talked in terms of fears and
regrets rather than communities and enemies.

Not so the men and boys. "At that moment we were enemies,"
said the man who was a child then. What was that moment? Why
did it come upon the people of Panipur when it did? How did they
see it, and why did they respond as they did? Let us go on to place
the moment of the riot in history and tease from the villagers'
actions and words the story of its reasons.

Chapter Nine

History and Ideology

3. The decision to riot was deeply informed by an awareness of history understood in terms of lived experience. The act of rioting integrated the village into a moment of national transformation which until then had been abstract and distant. In so doing, the rioters brought change home to the village and thus took their place in the making of their own history.

How people experienced themselves as members of communities, their community identities, was important not as static social facts but because they gave rise to, or served to justify, a set of ideas about the world, individuals' locations in that world, and a range of actions that could consequently be taken. They were important as part of an *ideology* that led to collective action.

In Chapter Seven I discussed the psychological role of cognition and argued that ideas and emotions are social constructs which are so thoroughly internalized that they come to appear as self-evident truths. The discussion that follows proceeds from the notion that it is a particular kind of society that is internalized, one organized into hierarchies that are accepted with some degree of unwillingness by those below. More accurately, they are not so much accepted as negotiated. Given a series of choices none of which is ideal, ordinary people, through a panorama of ordinary and dramatic transactions, negotiate the best bargain possible. By accepting inequities of power and at the same time resisting domination in myriad ways, people forgo as little well-being as possible. What clouds the process is that implicit ideologies of power are accepted along with the material fact of power, thus obscuring awareness of the bargain struck. That Golam held Sunil responsible not only for his own transgressions (treating Muslim children harshly when they fished in his stream; refusing to hire Muslim workers) but also for oppression by the upper-caste Hindus, who oppressed Sunil as well as Golam, reflects Golam's belief in a set of ideas about religious community: that all Hindus constitute a group, that each individual included in that group is responsible for the sins of all others. But even that idea, crude and inaccurate as it was, became a vehicle for Golam's mates to seize an edge of privilege that was truly in their interest. The competition, in other words, was both with Hindus of privilege, to take back dignity and advantage, and also with Hindus who were peers and therefore truly in competition for the scarce spoils of Partition. In the abstract, I argue here that unequally structured societies give rise to psychologically persuasive ideologies that operate on the level of assumptions and attitudes, and that these ideologies in turn provide the concepts with which to renegotiate power and rights within local communities.

Sources of Understanding

The Panipur riot was a good example of how new political realities on the state level contributed to changing assumptions about local life. More interesting than what may have happened in Delhi or Dhaka was how the villagers construed those events, drawing on them to construct new pictures of their world and new possibilities for action. Looking closely at the stories told in Panipur, we can see three sources of understanding, which flow in and out of each other, each altering the others over time and moving toward the specific event of the riot.[1]

The first source of consciousness grounds the others: it is *ordinary life*, the lived experiences of the individual participants in collective action. As I've said, most of life in the village was made up of friendly and banal transactions. But many people on both sides of the conflict also recounted grievances, and these complaints played an important role in the formulation of the riot:

They behave with us in that manner. . . . In the days before Partition, in the days of the British rulers, they did not treat us very well. We had to bow down before them. They caused a lot of trouble to us Mussalmans about our land and property. If our children went to catch fish in the nearby canal, they would beat them. Just the other day, they were still beating our children.

We have seen how grievances were evoked to justify the decision to riot (see Chapter Two). But these banal complaints did more than justify action. They also helped to define the battle lines and to define the nature of the battle itself.

When we pressed Golam, the man with the cow, to tell us who beat the children, he said, "They. Including Kumar." Sunil, the Hindu farmer, had mirror-image complaints about his Muslim neighbors:

Hindus were always under pressure from the Muslims. The Muslims always thought that they came first, they feel superior.

Did they express those feelings in how they behaved?

Often, they might break the borders of the field, or damage the *dhan* [paddy] in the neighboring field. They often attacked the women.

Both sets of grievances have to do with the sorts of everyday village friction that might also beset people of the same community. Both referred to incidents they themselves had suffered or witnessed. But time was an important part of the interpretations of the incidents. Clearly, the fact that the perpetrators belonged to the other community meant more at moments when relations were already highly charged. Sunil's examples, for instance, turned out to be set in the period after Partition, when Muslims had taken power:

When we sought justice from the responsible people, we didn't get it. They didn't take any interest in our troubles. . . . These leaders only offered vague words of consolation, but they never did a single thing to help. They would say, "Forget it, these things are natural. You are a minority, so you have to bear some troubles." They would pat our backs and send us away.

Earlier, speaking of the prelude to Partition, he had not recounted conflict but had spoken of his hopes for alliance with his Muslim neighbors. The grievances he remembered from those times had been the fault of landlords, who also happened to be Hindus. That "Hindu" (landlord) identified Sunil's oppressor before the creation of Pakistan, and "Muslim" (authority) after, suggests how fluid community identity is as a locus for animosity.

Golam's memories of the days before the British left were quite the reverse of Sunil's. His grievances from that time were heavily colored with indignities derived from Hindu religious ritual:

They did us many wrongs in those days. Suppose there was a fair anywhere. We went to that fair and they also went. We had to go along the same route. They carried their breakfast in paper packets or vessels on their heads. We also took ours with us. If somehow their vessels came in contact with us, they would beat us. Then they would throw away their rice, and ours also.

The picture Golam reconstructs here is nicely balanced between a shared village activity—going to a fair—and an asymmetrical imposition of religious principles by Hindus on Muslims. Imitating their caste brethren who enforced on Muslims—as well as on lower-caste Hindus like themselves—rules of food purity, the Namasudras would punish Muslims for "somehow" defiling their breakfast through proscribed contact. There was nothing comparably religion-based that Muslims did to Namasudras in Panipur, and such degradations were closely linked with Muslims' sense of grievance at the time of Partition and soon afterward.

That injustices personally and specifically experienced were couched as generalized attributions about the "other" community ("*They* behave with us in that manner"; "Hindus were *always* under pressure from the Muslims") suggests the second source of ideas about the world, what I call *community memory.* Often people recounted tales of injustice in great detail. Once pressed, however, they were unable to place themselves individually at the scene they had described. What they remembered were not events per se, but stories they had heard. Indeed, often they did not know who had told them the tales. Rather, they appeared as a shared culture of memories, a sort of stew of stereotypes and prototypical incidents about which everybody talked but which nobody in particular had witnessed. "The elderly Mussalmans had all suffered a lot of loss," said Golam. "It was the case with almost every Mussalman. We felt bitter, and we didn't care to compromise." A statement which begins with generalities in the third person ("The elderly Mussalmans had all . . . ") ends with a specific emotion in the first person ("We felt bitter") and a concrete shared decision ("we didn't care to compromise"). Clearly, not all elderly Mussalmans had the same experience. Golam suggests a piece of his worldview, however: the notion that Muslims had been long-suffering. As Jan Vansina has explained:

Collective memory simplifies by fusing analogous personalities or situations into one. Whole groups of traditions, now abraded to anecdotes, are set up and contrasted so that in every account details are sharpened, altered or left out to imprint the mark of their association to other accounts.[2]

As I suggested above, a particular kind of fusing characterized the Muslim villagers' complaints. The most vivid tales were of abuses combining class and religion: *zamindars* who made peasants squat in the hot sun outside their manor house lest they defile the interior or who forced the lone Muslim lad admitted to a *zamindari* school for elite Hindu youths to sit outside the classroom. As the stories multiplied and slipped back and forth between these injustices and the more banal—and reciprocated—injustices endured between peers, the evidence mounted that Muslims blamed peasant Hindus for the sins of their elite co-religionists, who, by virtue of their privilege, had been inaccessible to retaliation and, by virtue of Partition, had now all been humbled and many driven away. To say "Hindus oppressed us" was true. To say "Kumar Tarkhania oppressed us" was not—at least not more than we oppressed him. This merging of observation and stereotype powerfully reinforced an implicit ideology in which injustice resided in "the other community." To feel oneself to be victimized in general and actually to be victimized in very specific ways fuse together in the conviction that "they" victimize "us." The concrete details—who exactly is doing what precise wrong to whom, and what therefore is to be done about it?—are subsumed under the abstract sense of being wronged.

Grievance by association worked in the other direction, too: people took on injustices experienced by others of their extended community. I heard many stories about Muslims before Partition who had failed to find work in the city. Nobody could name a specific Muslim who had gone to town in search of employment, let alone one who had not succeeded. After Partition, Hindus told the same story about people of their own community, and again their tales lacked specificity. These anecdotes of people doing unfamiliar tasks and suffering discrimination in a setting foreign to the tellers took on an almost ritual air as they were told over and over in versions both similar and highly charged with indignation. Community memory is made up of such common-sense stories— nobody thinks to ask for specific examples because everybody "knows" they are true—heavily tinged with stereotype. They are a key component of implicit ideology, lying outside the realm of scrutiny and debate and all the more compelling for that inviolability. But what keeps them powerful is that they speak to a truth that *is* personally experienced. Golam *had* been treated badly by Hindu neighbors; Sunil *had* been belittled by Muslim authorities. The fact that Golam may have been treated badly by Muslim neighbors as well, or that villagers generally receive imperfect justice from town authorities, is eclipsed by the more generalized experience of community-based wrongs kept alive by community memory.

But most social beings have personal grievances, and community memories form a matrix for understanding them. What activates the brew and leads to decisions to act collectively is time-based: a new understanding of the historic moment and its potential for action. In Panipur, the recognition of that opportune moment was based on a third and more abstract source of understanding: *ideas about history and the state.*[3]

Said that perceptive old man, Mofizuddin:

These cows and plants are symbols. After Partition, the minority community didn't take it well. There was Hindu-Muslim tension. The Bengali year was 1360 [or 1362] when this happened. There was a big flood, even more than last year. There's a song, "Azad Pakistan," it says there is anger in us, even if we don't express it. That's internal talk, not something you speak about openly. Educated people don't ever mention that anger.

In our *rastriya* ["nation"], now it's Bangladesh, we all have to stay like Bangladeshis. In the British time, we had to obey the British laws. In the Pakistani time, we had to abide by those laws. There was no point in being angry. We felt it, but we didn't express our anger. Why couldn't they now accept our rules?

I wondered how those historic events, dotting the eighty-year-old Mofizuddin's life, had been experienced by him. That Mofizuddin should measure his fellow villagers' behavior with a different yardstick after the end of colonialism and the establishment of an independent state headed by Muslims may not seem surprising.

But between a Bengali villager and a government, *any* government, whether British or Pakistani, is a great distance.* Seven
years after Independence, not much had changed in practice for
the people of Panipur. The connecting link between villagers and
the state was still the same locally elected Muslim official. Cultivators continued to farm the same lands and faced all the same
problems, albeit with new hope. Some few had acquired a bit more
land, but others had grown poorer as the population increased.
Most Hindus in this area, even many caste Hindus, had not fled.
The *zamindar* was a well-liked man who still lived at Panipur. His
landholdings may have diminished on paper, but not substantially
in fact. Change, if any, was not dramatic.

But something decisive had changed in Mofizuddin's thinking.
His internal world had been rearranged. He still believed in obedience to the state, but his conception of the state was radically
altered. Now it was *his* state, not his Namasudra neighbor's, even
though the current state had at the time of the riot been dominated
by Pakistanis who spoke a language as foreign to him as English,
who came from a land for all intents and purposes as far away as
Britain, and who, as it turned out, exploited and oppressed Mofizuddin as brutally as had the European colonists before them.

State, Community, and Power

Conceptions of *state*, the most public of worlds, are also representations of inner worlds. I use the word *inner* in a psychological
sense; that is, statements about state power were emotionally
charged and were packed with meanings about a sense of self and
community. *Inner* also carries a social connotation. Bengali culture
draws very strong divisions between outer worlds and the inner
ones of village, community, and family. When Mofizuddin said,
"Now it's Bangladesh, we all have to stay like Bangladeshis," he

---

*It is a great distance measured in either direction. Remember Golam's story
that, when the riot was over, officials from town tried to camp in the village: "A
police officer . . . said that he had to visit the toilet. He asked whether there was
any *pukka* [brick, or "proper"] toilet in the village. But there was nothing like
that. . . . He asked where there was [one]. There were *pukka* toilets at Panipur
. . . half a mile away. He said, 'In that case, we will go there.' So, taking the
policemen with them, they went to . . . Panipur."

was expressing a very personal perception of his own place in the world and of new definitions of the "rules" ("our rules") governing how he expected Sunil, his Namasudra neighbor, to behave. The state was shorthand for Mofizuddin's complex beliefs, self-identities, and constructions of community, a merging of ideas into an ideology deeply enough felt to produce action.

A clue to that ideology is contained in the phenomenon of misnaming regimes. Wrote Vansina:

> Memory reorganizes the data it contains. It will put these in a sequential order which resembles an expression of measured duration but in fact is a creation of memory: the epoch. It places events or situations in one time frame or another and sometimes transposes them.[4]

Mofizuddin spoke as if Bangladesh had already existed at the time of the riot, when in fact Bangladesh was born seventeen years later. What he did was to reflect back in time his contemporary sense of identity with the state, forgetting that the state with which he felt identified then (at the time of the riot) later proved to be an alien state—a fact he implicitly acknowledged when he said, "In the Pakistani time, we had to abide by those laws." His historic memory leapt over a whole period, collapsing then into now because an emotional experience now echoed one from the past. He suggested a sentiment, perhaps more finely drawn once the state had become Bangladeshi but, in his recollection, operative then—so much so that he invoked it to explain motivations for a riot that occurred seventeen years before there was a Bangladesh. What Pakistan and Bangladesh had in common was their Muslim identity, and that is the quality with which Mofizuddin connected himself. "We" equaled Muslims; "they," Hindus.

In this sense, regimes are symbolic representations of communities. To be sure, Mofizuddin, wise and practical peasant that he was, understood the state in its practical manifestations as well. The state taxed him, redistributed (or, more often, failed to redistribute) land, sent the police to quell riots, and so on. But Mofizuddin had in his lifetime witnessed struggles for state power based on community identities, the communal politics of the nationalist period. He mapped those politics onto the little world of the village.

But the state played far more than a symbolic role. Although it appeared that officialdom took the stage only late in the drama, and then as peacekeeper and judge, in fact the interaction between populace and state involved both as contestants. Indeed, the structure of civil conflict is often framed as if two (or more) warring factions of civilians are pacified by a disinterested state that has only benevolent motivations. The riot in Panipur demonstrated the subtle ways that the state can be a party to the conflict.

Some of those ways are overt and obvious. Laws are passed, judicial rulings made, budgets enacted, employment policies created and rescinded, and on and on. These actions of state can serve as provocations for conflict between communities, although it may be more accurate to say that they embody struggles among peoples for power at the same time that they advance them.[5] Significant, too, are informal actions of agents of state, especially those individuals in direct contact with communities. In 1992 civil strife was evoked in Los Angeles by a sequence of official actions or actions by officials: the police beating of a black man, Rodney King; a court's decision to locate the officers' trial in a white suburb; the acquittal of the accused policemen. That drama well illustrates a second type of overt state action that frequently shapes community conflict: intervention. How and when force is exercised directly and simply affects the course of struggle. Several accounts suggested that in Panipur the police knew trouble was brewing for at least a day, and perhaps two, before they arrived. Without access to official archives or interviews, we could only speculate about why they delayed taking action. It is more useful to my inquiry about the villagers' formulation of conflict, however, to examine the role of the state through the prism of the rioters' experience. One way it appears from this angle is that *the nature of the state helped to define the moment as opportune for community struggle.*

How that process worked is implicit in Golam's reflections on the causes and consequences of the riot. I shall analyze his statement in some detail in order to show how all three levels of consciousness—personal grievances deriving from ordinary life, community memory of generalized wrongs, and abstract understandings of state and history—all come together in the construction of collective action:

They did us many wrongs in those days. . . . We were less strong because the state[6] belonged to them. The Hindus outnumbered us. So we were afraid of them.
But now the state belongs to you. Are they afraid of you now?

Yes, they are . . . they are afraid of us just as we were afraid of them in the past. They are afraid of us now because it is Pakistan now. But we don't beat them. We don't oppress them in any way. We try to live in peace, like brothers, with them. But there is a fear lurking in their minds, and there is a bit of envy, also.

But do you Mussalmans not entertain any envy of the Hindus?

No, we don't. Why should we envy them? We need not envy them.

What seems a simple description of change is not. Golam's statement contains a number of telling inaccuracies. "We were less strong because the state belonged to them," he said. But the state did not belong to Hindus "in those days"; it belonged to the British. Nor did it exactly "belong" to Golam at the moment when he was speaking. True, he was Muslim and most of the rulers were Muslim; in that sense he shared identity with the state. But only in that sense, for in truth the state "belonged" to a military dictatorship with very decided class biases. Affluent city-dwellers prospered at the extreme expense of people like Golam. In other contexts, Golam himself bitterly complained of that reality and saw himself as allied with his poor Namasudra neighbors in a battle for resources.

What Golam meant becomes a little clearer when we factor in the question of numbers. "The state belonged to them," he said, closely continuing with the observation: "The Hindus outnumbered us. So we were afraid of them." To equate state power with demographic numbers makes conceptual sense, although, again, for Golam that equation was not quite true. Hindus did not outnumber Muslims in Golam's own world of direct experience. They did in India as a whole, but in East Bengal Muslims were a large majority, and in Panipur itself Hindus and Muslims were about equal in numbers.

Wrong as they are, both statements—who owned the state and who outnumbered whom—shift into focus if by "state" Golam meant something more abstract, specifically, influence and power. For although the pre-Independence state belonged formally to the British, in fact Hindus were more influential than Muslims, both as civil servants and as leaders of nationalism. It seems obvious that Golam would fear that influence.

But in fact, it is not exactly obvious why it mattered to Golam

that leaders and bureaucrats—representatives of the state—were
Hindus. In his own village, the only elected official was, and always
had been, Altaf, a Muslim. Golam himself, a small landholder, had
virtually no contact with agents of state. No policeman had ever
visited his isolated village before the upheaval. Neither had a
single public official (according to popular lore). Taxes were collected as levies by the big landlord whose fields Golam tilled.

What did matter to Golam was that the landlord was a Hindu.
Class relations were defined by religious affiliation in ways that
affected daily life more significantly than did the nature of a distant
government. But the Namasudras of the village also felt those
effects. They, too, were economically disadvantaged and culturally
humiliated. Hindus may have outnumbered Muslims, therefore,
but all the peasants of Panipur of whatever affiliation also shared
important interests and struggles, as well as cultural and ritual
practices. Golam's statement that "we were afraid of them" because "they outnumbered us" was therefore not entirely ingenu-
ous. What he feared, no doubt, was the economic power of a very
small number of Hindu landlords, who were equally feared by
Golam's Namasudra neighbors.

The state did not "belong to them," nor did "they outnumber
us." Yet certain Hindus had enjoyed power and influence before
Independence, and to Golam's mind that power and influence
were symbolized by the state: "They are afraid of us just as we
were afraid of them in the past. They are afraid of us now because
it is Pakistan now."

Although at the moment we spoke it was not "Pakistan now" but
Bangladesh, another eliding of eras of some significance, it was
very true that Hindus feared Muslims now. I heard Hindus say
exactly that again and again in my conversations with them. It was
not true, however, that their fear was just the same as the Muslims'
fear in the past or that it derived in any simple way from the
existence of Pakistan. The Muslims' fear had been closely linked to
economic subservience. The Hindus feared their peers, as they had
not done at the time of the melee.

In fact, the fight had happened precisely because "they" were
not afraid. Golam, a Muslim, had set his cow in a field where it
could eat the plants of his neighbor Kumar, a Hindu. That was a
pretty cheeky thing to do. Kumar protested, as everyone, Golam

included, admitted he had a right to do. But he more than protested; he seized Golam's cow and held it hostage. That was an
enormously cheeky thing to do, not at all the behavior of a frightened man. The Hindus did become frightened, however, after the
whole business was concluded. The Muslims, in the wrong to begin
with, did not do what they normally would have done, which was
to posture a bit, finally apologize, and make amends for the injured
plants. Instead, they massed, sent word to Muslims in surrounding
villages, and "decided to riot." That they acted so atypically was
precisely because *they* knew it was Pakistan. But the Hindus were
taken by surprise. "It was totally counter to the social rules,"
complained Sunil. And indeed they did change the rules, because
they knew there now was a Muslim-dominated government and
they expected it to favor Muslims over Hindus.

Because the state had constituted itself in terms of religious
identity, these Muslim villagers enforced a new set of power relations on their Hindu neighbors. The new state symbolized a change
which so far in the village existed only as potential. By rioting, the
villagers made it actual.

As that process unfolded, the state continued to play a role.
Having by its nature helped to define the opportune moment, it
went on to *define the nature of the actions taken.* As we've seen,
the English word *riot* ill suits the formal and stylized possession of
territory that actually took place. Interestingly, the imposition of
the concept of *riot* on the villagers' consciousness had been accomplished by a colonial state against which the current government
had battled and against which it had defined itself in terms of
nationalism and Muslim statehood. Yet it accepted that label, used
it, and on its basis imposed punishments indistinguishable from
those the British had meted out in their day. That the villagers'
actions were treated as civil disorder and squelched rather than
adjudicated was on one level an inheritance from a colonial regime.
But on another level it demonstrated the capacity of institutions to
use the formal concepts of the past to define new situations. The
Pakistani government could not tolerate civil conflict any more
than its predecessor could, and, given recent history, especially not
conflict communally defined. Communal itself, in that everyone
knew real power resided with Muslims, the government accepted
the challenge of crafting its imposition in terms of communal eq-

uity: who gave the order, who fired the guns, what gestures it made, and who executed them were symbolically significant.

At the same time, this new state managed to convey meanings that were communally biased. The very equity of the punishment, I've argued, *defined a new set of power relations* among the villagers, and those relations replicated relations at the level of state.

An abstract understanding of a distant event, therefore, intersected the villagers' personal experiences to produce a particular construction of their community identities in the moment. When Golam and Mofizuddin talked about the state as "ours" or "theirs," they simplified a thick set of practical relationships and introduced a more abstract understanding of community. Community identity became a historicized fact of politics, serving to bond groups in order to pursue conflicts largely, but not entirely, unrelated to the defining religious signifiers. Who Golam "was"— that he worshipped in a mosque and not a temple—served to locate him in a group, not globally or forever, but situationally for the precise purpose of reconstructing village power relations. Identity became a means of guiding a contending group, in this case "the Muslims," along their course toward confrontation.

For it *was* the Muslims who set the course. It was they who made the decision, woven of the many strands I've outlined, to riot. In the early stages of the fight, there was criticism, widely shared, concerning both sides: Golam, a Muslim, should have taken more pains to secure his cow; the Namasudra brothers who seized the animal were too eager for a quarrel. That part of the story was clear and responsibilities easy to assign, albeit sympathetically, to a crew of young hotheads. But both Muslims and Hindus in Panipur agreed that the riot itself was a product of Muslim decision. "It was totally counter to the social rules," according to Sunil. Golam described the moment at which his community changed the rules:

That evening, we Mussalmans held a meeting. We thought we could not go on living like this. They often threatened us, they threatened to beat us.

For some hundreds of years, presumably, "we Mussalmans" had "gone on living like this." It was interesting to me that the complaint Golam evoked here to justify what was a very important decision by the Muslims to riot was such a mild one. He himself had just been injured, yet he spoke only of threats, not of violence. He had earlier reported his wound in a tone of prideful embarrassment, as incidental to the story of his own provocations: "Why do you want to keep the cow?" he had taunted the Hindus. "Do you want to eat it?" Golam was hard pressed to generate much outrage when such an insult triggered violent rage.

Lacking clear moral authority to justify their decision to move against their neighbors, the Muslims drew on personal grievances, community memories, and an abstract recognition that an opportune moment of history had arrived. Everybody now knew they were ruled by Pakistan, a Muslim-majority state. Yet the Namasudras did not exercise more caution as a result; their youths still seized cows and slashed arms provocatively. In other words, the mere fact of the change of government did not signify to the Hindus a change in local community relations. But the Muslims agreed that the moment had come to make that transformation.

Might change not have taken another form, though? All the pieces conspired to induce them to act in terms of Hindus and Muslims, in part because the framework within which they considered their options was constructed in those terms. The old ideology implicit in their view of the world as divided up into those particular communities disabled their ability to seize new opportunities in new ways. What might have overcome that ideological inertia were alternate ideologies and movements. Had there been, for instance, an energetic peasant land-reform movement, or a structure available for local political reorganization, or a locally active protest movement to challenge their implicit ideology, then the story's ending might have been different. Problematic as it is to speculate on what might have been, I do so because we are faced with a methodological dilemma. One can specify the role of implicit ideological structures only when they run against the grain of assumed worldviews. Once Jogen Mandal, the Namasudra leader, proposed an alliance with Muslim peasants on the basis of their shared material interests, Sunil could and did alter his relationship to his Muslim neighbors and therefore to his formulation of community. Had the possibility of alliance not appeared, had there been no Pakistan, he would have been less likely to have rethought that relationship, at least in that way. At the moment of the riot, other forms of alliance on the basis of which the villagers could change their world were absent. Therefore they relied on what they knew, choosing a path of action that was new and different, but organized along familiar lines.

Lacking other means, they gathered their forces, seized the field, and proved conclusively to the Namasudras just where power and justice would reside in future in the village of Panipur.

Chapter Ten

Bringing History Home

"Why couldn't they now accept our rules?" asked Mofizuddin quizzically. After the riot, "they" did in fact accept the new rules. The communal harmony which now reigns in Panipur, and possibly throughout Bangladesh, is the peace of defeat. A prominent and powerful Muslim politician said it clearly. We were talking about why communalism had abated in recent years. He asked that the tape recorder be turned off so he could speak confidentially, and then he said, "The Hindus are too weak to fight back, and they and we all know it." Sunil said much the same thing:

We keep silent, in fear that it might lead to a repeat of the riot. If something like that were to happen now, we couldn't defend ourselves. We wouldn't have any avenue of escape.

Moreover, Sunil believed that a change in power had been precisely the objective of the riot:

That incident expressed what was in the minds of the Muslims. They thought, "Even if we harm them, they have no right to protest."

Golam agreed that a change of power had been, if not the objective, certainly the outcome:

They are afraid of us just as we were afraid of them in the past. . . . But we don't beat them. We don't oppress them in any way. We try to live in peace, like brothers, with them. But there is a fear lurking in their minds.

Sunil linked power with the issue of rights. In any conflict now, he said, "we couldn't defend ourselves." Weakened in spirit, the Namasudras also faced harder odds. The social rules had changed

184

with the riot. Muslims did what they would never have done before: they refused to compromise in a fight over banal conflicts. The reason, in Sunil's view, is that Muslims now think Hindus "have no right to protest." Social justice is skewed.

If the riot was provoked by "wrongs," it made sense that people should speak of its consequences in terms of "rights." Rights to what, I wondered as I listened. The answers I got exactly paralleled the complaints I had heard in the beginning. They had to do with day-to-day village activities—fishing privileges in certain waterways, for instance, or access to unclaimed lands when riverbanks shifted—the same terrain on which wrongs were inflicted.

In a country so poor, there is a fairly constant competition for scarce resources: relief in famines, land when it becomes available, assistance in upgrading farming methods, and so on (see Appendix B for a discussion of land ownership in the area of Panipur). But that competition should divide along community lines is not to be assumed, and frequently it in fact does not so divide. Development workers form economic uplift cooperatives comprising both Hindus and Muslims, and people engage in mutual assistance harmoniously. I questioned people about contests over land, for instance, when the *zamindar*s emigrated and some slight redistribution occurred. It made sense to me that this might be a place where community would matter. But people assured me that land conflicts were as common with members of their own community as with others. Fights over land ownership more often mirrored class lines than community ones. I had asked a group of peasants what was going on in their area, and one Muslim man recounted a long and complex battle over land rights, a three-way struggle involving a wealthy Muslim, a wealthy Hindu, and himself. He lost out; without resources he was unable to pursue as lengthy a court battle as could his adversaries:

She wants to know what is going on in this area. This story makes it clear what's going on. He who is a moneyed man, he is strong and can do whatever he likes.

What makes you most angry, the Muslim who bought the land or the Hindu from whom he bought it?

I have no money, I have no strength. Otherwise I'd sue the man who bought the land.

But who are you angry at?

I have no complaint against anyone. It's the will of the Almighty.

Rights proceed from power. He who has the power to make things happen has rights. Yet the Muslims of Panipur asserted their power by flexing their muscle, confident—somewhat mistakenly as it turned out—that the new Muslim-majority state would side with them. Because of a new description of power relations on the state level, they played out an emotionally compelling show of strength on the local level. Even though by any objective standards there were no winners or losers in the Panipur riot, nonetheless everyone agreed that the Muslims emerged stronger, the Hindus weaker.

What had happened was clear: Muslims had asserted preeminent rights vis-à-vis Namasudras, and they had demonstrated their power to enforce those rights. The riot had been an expression of altered relations, and it also had altered them, bringing home something new from the level of state to the level of village.

Community Memory:
A Damn Good Story

Over thirty years had passed since the riot. Governments had come and gone. Nationhood had changed when Bengalis revolted against Pakistan and created Bangladesh. The more I listened to the stories, the more I sensed how the changed power relations between communities were reconstituted over time—through the act of storytelling. Each reconstruction of the event reasserted the truth: in a clash, Namasudras beware.

Storytelling is an act of creativity. Behind it lies a particular set of experiences, filtered through a set of decisions about what to say and to whom to say it. History is the life of memory, said Cicero, and memory is both an intensely personal experience and a thoroughly social one.[1]

On the individual level of perception, no two people's riots were precisely the same. Golam was dragged along with the most aggressive parts of the crowd, for he was the *shalar po shala* whose cow started the whole thing. Altaf, also in the forefront of the melee, sat in meetings, lurked near the Shiv temple with his gun, or ran about the field warning rioters that they would soon be shot. While Golam was off to the side of the field where people "chased and counter-chased," Altaf moved among the sitters, talking and pleading.

Even when the two men were in the same place at the same time, they perceived what happened differently. Both placed themselves at the Tarkhania household, for instance, when the haystack was set on fire, but they saw very different fires. Golam insisted the Hindus had torched their own structure: "We saw them starting the fire." Altaf "was taking the cows back, when all of a sudden I saw the Muslims attack the Hindus' house and set the haystack on fire."

But if their perceptions were unique, they nonetheless flowed directly from a social position, a slant on events determined by their vantage point, by who they were and what role they played. Altaf, from his vaunted class and political position, could afford to accuse the Muslims of the critical act of arson. Golam, the lowly cause of it all, could not.

Memory, too, is a composite of individual and social experience. "Individuals remember, in the literal, physical sense. However, it is social groups which determine what is 'memorable.'"[2] In another district a very old man recounted a piece of well-known history, an incident that had taken place sixty years earlier: a band of Muslim peasants had killed a Hindu moneylender and his family in a nearby village.[3] The storyteller was a town man, an attorney. What he knew of the incident was secondhand. He had been a socialist at the time and was sympathetic to the peasants. The moneylender had been a fierce usurer who regularly foreclosed on people's land. All the farmers had wanted was a fairer deal. They had seized weapons the moneylender produced only after he fired on them, and then, in bloody rage, had murdered the members of his household.

Was this incident communal, I asked, or was it a class revolt? It was about class, he answered definitively. But it was also communal.

What do you mean, exactly?

It became communal later. All the Muslims took the part of the Muslims. What was economic in the first place became communal.

As we talked on, he veered back and forth between descriptions of the killing as economic and as communal:

It wasn't communal. Most of the Muslims were in debt to these people. There were some Hindus, also, who borrowed from these moneylenders, but they were very few in number. The main purpose was to take away the documents. They looted only documents. . . . Afterward, there was a lot of torture. It continued for two or three months.

Who attacked whom?

Muslims attacked Hindus.

Muslims attacked Hindus in general?

No, they only attacked the moneylenders. That indicates it was not a communal riot.

Looking over the transcript of this confusing interview, I realized that there was a pattern to the elderly attorney's descriptions. Each time he spoke of events he had not personally witnessed—in other words, when his story was secondhand—his emphasis was on the rebellion of oppressed peasants against a greedy moneylender. But whenever I asked him what he himself had felt, what was happening in his own world, he tilted toward the communal element that was clearly there. At the time, nobody had been quite sure what had happened or why. My informant's own fear, and that of his fellow Hindus, had been that the killing, even if not communally motivated, would have communal consequences. Over the distance of time, he knew full well that violence had remained contained within very specific limits, directed only against the most hated landlords and moneylenders. But even over time, when he remembered his own discomfort back then, he classified the facts as communal. His emotional relationship to the history he recounted shaped the way he remembered and recited it.

Shared and personalized histories also interact in the process of locating events in time according to the markers in people's personal lives, a method familiar to illiterate peoples (and not unknown to literate ones). Basantibala, for instance, had thrown everyone into confusion by insisting that the riot had happened before Independence. She linked it to her own youth, before her first child was born. She claimed she was in her seventies, and she certainly looked that old. Her husband, who had died within the year, was known to have been around eighty. We were hearing about the riot for the first time, so we had nothing but her account to go on. The personal and public dates she proposed were consistent with a riot in the mid-1930s, a time when trouble was afoot in the area; I had found archival references to conflict between the communities in the vicinity around then.

But the men in the room were incredulous. Although nobody was as old as everybody believed Basantibala to be, nobody could believe that so massive an event could have escaped their knowledge. In addition, the more she said about the riot, the more it resembled the riot they had all known firsthand.

The mystery was cleared up when Basantibala's son arrived. "How old are you?" we promptly asked. "Thirty," he replied, bewildered by the interest. A quick calculation told us that Basantibala, who was known to have been a young woman when that son was born, must be in her fifties, not her seventies. Not only had she misdated the riot, but she saw herself as a generation older than she actually was, a mistake that may say something about the social dislocation of women as individuals in Bengali society. Twenty years her husband's junior, aged by illness and adversity, she had accepted her membership in his age group. Quite literally, she had lost her youth somewhere in the social landscape.

Where people placed the story in time was revealing, and so were the specific stories they told. The number of people rioting, for instance, varied enormously from one telling to another. Nobody could possibly have estimated the size of the crowd accurately, but what they suggested instead was a sense of drama. I wondered if it were coincidence that each successive informant we interviewed presented us with a larger number than the one before, even though none had heard his predecessors' estimates. This phenomenon, I believe, attests to a transaction between storytellers and listeners. Our questions grew more detailed, more informed, with each conversation. Perhaps the tellers, sensing our increasing sophistication, wished to top the previous fellow's dramatic effect. I wondered, too, if the stories became more forthright over time, as people figured out we already knew the worst and were not shocked or disapproving. Perhaps our manner gave the villagers permission to express ever fuller degrees of their own wonderment at the event, couched in the idiom of numbers.

Other differences in tales indicated a creative human facility for self-serving recollection. Take, for example, Golam's and Altaf's differing accounts of peace-making. Altaf consistently reported himself as mediating the conflict, exhorting both Hindus and Muslims to think better of the call to gather, running from side to side at considerable risk to himself to cool things out, begging people to disperse rather than be targeted by the police marksmen. But Golam remembered Altaf covertly giving the nod to the Muslim community's plan to "teach the Hindus a lesson":

Altaf-uddin was then the chairman of the Union Board, and we thought we could not start the fight without informing him. So we went to his house. There were about twenty-five of us. He said it was quite okay.

If what people remember is shaped according to a mixture of social and individual forces, whom they tell is similarly selective. As I have said, people who had lived and worked in the area all their adult lives had never heard about the riot. Yet everyone we asked in the village or the surrounding villages knew about it in some detail:

How did you hear about this riot? In what context?
[A man in his thirties:] There wasn't any particular moment that I heard. It was just random storytelling by my father and uncles.
[To two young peasants:] You two must have been too young to see it yourselves. How do you know so much about the riot?
[First young man:] We heard about it.
[Second young man:] I heard from my grandfather.
What did you hear?
[Second young man:] That there was a riot between Hindus and Muslims. That there was firing, and people came from far away on horseback. These things we heard.
Did he say anything about whose fault it was?
No, nothing.

In general, people sought to reassure me that the telling of the story did not imply any animosity toward the other community. Everyone suggested that it was told neutrally, simply as an interesting tale. I asked one old man:

How many times have you told this story to people?
I tell it to those people who ask me.

Do your children know about it?

They have heard it.

What do they say about it? Do they ask questions? Do they say you did well, or badly? Did they ever ask you why you fought?

They don't make any such question or remark.

I found it hard to believe that more was not being communicated than a good old tale. For one thing, the telling was so selective. Over and over I asked people why they told their own youngsters, but not people with whom they had friendly relations from outside, people like those from the development project. Most answered with a shrug and a sheepish smile. One man proposed that, had relations been tense between the communities, the story would have been told more widely.

In fact, I came to believe that the story had become a cautionary tale, to teach the younger generation about social topography:

Every traditional message has a particular purpose and fulfills a particular function, otherwise it would not survive. The significance of its content in relation to community or society at large is what I call a function. But we cannot observe functions. . . . We can deduce these only by seeing how messages are . . . in fact used or whom the message benefited.[4]

The story conveyed information: We/they are in charge here. We/they have the right to protest, they/we do not. The story was a mechanism for enforcing particular power relations and the conveyance of a particular set of ideas. It is precisely through such experiences that implicit ideology is conveyed. There was no need to tell the story to gentlefolk, either outsiders or local people of a higher class, because *their* power position was ascertained by different means: economics, control of government posts, and so on. The telling, moreover, was somewhat surreptitious. If Basantibala had not mentioned the riot, I might never have heard of it. In many cases people told the story only once I had asked them. They started out discreetly, their narrative gaining in detail as we revealed our sympathy and explained our motivation for asking. There may have been some shame in the memories, but it was not my sense that anyone was deeply ashamed. What their manner suggested instead was caution. Those who made their fears explicit were Namasudras who worried about reprisals from their neighbors, particularly from those with political power. Understandably, they hesitated to say anything inflammatory, seeking reassurance about confidentiality from us first, and even then they usually remained cautious in their statements.

As we followed the trails of storytelling, a map of this community's public memory began to emerge. Boundaries were composed of lines of power, complexly interwoven with community. Within one's own world, a point was made of telling the young. Even if we accept that the stories told were as objective and friendly as people claimed, they nonetheless conveyed important information: Muslims are prepared to rally, and when they do they are a formidable force. Whatever protection may have been referred their way from the light of caste-Hindu domination in the past, after the state became Muslim, Namasudras could no longer resist the assertion of superior Muslim rights.

The young learned the lesson. New ideas joined the ideology of their fathers, reshaping the landscape of community relations in Panipur. How the riot was remembered conveyed both to teller and to listener a prevailing view of the world.

Conclusion

A cow ate some plants, and many people fought each other: on the surface a simple story, easy to pigeonhole, easy to dismiss. The trouble is, it is a story so oft repeated in so many languages that we can dismiss it only at great peril.

In whatever tongue spoken, the tale of the cow and the plants is meaningful. "These cows and plants are symbols," as Mofizuddin said. What they stand for is a day-to-day experience rarely expressed. "There is anger in us," he continued, "even if we don't express it. That's internal talk, not something you speak about openly." When those many thousand men took the field in Bangladesh, they spoke openly about their internal griefs and desires. Each side heard the other. "Internally," within the world of the village, the sons and daughters of the fighters heard the story of the conflict as a continuing lesson in community relations.

Outside, however, who was listening? I do not believe that a riot had been inevitable in Panipur. It seemed to me that people strongly felt the need for change, and that the options they saw for enacting it were severely limited. Nationalist revolt had created new possibilities in the form of nation-states, but no effective means for local improvement. Popular political parties were in disarray, exhausted by upheaval or suppressed by the new state. To redress old wrongs and create new opportunities, the means at hand were crude and obvious.

That conclusion was implicit in the terms in which the villagers thought out their problem. Seeing their world through the effective constructs of religious communities, the groupings most reliably mobilized in times of trouble, the act of community confrontation followed easily. There was a certain integrity to the riot, for it related to the true experience of the rioters in a way little else happening at that moment on grander scales did. Even when that experience was wrongly formulated, when stereotypes of the others' behavior did grave injustice to reality, nonetheless their complaints—"*they* beat our children," "*they* threw away food we had touched," "*they* won't hire us to work within their homes"—all contained elements of truth more profound and important than the misconceptions. Their grievances deserved redress. When new forces took power on the state level and failed to right the wrongs most deeply felt on the local level, people took matters into their own hands.

The experiences of villagers in Bangladesh are foreign to outsiders. We cannot know their history unless we listen to their stories. So, too, the people of Panipur were unaware of what "others" felt within their shared village. Hindus over and over told us they were frightened, that they would leave if they could, that they believed the currently peaceful conditions masked danger. Pressed, most said that there were many kindly Muslims, that the people they knew personally would protect them, and that nothing in fact was happening that constituted a threat. But underneath lurked a profound mistrust of the future. As one man said:

> Though apparently there is no tension here at present, nonetheless Hindus, especially cultivators, are suffering from apprehension and tension. At least, this is my feeling, though nobody talks about these things openly.

When I told Muslim friends, people who are the essence of goodness and well-meaning, that Hindus were wary, they were incredulous. They believed themselves to harbor no ill will, and they experienced no tension. But from the other side of the divide, from a position of powerlessness, life looked quite different.

To talk across such a gulf we must first understand the language spoken. Couched in terms both abstract and immediate, in a vocabulary of cows and states, of crops and rage, the story told in Panipur was clear for the hearing.

Appendix A

Chronology

Mid 7th century	Arab traders visit India
Early 13th century	Muslim rule established at Gaur in Bengal
1757	Battle of Plassey marks beginning of British rule in Bengal
1857	Great Mutiny; direct British rule replaces last Moghul emperor
1885	Indian National Congress founded
1905	Partition of Bengal
1905–9	Swadeshi movement and boycott of British goods
1906	Muslim League founded
1911	Repeal of the Partition
	Government of India moved from Calcutta to New Delhi
1919–21	Khilafat Movement (alliance between Muslim activists and Congress which came under Gandhi's leadership); first all-India mass agitation
1923–27	Upsurge of Hindu-Muslim riots throughout north India
1930	Anti-moneylender uprising in Kishoreganj, East Bengal
1930–33	Congress organizes All-India Civil Disobedience Movement and Salt Satyagraha, a protest against British taxation of necessities like salt; masses of protestors, led by Gandhi, march to the sea and make salt from seawater
	Terrorist anti-British movement in Bengal
1940	Muslim League first demands separate homeland
1942–43	Quit India Movement; Gandhi and established Congress leaders arrested; younger Congress leadership conducts underground campaign of sabotage

1943	Famine in Bengal; six million die
1946	Muslim League Direct Action Day in August sparks Hindu-Muslim riots in Bengal in which thousands die
1947	Subcontinent is partitioned, and India and Pakistan become independent; migrations across new borders lead to massacres
1950	Massacre of Hindus at Muladi in Barisal, East Pakistan
1954	Riot at Panipur
1971	East Bengal rebels against Pakistan and forms new nation of Bangladesh

Appendix B

Land Relations in Panipur

How had the peasants of Panipur fared economically during the period between Independence and the riot? Statistics that reflect specific localities are hard to come by, especially for the years in question. It was a time of major upheaval, not good conditions for demographers. Nonetheless, we can get something of a crude statistical profile which supports the idea that life was slowly growing somewhat better for some people. Let us start with (reasonably) contemporary times—sizes of farm holdings in 1983–84:[1]

	Small (.05–2.49 acres)	Medium (2.5–7.49 acres)	Large (7.5 acres and above)
Faridpur District (old)	71%	25%	4%
All Bangladesh	70	25	5
Panipur Vicinity	76	21	3

Overall, the proportion of landless families in Panipur was relatively small (21 percent as compared to a national average of 27 percent, with a rural range from 18 to 40 percent).[2] To be sure, one in five families in Panipur was landless, and the size of the small-holdings was very small indeed. More significant, however, is the degree of change over recent time. If we bracket the date of the riot and compare landholdings, the change becomes apparent. In 1940, 81.5 percent of Faridpur's families held less than 2 acres,[3] whereas somewhat fewer than 70 percent were that land-poor by

197

1983. The most impressive change happened in the middle range
of holdings. About 13 percent of all families farmed from 2 to 10
acres in 1940.[4] By 1983 that number had increased to approximately 25 percent.* A statistical hole exists during the relevant
years, so we cannot know exactly when the increase occurred, but
there is anecdotal evidence that it accelerated in the late 1940s and
early 1950s.

*We are comparing holdings between 2 and 10 acres in 1940 to farms between
2.5 and 7.49 acres in 1983. Had we statistics for the same acreage in the two
periods, the contrast could only be more striking.

Notes

Introduction

1. "Attention needs to be paid," wrote Daniel L. Horowitz in another approach to the same problem, "to developing theory that links elite and mass concerns and answers the insistent question of why the followers follow" (*Ethnic Groups in Conflict* [1985], p. 140). Horowitz's agenda is a worthy one, and his formulation contains a controversial assumption which, once questioned, deepens the inquiry. Do leaders lead and followers follow? I would suggest that leaders often voice what masses feel and, through a complex interaction with their followers, set the direction in which they lead.

2. Scholars debate just how and when antagonism between the communities appeared at the grass-roots level. Some believe it occurred early on (for instance, see C. A. Bayly, "The Pre-History of 'Communalism'?" [1985]), but others contest that view: "The dominant picture of the eighteenth century is not of the Hindus and the Muslims forming exclusive and antagonistic groups but of their cooperating in cultural life and social affairs" (Mushirul Hasan, *Nationalism and Communal Politics in India, 1885–1930* [1991], pp. 4–5).

3. Gyanendra Pandey, *The Construction of Communalism in Colonial North India* (1990).

4. The archives I searched were housed in the West Bengal Secretariat in Calcutta. They were reports from district officers, records of judicial proceedings, and police records.

5. In fact, some intensive detective work might yield an archival trail. Frequent changes of rule since the riot have scattered official papers to a variety of resting places. It is possible that records of the Panipur riot were not among the many destroyed and that, with more time and help, I could locate them somewhere within the fifteen hundred miles between

the Bangladeshi district and Islamabad. Alas, scholars must make choices dictated by limited means, and I chose to immerse myself in the subjective record rather than pursue a written one.

6. Katharine Galloway Young, *Taleworlds and Storyrealms* (1987), p. viii. See also Jan Vansina, *Oral Tradition as History* (1985), p. 111: "Informants wonder to what uses the testimony will be put. . . . The behavior of the informant depends largely on the impression he or she has formed of the researcher."

7. I am indebted to Benjamin Orlove for elaborating this formulation of stories within stories, in a private communication.

8. I choose this example thinking of Theda Skocpol's excellent study, *States and Social Revolutions* (1979).

9. See James Scott, *Domination and the Arts of Resistance* (1990), for an intriguing discussion of secrecy as a political act.

1. The Quarrel

1. Therein lies another story. My husband's family lived on the Indian side of the border in another village called Panipur. During my first visit to Bangladesh, I went to India to visit my in-laws and commented on the coincidence of two villages named Panipur in what were now two separate countries. They exclaimed that the coincidence was greater than I knew.

When I had first gone to India as a newlywed, there had been an old man living as part of my in-laws' family. Known to everyone as Mastada, or elder-brother-teacher, in his youth he had been hired to tutor my husband and his siblings, who were then children. Eventually, as his private students grew up and moved on, Mastada started a school for village youngsters and came to be beloved by a wider circle. When I first arrived, he was a glowing old man, still living with my husband's family, the soul of gentleness, an elder to whom everyone referred and who spent his days cooing to the babies and making occasional comments on the life of the family like a loving guardian spirit.

Now, when I told my mother-in-law I had found a village called Panipur in Bangladesh, she said that Mastada, by then many years dead, had come from *that* Panipur, a coincidence cherished in the family for many years. With great excitement she said Mastada had had a brother there, a man he visited on rare occasions and who must be ancient by now, if he survived at all. "Go see if he's still living," she instructed me, "and, if so, give him our respects."

I did, he was, and we had a tearful and touching meeting. It was this man who had in the interim died, and Basantibala was his widow.

2. Jawaharlal Nehru, *The Discovery of India* (1961), p. 261.

3. Partha Chatterjee contends that caste is inadequately described by notions of either class or superstructure; he tries to construct a Gramscian conception of caste as practical community. "Caste and Subaltern Consciousness" (1989).

4. Sugata Bose, *Agrarian Bengal* (1987), p. 21.

5. Nirad C. Chaudhuri, *The Autobiography of an Unknown Indian* (1969), p. 38.

6. An interest in experience appears in many literatures, existential, psychological, feminist, and others. R. D. Laing wrestled with a notion of experience when he formulated an approach to madness based on respect rather than cure. See his *The Politics of Experience* (1967).

7. Paul Connorton, *How Societies Remember* (1989); Stephen William Foster, *The Past Is Another Country* (1988); Fernando Coronil and Julie Skurski, "Dismembering and Remembering the Nation" (1991).

8. Peter Hardy, *The Muslims of British India* (1972), p. 5.

9. R. Ahmed, p. 8.

10. Ibid., p. 2.

11. Hardy, p. 5.

12. R. Ahmed, p. 6.

13. Census of Bengal, 1881, from R. Ahmed, p. 27.

14. R. Ahmed, p. 27.

15. Ibid., pp. 134 ff.; Hardy, pp. 92 ff. Hardy emphasizes more a religious disinclination to participate in British-sponsored education than a political one.

16. R. Ahmed, p. 135.

17. Ibid., p. 110.

18. Lord Risely, quoted in Rajat Kanta Ray, *Social Conflict and Political Unrest in Bengal* (1984), pp. 149–50.

19. Risely, quoted in Ray, p. 150.

20. Gail Minault, *The Khilafat Movement* (1982).

21. Sekhar Bandyopadhyay, "Social Protest or Politics of Backwardness?" (1989) p. 174.

22. Annette and Henry Beveridge Collection, MSS. Eur. C. 176, India Office Library, London. It is an interesting sidelight that this document is typed. Since it was clearly written in transit, I wondered whether Lady Beveridge had ordered her bearers to carry her nineteenth-century typewriter along in her baggage.

23. Lt. Col. L. N. Bavin, "Lt. Col. L. N. Bavin, I.P. Bengal 1912–36," MSS. Eur. D 1152, India Office Library, London.

24. Ray, p. 177.

25. Ibid., pp. 180–81.

26. Tajul Islam Hashmi, "Peasants and Politics in East Bengal, 1920–47" (1986), p. 177.

27. Ibid., p. 183.
28. Ray, pp. 78-79.
29. Ibid., p. 47.

2. The Decision

1. James Scott, *Weapons of the Weak* (1985); Karen Brodkin Sacks and Dorothy Remy, eds., *My Troubles Are Going to Have Trouble with Me* (1984). See especially Sacks and Remy, chap. 11, "Resistance Strategies: The Routine Struggle for Bread and Roses," by Nina Shapiro-Perl, for an excellent description of women's everyday activism against oppression. Amrita Basu provides a very helpful history of women's overt political activism in *Two Faces of Protest* (1992).

2. Discussion of the Union Board controversy appears in a fine dissertation by Tajul Islam Hashmi, "Peasants and Politics in East Bengal, 1920-47" (1986). See, for instance, p. 91. See also Partha Chatterjee, *Bengal 1920-1947* (1984).

3. The Riot

1. "A riot is the language of the unheard," said Martin Luther King; quoted in Lewis Killian, *The Impossible Revolution?* (1968), p. 109.

2. Sandria B. Freitag, *Collective Action and Community* (1989), pp. 16-17.

3. Gustave Le Bon, *The Crowd* (1960), p. 18.

4. Sigmund Freud, *Group Psychology and the Analysis of the Ego* (1960), p. 9. More modern scholars, eschewing such normative approaches to sociology, nonetheless continue the tradition of analyzing and categorizing crowds rather than understanding their actions. In *Theory of Collective Behavior* (1963), Neil Smelser, a highly regarded sociologist, theorized collective behavior with careful models of the components and structure of social action. But he did not speculate about the specifics or significances of that action.

5. The study of crowds has interested historians and sociologists over the last four decades, especially those trying to rewrite history "from the bottom up"—people like E. P. Thompson, George Rudé, and Eric Hobsbawm in England (E. P. Thompson, *The Making of the English Working Class* [1966]; George Rudé, *The Crowd in the French Revolution* [1959] and *The Crowd in History* [1964]; Eric Hobsbawm, *Primitive Rebels* [1969] and *Bandits* [1969]), students of the French Revolution clustered around Lefebvre in France (George Lefebvre, *The Coming of the French Revolution* [1947]; Albert Soboul, *The Parisian Sans-Culottes and the*

French Revolution [1958; English trans. 1964]; Richard Cobb, *The People's Armies* [1961; English trans. 1987]); and Louise and Charles Tilly in the United States (Charles Tilly, *From Mobilization to Revolution* [1978] and *The Contentious French* [1986], and, with Louise Tilly and Richard Tilly, *The Rebellious Century* [1975]). Crowds have continued to fascinate social scientists working in a variety of traditions: political scientists theorizing reasons for rebellion (Ted Robert Gurr, *Why Men Rebel* [1970]; Harry Eckstein, "Explaining Collective Political Violence," in *Handbook of Political Conflict*, ed. Gurr [1980]); social psychologists working out the dynamics of mass behavior (Stanley Milgram and Hans Toch, "Collective Behavior: Crowds and Social Movements," in *Handbook of Social Psychology*, ed. Gardner Lindzey and Elliot Aronson [1969]); and sociologists looking for an integration of behaviors and attitudes in collective action (Lewis Coser, *The Functions of Social Conflict* [1956]; Talcott Parsons, R. F. Bales, and E. A. Shils, *Working Papers in the Theory of Action* [1953]; Neil J. Smelser, *Theory of Collective Behavior* [1963]; Herbert Blumer, *Symbolic Interactionism* [1969]).

6. A. J. P. Taylor in *The Guardian* (9 February 1962), quoted in George Rudé, *The Face of the Crowd* (1988), p. 63.

7. James Scott, *Domination and the Arts of Resistance* (1990). Was their telling the story to me an act of rebelliousness? It would be interesting to know whether something was happening locally in that moment of narration that contributed to the villagers' willingness to speak.

8. George Rudé, *The Crowd in History* (1964), p. 255.

9. Sandria B. Freitag, "Hindu-Muslim Communal Riots in India" (1977).

10. *Report of the National Advisory Commission on Civil Disorders* (1968), p. 110.

11. Martin Kettle and Lucy Hodges, *Uprising!* (1982), pp. 106–14.

12. See Gyanendra Pandey, "Rallying Round the Cow" (1983).

4. Intervention and Punishment

1. Sandria B. Freitag, "Hindu-Muslim Communal Riots in India" (1977), p. 443.

2. *Amrita Bazar Patrika*, 29 March 1907.

3. B. B. Chatterjee, P. N. Singh, and G. R. S. Rao, *Riots in Rourkela* (1967), p. 35.

4. Ghanshyam Shah, "The 1969 Communal Riots in Ahmedabad" (1984), pp. 201, 203. See also M. J. Akbar, *Riot after Riot* (1988).

5. *Report of the National Advisory Commission on Civil Disorders*, pp. 124 ff.

6. I. F. Stone, *The Killings at Kent State* (1971).

7. Willard A. Heaps, *Riots, U.S.A.* (1966), pp. 166, 161.

8. Note by H. L. Stephenson, acting governor, 7 July 1926, quoted in Chatterjee et al., p. 72.

9. Sandria B. Freitag analyzes these relationships in her essay on "State and Community" in Sandria B. Freitag, ed., *Culture and Power in Banares* (1989), pp. 214–15.

5. Reconciliation and Thereafter

1. Hugh Tinker, *India and Pakistan* (1962), pp. 143–44.

2. Compiled from a variety of sources: *Statistical Yearbook of Bangladesh 1982* (1983), p. 76; East Pakistan Bureau of Statistics, *Statistical Abstract for East Pakistan*, vol. 5: *1950–51 to 1959–60* (1964), p. 52; Government of India, *India, District & Provincial Gazetteers, Bengal, Faridpur, 1905*, p. 6; Government of Bengal, *Bengal District Gazetteer, B. Volume, Faridpur District, Statistics, 1921–1922 to 1930–1931* (1933), p. 5; Bangladesh Bureau of Statistics, *Statistical Pocket Book of Bangladesh* (1989), pp. 69–70; Bangladesh Bureau of Statistics, *Upazila Statistics of Bangladesh* (1988), p. 140.

3. *Bangladesh District Gazetteers: Faridpur* (1977), p. 60.

6. Lessons of Panipur

1. For a sampling from a variety of perspectives see Barrington Moore, Jr., *Injustice* (1978); Ted Robert Gurr, *Why Men Rebel* (1970); William A. Gamson, Bruce Fireman, and Steven Rytina, *Encounters with Unjust Authority* (1982).

2. See Donald L. Horowitz, *Ethnic Groups in Conflict* (1985).

3. Sir Henry Joseph Twynam, "Golden Years and Times of Stress," unpublished manuscript (India Office Library, Photo. Eur. 53), pp. 92–93

4. P. Hardy, *The Muslims of British India* (1972).

5. Governor-General Canning, in a letter written in 1857, quoted in Hardy, p. 72.

6. In his autobiography, *Toward Freedom* (1941), p. 289, Nehru writes: "It is interesting to trace British policy since the Rising of 1857 in its relation to the communal question. Fundamentally and inevitably it has been one of preventing the Hindu and Moslem from acting together, and of playing off one community against another." Nehru did not accuse the British alone. He added a hearty condemnation of communalist politicians as well, and he understood that there was something to be accounted for in the behavior of the masses for following them (see pp. 115–16). But he believed the British government to be a key player in

promoting communalism. After the 1930 Round Table Conference in which communalists were seated over the objections of the Congress Party, Nehru commented: "The British Government . . . demonstrated that it still has . . . the cunning and statecraft to carry on the imperial tradition for a while longer" (p. 209). Even that super-reasonable historian V. P. Menon suggests the same idea. Relating Viceroy Lord Minto's 1909 assurances to a delegation of Muslims that they should be guaranteed government representation as a community, Menon quotes Lady Minto, who congratulated her husband for doing "nothing less than the pulling back of sixty-two millions of people from joining the ranks of the seditious opposition" (*The Transfer of Power in India* [1957], p. 9).

7. Bipan Chandra, *Communalism in Modern India* (1984), pp. 22–23, 17.

8. A. B. Siddique, private communication.

9. N. C. Saxena, "Historiography of Communalism in India" (1985), p. 307. The quote within this quote is taken from M. S. A. Rao, ed., *Social Movements in India*, vol. 1 (1978), p. 2.

10. "Groups require disharmony as well as harmony, dissociation as well as association; and conflicts within them are by no means altogether disruptive factors," wrote Lewis Coser in *The Functions of Social Conflict* (1956), p. 31.

11. Marxists have spent much time on the question. See, for instance, Karl Marx and Friedrich Engels, *The Communist Manifesto;* V. I. Lenin, *What Is to Be Done?* (1902/1961); Antonio Gramsci, *Selections from the Prison Notebooks* (1980). Social historians approach their subject from the premise that ordinary people are historically relevant actors. See E. P. Thompson, *The Making of the English Working Class* (1966); George Rudé, *The Crowd in History* (1964); Stree Shakti Sanghatana, *"We Were Making History"* (1989).

12. See Karl Marx and Friedrich Engels, *Capital* and *The Communist Manifesto*.

13. Ranajit Guha, *Elementary Aspects of Peasant Insurgency in Colonial India* (1983), pp. 3–4.

14. Gramsci. The word *subaltern* is taken from Gramsci. Imprisoned by Mussolini in the 1920s, Gramsci wrote his notebooks in code, using words like *subaltern* instead of the more politically revealing *workers* or *proletariat*. South Asian scholars use the word because it collapses more familiar categories such as class, caste, and communal distinctions, allowing the overarching commonalities among all those groups to be highlighted. That goal becomes important when analyzing layers of domination in a colonialized nation, since all masses are subordinate to the elite groups the Subalternists delineate.

15. Marx, "The German Ideology," in his *Selected Writings* (1977), p. 176.

16. Clifford Geertz, *The Interpretation of Cultures* (1973) and *Local Knowledge* (1983).

17. Geertz, "Religion as a Cultural System," in his *The Interpretation of Cultures*.

18. Sandria B. Freitag, *Collective Action and Community* (1989), p. 14. For discussions of the methodological problem of social history, see E. P. Thompson; Rudé; Stree Shakti Sanghatana.

19. Sandria B. Freitag, "Hindu-Muslim Communal Riots in India" (1977), pp. 429–65.

20. See Jan Vansina, *Oral Tradition as History* (1985), for an elaboration of this dynamic.

7. Self and Decision

1. Similar ideas are found in cognitive psychology, and I shall return to those views in more detail below. See George Mandler, *Cognitive Psychology* (1985), and Andrew Ortony, Gerald L. Clore, and Allan Collins, *The Cognitive Structure of Emotions* (1988).

2. Nancy Chodorow, *The Reproduction of Mothering* (1978), p. 51.

3. Sigmund Freud, *Civilization and Its Discontents* (1962), p. 69. See also Eli Sagan, *Cannibalism* (1974), for an application of Freudian theory to history which, in its reductionism, highlights underlying assumptions.

4. There is a large and varied literature on the question of rationality. Those interested in pursuing it would do well to begin with Adam Smith's *The Wealth of Nations* (1776/1982) and proceed to game theorists such as Anatol Rapoport and Albert M. Chammah, *Prisoner's Dilemma* (1965). Psychological theories of rationality have largely dwelt in the realm of cognitive psychologists, whose work I shall discuss later in this chapter.

5. See the critique of William A. Gamson, Bruce Fireman, and Steven Rytina in *Encounters with Unjust Authority* (1982).

6. For an excellent summary of other approaches to social conflict, see James B. Rule, *Theories of Civil Violence* (1988). Some broad theories of collective action nod in the direction of the psychological, but they offer only a superficial integration. See, for instance, Neil Smelser, *Theory of Collective Behavior* (1963). Gamson and his colleagues, who use a resource-mobilization approach to collective action, noted the lack and called for a more sophisticated approach: "Resource mobilization theory needs its own, more appropriate social psychology, focusing less on sources of frustration and more on mobilizing for collective action. Social

psychology is an indispensable component of an adequate theory of resource mobilization, not an antagonist of it" (p. 9).

7. For other psychological approaches to social matters, see the Frankfurt School's masterful study, T. W. Adorno, Else Frenkel-Brunswik, Daniel J. Levinson, and R. Nevitt Sanford's *The Authoritarian Personality* (1950), and Wilhelm Reich's classic *The Mass Psychology of Fascism* (1970).

8. Chodorow, p. 32.

9. Raymond J. Corsini and Danny Wedding, *Current Psychotherapies* (1989), p. 285.

10. Mandler, p. 11.

11. Ortony et al., p. 13.

12. Arlie Hochschild, *The Managed Heart* (1983). Another contribution to the establishment of this point of view is Thomas J. Scheff, *Microsociology* (1990).

13. Hochschild, p. 18.

14. Ibid., p. 219.

15. See Frantz Fanon, *The Wretched of the Earth* (1963); Phyllis Chesler, *Women and Madness* (1972); Claude Steiner, "The Pig Parent" (1978).

16. Antonio Gramsci defines common sense as the "philosophy of non-philosophers," or, with more precision, "the conception of the world which is uncritically absorbed by the various social and cultural environments in which the moral individuality of the average man is developed" (*Selections from the Prison Notebooks* [1980], p. 419). According to Clifford Geertz, common sense "can be questioned, disputed, affirmed, developed, formalized, contemplated, even taught, and it can vary dramatically from one people to the next. It is, in short, a cultural system" (*Local Knowledge* [1983], p. 76).

17. See Gramsci's theory of cultural hegemony.

18. Carol Gilligan's new work on the development of preadolescent girls is very relevant to this discussion: Lyn Mikel Brown and Carol Gilligan, *Meeting at the Crossroads* (1992).

19. Chesler, p. 18.

20. Wilhelm Reich, *Character Analysis* (1972), pp. 155ff.

21. Jan Vansina notes the role of clichés in transmitting the essence of experience. "Clichés are deliberate and purposeful simplifications" (*Oral Tradition as History* [1985], p. 139). Vansina is well attuned to the ideological function of traditions.

22. I see this analysis as a restatement of George Rudé's formulation: "There are three factors . . . to be taken account of: the 'inherent' element

which . . . was the common base; the 'derived', or outside, element, which could only be effectively absorbed if the ground was already prepared; and the circumstances and experience which, in the final analysis, determined the nature of the final mixture" (*Ideology and Popular Protest* [1980], p. 35).

8. Community and Identity

1. Sandria B. Freitag, *Collective Action and Community* (1989), p. 4.
2. Ibid., p. 5.
3. *The Exploratorium Quarterly* 14, no. 2 (Summer 1990): 24.
4. The following discussion owes much to Clifford Geertz, "Religion as a Cultural System" in his *The Interpretation of Cultures* (1973), pp. 87–125.
5. Geertz, pp. 121–22.
6. Ibid., p. 123.
7. Freitag, p. 6.

9. History and Ideology

1. See George Rudé, *Ideology and Popular Protest*, p. 35.
2. Jan Vansina, *Oral Tradition as History* (1985), p. 21.
3. "Historical tradition established group consciousness," according to Vansina (p. 105).
4. Ibid., p. 176.
5. See Dionne Jones and Monica Jackson's work on "Levels of Interracial Conflict" (unpublished paper, 1992).
6. There are three words in Bengali that Golam might have chosen to express his meaning. *Des* translates as "land" or "country." It is the most personal of the choices, a designation that endures well beyond regimes. *Sarkar*, the most formal, means "government" and is used in conjunction with the present regime. The word Golam used was *rastriya*, usually translated as "state." These shades of meaning are subtle but important. *Rastriya* suggests an entity that combines a sense of nationality with a conception of law. The *Samsad Bengali English Dictionary* (1968) defines *rastriya* as "a state, a kingdom; a country." According to the *Samsad English Bengali Dictionary* (1987), a "civil community having its own government or law" is *rastriya*.

10. Bringing History Home

1. Jan Vansina's work on oral traditions is a fine theoretical basis for exploring notions of the social nature of memory (*Oral Tradition as History* [1985]).

2. Peter Burke, "History as Social Memory," in Thomas Butler, ed., *Memory* (1989).

3. There is a relatively large literature about the event, which took place in 1930 in Kishoreganj. See, for instance, Sugata Bose, *Agrarian Bengal* (1987), pp. 190–94; Partha Chatterjee, *Bengal 1920–1947* (1984), pp. 135–39; Tajul Islam Hashmi, "Peasants and Politics in East Bengal, 1920–47" (1986), pp. 207–19; Tanika Sarkar, *Bengal 1928–1934* (1987), pp. 107–14.

4. Vansina, p. 101.

Appendix B

1. I have combined a variety of sources to construct these crude figures. Since I was aiming at a comparison over time, the first problem I encountered was the lack of comparable categories. Not only did differing definitions of landholding sizes appear at different times, but what lands were included within district boundaries also changed dramatically. By 1983, the administrative unit of Faridpur had become much diminished compared to its extent before the 1980s. I have combined figures for all the localities included in the old definition of Faridpur to calculate this table.

The old Faridpur district figures are derived from Table 12, "Number of Farms and Area 1983–84," Bangladesh Bureau of Statistics, *Upazila Statistics of Bangladesh* (1988), p. 153; the all-Bangladesh figures come from "Number of Households in 1983–84 by Type of Farm," Bangladesh Bureau of Statistics, *Statistical Pocket Book of Bangladesh* (1989), p. 101; and the Panipur Vicinity figures are taken from Table 12, *Upazila Statistics* (Rajoir and Madaripur Upazilas), p. 153.

2. Bangladesh Bureau of Statistics, *Statistical Pocket Book*, pp. 101–2.

3. Table 1.1, "Distribution of Areas Held by a Family" (1940), in Sugata Bose, *Agrarian Bengal* (1987), p. 24.

4. Ibid.

Names and Terms

Akrosh	Desire for revenge
Ashraf	Muslim descendant of immigrants from Persia or Arabia
Atanka	Panic
Atrap	Muslims converted in India
Baba	Father
Babu	Bengali Hindu term of respect for a man, sometimes appended to his name
Bazar	Marketplace
Bhadralok	Bengali gentlefolk, usually but not always Hindus
Bigha	Unit of area, in the Panipur region about half an acre
Bil	Marsh or canal
Bolum	Sword, formerly used by peasants in defending the *zamindar;* many families continue today to hide a *bolum* and a *dhal* in the rafters of their houses, bringing them out on ceremonial occasions
Caste	Hindu system of social categorization, thought originally to correspond roughly to occupations; there are four major castes and outcastes (those

	who perform impure work), and within those categories are many thousands of subcastes
Chacha	Uncle; a Muslim term
Chadar	Shawl worn by Bengali, mostly Hindu, men with the *dhoti*
Chak	Field
Chal	Uncooked rice
Char	Sand bar, often land exposed when a river shifts course
Chirra	Flattened rice, eaten either raw, or fried and sweetened
Communalism	Conflict between or among communities; a term used especially (although not exclusively) in referring to South Asia
Congress Party	Formally known as the Indian National Congress, an organization that campaigned for independence from England; after Independence, it became the ruling political party in India
Dacoit	Bandit
Dal	Lentils
Dhal	Shield, formerly used by peasants in defending the *zamindar*
Dhan	Mature rice plant
Dhoti	Man's garment, usually five yards of unstitched fabric worn draped from the waist to create pants; it is associated particularly with Bengali Hindus
Harijan	Gandhi's name for an Untouchable, literally "child of god"
Jinnah, Mohammed Ali	A leader of the Muslim League, first president of Pakistan
Jotedar	Landholder of an estate smaller than a *zamindar*'s, but nonetheless substantial

Kachi	Large sickle
Kalibari	Literally, "house of Kali," the goddess of war; a Hindu temple
Kameez	Flowing scarf worn with the *kurta* and *salwar*
Katra	Barbed spear used in fishing
Kheshari dal	Type of small, brown lentil grown in Panipur
Koch	Fishing spear without barbs
Kolai	Variety of lentil
Kopiruddin	Muslim village doctor
Krishak	Bengali tiller
Kurta	Loose-fitting, knee-length shirt worn by men and women in Western India and Pakistan, and in modern times by many Muslim women in Bangladesh as well
Lakh	Unit of measure, equaling 100,000
Lathi	Stick used for herding and tethering cattle
Lungi	Circular, ankle-length, skirt-like garment worn by men; it is tied around the waist and sometimes pulled between the legs
Mandal, Jogen	Representative of tribal and Scheduled Caste groups, he negotiated an alliance with Muslim tillers and supported the formation of Pakistan
Mashima	Aunt
Mastan	A criminal
Matabbar	Bengali village headman
Maund	Measure of weight, about eighty pounds but varying slightly from place to place
Mela	Fair or celebration
Moori	Puffed rice, eaten plain or with oil and spices
Moghul	Islamic Empire in India from the sixteenth to the nineteenth century

Muke muke	Literally, from mouth to mouth; used to describe the spread of news or rumors
Muladi	Town in East Bengal, not far from Panipur, where Hindus were massacred by Muslims in the early 1950s
Muslim League	Party formed at Dacca in 1906 to represent Muslim nationalist interests; it formulated and led the movement for a separate Muslim state in 1940 and became the ruling party in independent Pakistan after Independence in 1947
Namasudra	Member of a low-caste group of farmers and fishermen, once a tribe but Hinduized some hundreds of years ago
Nehru, Jawaharlal	Leader of the National Congress and first president of India
Nishputi	Compromise
Para	Village neighborhood
Partition	Creation in 1947 of two independent states—India, with a Hindu majority, and Pakistan, with a Muslim majority—out of the territory formerly ruled by the British
Puja	Hindu worship
Pukka	Literally "ripe," used to mean a brick or "proper" building
Purdah	Literally, a curtain; refers to the isolation of women within the home, a common Islamic practice and imposed on some upper-class Hindu women as well; when women do appear in public, they wear robes and masks
Ram deo	Large curved knife, used for animal sacrifice in Muslim ritual, as well as for mundane functions
Rastriya	Nation or state
Sahib	Term of respect

Salwar	Loose-fitting trousers worn by women with the *kurta*
Saree	Woman's garment, usually six yards of unstitched fabric worn draped in ways particular to a region
Scheduled Castes	Name given to Untouchables and low castes after Independence
Seer	Measure of weight, about twenty pounds
Shaha	Subcaste associated with money-lending
Shalar po shala	A curse, literally "brother-in-law who is the son of my brother-in-law," suggesting an incestuous relationship
Talukdar	Petty landholder
Tetul	Tamarind, a sour fruit, used in chutneys and eaten during the riot to diminish thirst
Thana	Unit of police administration, usually comprising several villages
Til	Linseed
Toupee	Cap, in particular a cap worn by religious Muslim men
Upazila	Administrative subdistrict in Bangladesh, usually containing a number of *thana*
Wallah	Literally "one," appended to another word to mean "one who . . . "; e.g., Congress-*wallah* means a member of the Congress Party
Zamindar	In Bengal, holder of a large estate, usually one farmed by sharecroppers or subtenants; created by the British administration as part of a feudal system of revenue collection

Bibliography

South Asia

Bengal

Ahmed, Rafiuddin. *The Bengal Muslims 1871–1906*. Delhi: Oxford University Press, 1981.

Ahmed, Rafiuddin, ed. *Bangladesh: Society, Religion and Politics*. Chittagong: South Asia Studies Group, 1985.

Ahmed, Sufia. *Muslim Community in Bengal 1884–1912*. Dacca: Oxford University Press, 1974.

Bandapadhyay, Atin. *Nilakast Pakhir Khoje* (Books 1 and 2). Calcutta: Karuna Prakashni, 1988.

Bandyopadhyay, Sekhar. "Social Protest or Politics of Backwardness? The Namasudra Movement in Bengal, 1872–1911." In Basudeb Chattapadhyay, Hari S. Vasudevan, and Rajat Kanta Ray, eds., *Dissent and Consensus: Protest in Pre-Industrial Societies*. Calcutta: K. P. Bagchi, 1989.

Bhattacharya, Buddhadeva. *Satyagrahas in Bengal: 1921–39*. Calcutta: Minerva Associates, 1977.

Bose, Sugata. *Agrarian Bengal: Economy, Social Structure and Politics 1919–1947*. Hyderabad: Orient Longmans, 1987.

Broomfield, John. *Elite Conflict in a Plural Society: Twentieth-Century Bengal*. Berkeley: University of California Press, 1968.

———. *Mostly About Bengal: Essays in Modern South Asian History*. New Delhi: Manohar, 1982.

Chaddapadhyaya, Kulam. *Tebhaga Andolanera Itihasa*. Calcutta: Progressive Publishers, 1987.

Chatterjee, Partha. *Bengal 1920–1947: The Land Question*. Calcutta: K. P. Bagchi, 1984.

Bibliography

Das, Suranjan. *Communal Riots in Bengal: 1905–1947.* Delhi: Oxford University Press, 1991.

Datta, Sekhara. *Tebhaga Andolana.* Dhaka: Bamla Ekademi, 1985.

Gordon, Leonard A. *Bengal: The Nationalist Movement, 1876–1940.* New York: Columbia University Press, 1974.

Hunter, W. W. *The Annals of Rural Bengal.* Calcutta: Indian Studies Past and Present, 1965.

Islam, Ajaharul. "Kishoreganj! Amar Kishoreganj." *Srishti,* 2nd Year, vol. 3–4, Dhaka, January–March 1988.

———. "Kishoreganj! Amar Kishoreganj." *Srishti,* 4th Year, vol. 1, April–June 1989.

———. "Kishoreganj! Amar Kishoreganj: Purba Prakashiter Pare." *Srishti,* 3rd Year, vol. 1, April–June 1988.

Islam, Mustafa Nurul. *Bengali Muslim Public Opinion as Reflected in the Bengali Press 1901–1930.* Dacca: Bangla Academy, 1973.

Kaviraj, Narahari. *Wahabi and Farazi Rebels of Bengal.* New Delhi: People's Publishing House, 1982.

Khan, Tamizuddin. *The Test of Time: My Life and Days.* Dhaka: University Press Limited, 1989.

McPherson, Kenneth. *The Muslim Microcosm: Calcutta, 1918 to 1935.* Wiesbaden: Franz Steiner, 1974.

Maniruzzaman, Talukdar. *The Bangladesh Revolution and Its Aftermath.* Dhaka: University Press Limited, 1988.

al Mujahid, Firoz. *Life and Philosophy of Maulana Vhasani.* Dhaka: Priya Prakasani, 1982.

Rahman, Atiur. *Peasants and Classes.* London: Zed Books, 1986.

Ray, Rajat Kanta. *Social Conflict and Political Unrest in Bengal: 1875–1927.* Delhi: Oxford University Press, 1984.

Sarkar, Sumit. *The Swadeshi Movement in Bengal: 1903–1908.* New Delhi: People's Publishing House, 1973.

Sarkar, Tanika. *Bengal 1928–1934: The Politics of Protest.* Delhi: Oxford University Press, 1987.

Sen, Rangalal. *Political Elites in Bangladesh.* Dhaka: University Press Limited, 1986.

Sen, Sunil. *Agrarian Struggle in Bengal: 1946–47.* New Delhi: People's Publishing House, 1972.

Suhrawardy, Huseyn Shaheed. *Memoirs.* Dhaka: University Press Limited, 1987.

Communalism

Akbar, M. J. *Riot After Riot.* New Delhi: Penguin Books, 1988.

Bayly, C. A. "The Pre-History of 'Communalism'? Religious Conflict in India, 1700–1860." *Modern Asian Studies* 19, no. 2 (1985).

Chandra, Bipan. *Communalism in Modern India*. New Delhi: Vikas, 1984.

Chatterjee, B. B., P. N. Singh, and G. R. S. Rao. *Riots in Rourkela: A Psychological Study*. New Delhi: Popular Book Services, 1967.

Das, Veena, ed. *Mirrors of Violence: Communities, Riots and Survivors in South Asia*. Delhi: Oxford University Press, 1990.

Engineer, Asghar Ali, ed. *Communal Riots in Post-Independence India*. Hyderabad: Sangam Books, 1984.

Freitag, Sandria B. *Collective Action and Community: Public Arenas and the Emergence of Communalism in North India*. Berkeley: University of California Press, 1989.

————. "Hindu-Muslim Communal Riots in India: A Preliminary Overview." In *Berkeley Working Papers on South and Southeast Asia*. Berkeley: Center for South and Southeast Asia Studies, University of California at Berkeley, 1977.

Hasan, Mushirul. *Nationalism and Communal Politics in India, 1916–1928*. New Delhi: Manohar, 1979.

————. *Nationalism and Communal Politics in India, 1885–1930*. New Delhi: Manohar, 1991.

Hasan, Mushirul, ed. *Communal and Pan-Islamic Trends in Colonial India*. New Delhi: Manohar, 1985.

Pandey, Gyanendra. *The Construction of Communalism in Colonial North India*. Bombay: Oxford University Press, 1990.

————. "Rallying Round the Cow." In Ranajit Guha, ed., *Subaltern Studies II: Writings on South Asian History and Society*. Delhi: Oxford University Press, 1983.

Saxena, N. C. "Historiography of Communalism in India." In Mushirul Hasan, ed., *Communal and Pan-Islamic Trends in Colonial India*. New Delhi: Manohar, 1985.

Shah, Ghanshyam. "The 1969 Communal Riots in Ahmedabad: A Case Study." In Asghar Ali Engineer, ed., *Communal Riots in Post-Independence India*. Hyderabad: Sangam Books, 1984.

Thapar, Romila, Harbans Mukhia, and Bipan Chandra. *Communalism and the Writing of Indian History*. New Delhi: People's Publishing House, 1969.

History and Culture of South Asia

Azad, Maulana Abul Kalam. *India Wins Freedom*. New York: Longmans, Green, 1960.

Basu, Amrita. *Two Faces of Protest: Contrasting Modes of Women's Activism in India*. Berkeley: University of California Press, 1992.

Brown, Judith M. *Gandhi's Rise to Power*. London: Cambridge University Press, 1972.

Carritt, Michael. *A Mole in the Crown*. Calcutta: Rupa, 1986.

Carstairs, R. *The Little World of an Indian District Officer*. London: MacMillan, 1912.

Chatterjee, Partha. "Caste and Subaltern Consciousness." In Ranajit Guha, ed., *Subaltern Studies VI: Writings on South Asian History and Society*. Delhi: Oxford University Press, 1989.

Chatterjee, Saratchandra. *Shrikant*. Bombay: Jaico Publishing House, 1969.

Chaudhuri, Nirad C. *The Autobiography of an Unknown Indian*. Bombay: Jaico Publishing House, 1969.

Das Gupta, Jyotirindra. *Language Conflict and National Development*. Berkeley: University of California Press, 1970.

De, Barun, ed. *Perspectives in Social Sciences*. Vol. 1: *Historical Dimensions*. Calcutta: Oxford University Press, 1977.

Dhanagare, D. N. *Peasant Movements in India 1920–1950*. Delhi: Oxford University Press, 1983.

Douglas, Ian Henderson. *Abul Kalam Azad: An Intellectual and Religious Biography*. Delhi: Oxford University Press, 1988.

Freitag, Sandria B., ed. *Culture and Power in Banares: Community, Performance and Environment, 1800–1980*. Berkeley: University of California Press, 1989.

Guha, Ranajit. *Elementary Aspects of Peasant Insurgency in Colonial India*. Delhi: Oxford University Press, 1983.

Guha, Ranajit, ed. *Subaltern Studies I: Writings on South Asian History and Society*. Delhi: Oxford University Press, 1982.

———. *Subaltern Studies II: Writings on South Asian History and Society*. Oxford University Press, 1983.

———. *Subaltern Studies III: Writings on South Asian History and Society*. Delhi: Oxford University Press, 1984.

———. *Subaltern Studies IV: Writings on South Asian History and Society*. Delhi: Oxford University Press, 1985.

———. *Subaltern Studies V: Writings on South Asian History and Society*. Delhi: Oxford University Press, 1987.

———. *Subaltern Studies VI: Writings on South Asian History and Society*. Delhi: Oxford University Press, 1989.

Hardy, Peter. *The Muslims of British India*. London: Cambridge University Press, 1972.

Low, D. A. *Soundings in Modern South Asian History*. Berkeley: University of California Press, 1968.

Masselos, Jim. *Indian Nationalism: An History*. New Delhi: Sterling Publishers, 1985.

Menon, V. P. *The Story of the Integration of the Indian States*. Bombay: Orient Longmans, 1956.

————. *The Transfer of Power in India.* Bombay: Orient Longmans, 1957.

Minault, Gail. *The Khilafat Movement: Religious Symbolism and Political Mobilization in India.* Delhi: Oxford University Press, 1982.

Nehru, Jawaharlal. *The Discovery of India.* Bombay: Asia Publishing House, 1961.

————. *Toward Freedom.* Boston: Beacon Press, 1941.

Panikkar, K. M. *India Through the Ages.* Delhi: Discovery Publishing House, 1985.

Rao, M. S. A., ed. *Social Movements in India.* Vols. 1, 2. New Delhi: Manohar, 1978, 1979.

Sarkar, Sumit. *"Popular" Movements and "Middle Class" Leadership in Late Colonial India.* Calcutta: K. P. Bagchi, 1983.

Sen, Sunil Kumar. *An Economic History of Modern India, 1848–1939.* Calcutta: Progressive Publishers, 1981.

————. *Peasant Movements in India Mid-Nineteenth and Twentieth Centuries.* Calcutta: K. P. Bagchi, 1982.

Smith, Wilfred Cantwell. *Modern Islam in India: A Social Analysis.* Lahore: Minerva Book Shop, 1943.

Spear, Percival. *A History of India.* Vol. 2. Harmondsworth: Penguin Books, 1978.

Stree Shakti Sanghatana. *"We Were Making History": Women and the Telangana Uprising.* London: Zed Books, 1989.

Tinker, Hugh. *India and Pakistan: A Political Analysis.* New York: Frederick A. Praeger, 1962.

Wolpert, Stanley. *A New History of India.* Oxford: Oxford University Press, 1979.

Conflict in Other Cultures

Alba, Richard D. *Ethnic Identity: The Transformation of White America.* New Haven: Yale University Press, 1990.

Bills, Scott L. *Kent State/May 4: Echoes Through a Decade.* Kent, Ohio: Kent State University Press, 1982.

Brown, Terence. *Ireland: A Social and Cultural History, 1922 to the Present.* Ithaca: Cornell University Press, 1985.

Conot, Robert. *Rivers of Blood, Years of Darkness.* New York: William Morrow, 1968.

Crump, Spencer. *The Story of the Watts Tragedy.* Los Angeles: Trans-Angle Books, 1966.

Davies, Peter. *The Truth About Kent State.* New York: Farrar Straus Giroux, 1973.

Diuk, Nadia, and Adrian Karatnycky. *The Hidden Nations: The People Challenge the Soviet Union.* New York: William Morrow, 1990.

Doumitt, Donald P. *Conflict in Northern Ireland.* New York: Peter Lang, 1985.

Fanon, Frantz. *The Wretched of the Earth.* New York: Grove Press, 1963.

Finnegan, Richard B. *Ireland: The Challenge of Conflict and Change.* Boulder: Westview Press, 1983.

Fogelson, Robert M., comp. *The Los Angeles Riots.* New York: Arno Press and the New York Times, 1969.

Gilmore, David D. *Aggression and Community: Paradoxes of Andalusian Culture.* New Haven: Yale University Press, 1987.

Governor's Commission on the Los Angeles Riots. *Violence in the City—an End or a Beginning?* Los Angeles: State of California, 1965.

Heaps, Willard A. *Riots, U.S.A.* New York: Seabury Press, 1966.

Heirich, Max. *The Spiral of Conflict.* New York: Columbia University Press, 1971.

Horowitz, Donald L. *Ethnic Groups in Conflict.* Berkeley: University of California Press, 1985.

Kelner, Joseph, and James Munves. *The Kent State Coverup.* New York: Harper and Row, 1980.

Kettle, Martin, and Lucy Hodges. *Uprising!* London: Pan Books, 1982.

Khalaf, Samir. *Lebanon's Predicament.* New York: Columbia University Press, 1987.

Killian, Lewis. *The Impossible Revolution?* New York: Random House, 1968.

Rabinovitch, Itamar. *The War for Lebanon: 1970–1985.* Ithaca: Cornell University Press, 1985.

Report of the National Advisory Commission on Civil Disorders. New York: The New York Times, 1968.

Stone, I. F. *The Killings at Kent State: How Murder Went Unpunished.* New York: New York Review, 1971.

Theory

Adorno, T. W., Else Frenkel-Brunswik, Daniel J. Levinson, and R. Nevitt Sanford. *The Authoritarian Personality.* New York: Harper and Row, 1950.

Allport, Gordon W., and Leo Postman. *The Psychology of Rumor.* New York: Henry Holt, 1947.

Bettelheim, Bruno, and Morris Janowitz. *Social Change and Prejudice.* New York: Free Press, 1950.

Blumer, Herbert. *Symbolic Interactionism: Perspective and Method.* Englewood Cliffs, N.J.: Prentice-Hall, 1969.

Boulding, Kenneth E. *Conflict and Defense: A General Theory*. New York: Harper and Row, 1962.

Brown, Lyn Mikel, and Carol Gilligan. *Meeting at the Crossroads: Women's Psychology and Girls' Development*. New York: Ballantine, 1992.

Burke, Peter. "History as Social Memory." In Thomas Butler, ed., *Memory*. Oxford: Basil Blackwell, 1989.

Chesler, Phyllis. *Women and Madness*. New York: Avon Books, 1972.

Chodorow, Nancy. *The Reproduction of Mothering: Psychoanalysis and the Sociology of Gender*. Berkeley: University of California Press, 1978.

Cicourel, Aaron V. *Cognitive Sociology: Language and Meaning in Social Interaction*. New York: Free Press, 1974.

Cobb, Richard. *The People's Armies*. 1961; English trans. by Marianne Elliott. New Haven: Yale University Press, 1987.

Coles, Robert. *The Moral Life of Children*. Boston: Houghton Mifflin, 1986.

Connorton, Paul. *How Societies Remember*. Cambridge: Cambridge University Press, 1989.

Coronil, Fernando, and Julie Skurski. "Dismembering and Remembering the Nation: The Semantics of Political Violence in Venezuela." *Comparative Studies in Society and History* 33, no. 2 (April 1991).

Corsini, Raymond J., and Danny Wedding. *Current Psychotherapies*. Fourth edition. Itasca, Ill.: F. E. Peacock Publishers, 1989.

Coser, Lewis. *Continuities in the Study of Social Conflict*. New York: Free Press, 1970.

———. *The Functions of Social Conflict*. New York: Free Press, 1956.

de Beauvoir, Simone. *The Second Sex*. Trans. and ed. H. M. Parshley. New York: Vintage Books, 1989.

de Reuck, Anthony, and Julie Knight, eds. *Conflict in Society*. Boston: Little, Brown, 1966.

Deutsch, Karl W. *Nationalism and Social Communication*. Cambridge: M.I.T. Press, 1953.

Deutsch, Morton. *The Resolution of Conflict*. New Haven: Yale University Press, 1973.

Erikson, Erik H. *Childhood and Society*. New York: W. W. Norton, 1963.

———. *Identity, Youth and Crisis*. New York: W. W. Norton, 1968.

Feierabend, Ivo K., Rosalind L. Feierabend, and Ted R. Gurr, eds. *Anger, Violence and Politics*. Englewood Cliffs, N.J.: Prentice-Hall, 1972.

Finlay, David J., Ole R. Holsti, and Richard R. Fagen. *Enemies in Politics*. Chicago: Rand McNally, 1967.

Foster, Stephen William. *The Past Is Another Country: Representation,*

Historical Consciousness, and Resistance in the Blue Ridge. Berkeley: University of California Press, 1988.

Freud, Sigmund. *Civilization and Its Discontents*. Trans. James Strachey. New York: W. W. Norton, 1962.

———. *Group Psychology and the Analysis of the Ego*. Trans. James Strachey. New York: Bantam Books, 1960.

Gamson, William A., Bruce Fireman, and Steven Rytina. *Encounters with Unjust Authority*. Homewood, Ill.: Dorsey Press, 1982.

Gay, Peter. *Freud for Historians*. Oxford: Oxford University Press, 1985.

Geertz, Clifford. *The Interpretation of Cultures*. New York: Basic Books, 1973.

———. *Local Knowledge: Further Essays in Interpretive Anthropology*. New York: Basic Books, 1983.

Gilligan, Carol. *In a Different Voice: Psychological Theory and Women's Development*. Cambridge: Harvard University Press, 1982.

Goffman, Erving. *Strategic Interaction*. Oxford: Basil Blackwell, 1970.

Gramsci, Antonio. *Selections from the Prison Notebooks*. Ed. and trans. Quintin Hoare and Geoffrey Nowell Smith. New York: International Publishers, 1980.

Gurr, Ted Robert, ed. *Handbook of Political Conflict: Theory and Research*. New York: Free Press, 1980.

———. *Why Men Rebel*. Princeton: Princeton University Press, 1970.

Hardin, Russell. *Collective Action*. Baltimore: Johns Hopkins University Press, 1982.

Hartmann, Frederick H. *The Conservation of Enemies: A Study in Enmity*. Westport, Conn.: Greenwood Press, 1982.

Hobsbawm, Eric. *Bandits*. New York: Pantheon Books, 1969.

———. *Primitive Rebels*. New York: Pantheon Books, 1969.

Hochschild, Arlie. *The Managed Heart*. Berkeley: University of California Press, 1983.

Jessel, Levic. *The Ethnic Process: An Evolutionary Concept of Languages and Peoples*. The Hague: Mouton, 1978.

Kanter, Rosabeth Moss. *Men and Women of the Corporation*. New York: Basic Books, 1977.

Laing, R. D. *The Politics of Experience*. New York: Pantheon Books, 1967.

Le Bon, Gustave. *The Crowd*. New York: Viking Press, 1960.

Lefebvre, George. *The Coming of the French Revolution*. Princeton: Princeton University Press, 1947.

Lenin, V. I. *What Is to Be Done?* New York: International Publishers, 1902; reprint ed. 1961.

Lindzey, Gardner, and Elliot Aronson, eds. *The Handbook of Social Psy-*

chology. Second edition, vol. 4. Reading, Mass.: Addison-Wesley, 1969.

Lofland, John. *Protest: Studies of Collective Behavior and Social Movements.* New Brunswick, N.J.: Transaction Books, 1985.

McBroom, Patricia. *The Third Sex: The New Professional Woman.* New York: William Morrow, 1986.

Mandler, George. *Cognitive Psychology: An Essay in Cognitive Science.* Hillsdale, N.J.: Lawrence Erlbaum Associates, 1985.

Marx, Karl. *Selected Writings.* Ed. David McLellan. Oxford: Oxford University Press, 1977.

Marx, Karl, and Friedrich Engels. *Capital: A Critique of Political Economy.* Trans. from the 3d German ed. by Samuel Moore and Edward Aveling. New York: Modern Library, 1906.

————. *The Communist Manifesto.* In Marx, *Selected Writings.*

Moore, Barrington, Jr. *Injustice: The Social Bases of Obedience and Revolt.* Armonk, N.Y.: M. E. Sharpe, 1978.

Morgan, David L., and Michael L. Schwalbe. "Mind and Self in Society: Linking Social Structure and Social Cognition." *Social Psychology Quarterly* 53, no. 2 (June 1990).

Nandy, Ashis. *Traditions, Tyranny, and Utopias: Essays in the Politics of Awareness.* Bombay: Oxford University Press, 1987.

Oliner, Samuel P., and Pearl M. Oliner. *The Altruistic Personality: Rescuers of Jews in Nazi Europe.* New York: Free Press, 1988.

Ortony, Andrew, Gerald L. Clore, and Allan Collins. *The Cognitive Structure of Emotions.* Cambridge: Cambridge University Press, 1988.

Parsons, Talcott. *Social Structure and Personality.* New York: Free Press, 1964.

Parsons, Talcott, R. F. Bales, and E. A. Shils. *Working Papers in the Theory of Action.* New York: Free Press, 1953.

Piven, Frances Fox, and Richard A. Cloward. *Poor People's Movements: Why They Succeed, How They Fail.* New York: Vintage Books, 1979.

Rapoport, Anatol, and Albert M. Chammah. *Prisoner's Dilemma.* Ann Arbor: University of Michigan Press, 1965.

Reich, Wilhelm. *Character Analysis.* Third edition. Trans. Vincent R. Carfagno. New York: Farrar Straus Giroux, 1972.

————. *The Mass Psychology of Fascism.* Trans. Vincent R. Carfagno. New York: Farrar Straus Giroux, 1970.

Rogin, Michael Paul. *The Intellectuals and McCarthy: The Radical Specter.* Cambridge: M.I.T. Press, 1967.

Rokeach, Milton. *The Open and Closed Mind.* New York: Basic Books, 1960.

Rudé, George. *The Crowd in the French Revolution.* London: Oxford University Press, 1959.

———. *The Crowd in History.* London: Lawrence and Wishart, 1964.

———. *The Face of the Crowd,* ed. Harvey J. Kaye. Atlantic Highlands, N.J.: Humanities Press International, 1988.

———. *Ideology and Popular Protest.* New York: Pantheon Books, 1980.

Rule, James B. *Theories of Civil Violence.* Berkeley: University of California Press, 1988.

Rummel, R. J. *Understanding Conflict and War.* Vol. 3: *Conflict in Perspective.* Beverly Hills: Sage Publications, 1977.

Sacks, Karen Brodkin, and Dorothy Remy, eds. *My Troubles Are Going to Have Trouble with Me: Everyday Trials and Triumphs of Women Workers.* New Brunswick, N.J.: Rutgers University Press, 1984.

Sagan, Eli. *Cannibalism: Human Aggression and Cultural Form.* London: Psychohistory Press, 1974.

Scheff, Thomas J. *Microsociology: Discourse, Emotion, and Social Structure.* Chicago: University of Chicago Press, 1990.

Scott, James. *Domination and the Arts of Resistance.* New Haven: Yale University Press, 1990.

———. *Weapons of the Weak.* New Haven: Yale University Press, 1985.

Simmel, Georg. *Conflict and the Web of Group-Affiliations.* New York: Free Press, 1955.

Skocpol, Theda. *States and Social Revolutions.* Cambridge: Cambridge University Press, 1979.

Smelser, Neil J. *Theory of Collective Behavior.* New York: Free Press, 1963.

Smith, Adam. *The Wealth of Nations.* Harmondsworth: Penguin Books, 1982.

Soboul, Albert. *The Parisian Sans-Culottes and the French Revolution.* Paris, 1958; English trans. by Gwynne Lewis. Oxford: Clarendon Press, 1964.

Steiner, Claude. "The Pig Parent." *Issues in Radical Therapy,* no. 23 (Summer 1978).

Thompson, E. P. *The Making of the English Working Class.* New York: Vintage Books, 1966.

Thompson, John B. *Studies in the Theory of Ideology.* Berkeley: University of California Press, 1984.

Thompson, Kenneth. *Beliefs and Ideology.* London: Tavistock Publications, 1986.

Tilly, Charles. *The Contentious French.* Cambridge: Harvard University Press, 1986.

———. *From Mobilization to Revolution.* Reading, Mass.: Addison-Wesley, 1978.

Tilly, Charles, and Louise Tilly, eds. *Class Conflict and Collective Action.* Beverly Hills: Sage Publications, 1981.

Tilly, Charles, Louise Tilly, and Richard Tilly. *The Rebellious Century.* Cambridge: Harvard University Press, 1975.

Vansina, Jan. *Oral Tradition as History.* Madison: University of Wisconsin Press, 1985.

Weber, Max. *The Protestant Ethic and the Spirit of Capitalism.* New York: Charles Scribner's Sons, 1976.

Wright, Sam. *Crowds and Riots.* Beverly Hills: Sage Publications, 1978.

Young, Katharine Galloway. *Taleworlds and Storyrealms.* Dordrecht: Martinus Nijhoff, 1987.

Government Publications

Bangladesh Bureau of Statistics. *Population Census of Bangladesh 1974. District Census Report, Faridpur.* Dacca, 1974.

———. *Statistical Pocket Book of Bangladesh.* Dhaka, 1989.

———. *Statistical Yearbook of Bangladesh 1974.* Dhaka: Government of the People's Republic of Bangladesh, 1975.

———. *Statistical Yearbook of Bangladesh 1982.* Dhaka: Government of the People's Republic of Bangladesh, 1983.

———. *Upazila Statistics of Bangladesh.* Dhaka: Government of the People's Republic of Bangladesh, 1988.

Bangladesh District Gazetteers: Faridpur. Bangladesh Government Press, Dacca, 1977.

East Pakistan Bureau of Statistics. *Statistical Abstract for East Pakistan.* Vol. 5: *1950–51 to 1959–60.* Dacca: Government of East Pakistan, 1964.

Government of Bengal. *Bengal District Gazetteer, B. Volume, Faridpur District, Statistics, 1921–1922 to 1930–1931.* Calcutta: Bengal Secretariat Book Depot, 1933.

———. *Bengal District Gazetteers, Mymensingh District, Vol. B.* Calcutta: Bengal Secretariat Book Depot, 1923.

———. *Report on the Administration of Bengal.* Calcutta: Bengal Secretariat Book Depot, 1927.

Government of India. *India, District and Provincial Gazetteers, Bengal, Faridpur,* 1905.

Government of Pakistan. *Population Census of Pakistan 1961. District Census Report, Faridpur.* Ministry of Home and Kashmir Affairs, 1961.

Sachse, F. A. *Bengal District Gazetteers, Mymensingh.* Calcutta: Bengal Secretariat Book Depot, 1917.

Scholberg, Henry. *The District Gazetteers of British India: A Bibliography.* Ag Zug, Switzerland: Inter Documentation, 1970.

Unpublished Materials

Bandyopadhyay, Sekhar. "A Namasudra-Muslim Riot in Jessore-Khulna, May 1911: A Case Study in Community Formation and Communal Conflict." Paper presented at Indian History Congress, Gorakhpur, 1989.

Bavin, L. N. "Lt. Col. L. N. Bavin I.P. Bengal 1912–36." Written about 1920 of a conference at Khulna, East Bengal. 1912–36.

Bell, Frank Owen. "Notes on Rural Travels in Dinajpur 1939." 1939.

Beveridge, Annette. Annette and Henry Beveridge Collection. 1884.

Carritt, Michael. "The Carritt Papers." 1930–39.

Casey, Richard Cardiner. "Personal Diaries." January 1944–February 1946.

Cooper, Adrienne. "Sharecropping and Sharecroppers' Struggles in Bengal, 1930–50." Thesis, University of Sussex, March 1984.

Das, Suranjan. "Communal Riots in Bengal 1905–1947." Ph.D. dissertation in history, Oxford University, 1987.

Dash, Sir Arthur Jules. "Memoirs." 1919–27.

———. "Rural Public Opinion in Bengal: A Close-Up." Paper presented at postgraduate seminar, Bengal: Past and Present, Institute of Commonwealth Studies, University of London, 15 March 1972.

Dundas, Lawrence John Lumley. "My Bengal Diary." Vol. 2. 1919–22.

Finney, Philip Edmund Stanley. Papers. 1927–47.

Hashmi, Tajul Islam. "Peasants and Politics in East Bengal, 1920–47." Ph.D. thesis, dept. of history, University of Western Australia, 1986.

Home Political Files. West Bengal Government Archives, Calcutta.

Jones, Dionne, and Monica Jackson. "Levels of Interracial Conflict: Manifestations of Symbolic and Competitive Racism." Paper presented at annual conference on Law and Society, Philadelphia, 1992.

Lambert, Richard D. "Hindu-Muslim Riots." Ph.D. dissertation, University of Pennsylvania, dept. of sociology, Philadelphia, 1951.

Phillips, John Roland. Tour diaries. 1911–1935.

Twynam, Sir Henry Joseph. "Golden Years and Times of Stress." (Memoirs and speeches.) 1909–46.

Index

229

process; Methodology; Police intervention; *specific people and groups*
Police intervention, 89–90, 91–110; camp
establishment, 104–5; and caste bias,
23; and haystack fire, 35; history of,
92–93; lack of indignation, 100–103;
police hierarchy, 94n; punishment,
105–10; and Union Board chairman,
34, 35, 94, 97; United States, 101–2
*The Protestant Ethic and the Spirit of
Capitalism* (Weber), 162
Psychology, 138–39, 206–7n6; and gender identity, 140–42; and ideology,
145–52, 207–8n22; vs. structural
forces, 6–7

Ray, Rajat Kanta, 41
Reich, Wilhelm, 148
Riots, U.S.A., 101
Rudé, George, 74, 81–82, 207–8n22

Saxena, N. C., 129, 130, 131, 132
Scheduled Castes, 43n, 45–46. *See also*
Caste

Scott, James, 75
Smelser, Neil, 202n4
Social location, 21
State, 165, 174–83. *See also* Bangladesh;
Police intervention
Storytelling, 186–92
Subalternists, 130–32, 205n14
Swadeshi movement, 32

Tagore, Rabindranath, 158

Union Board chairman, 24–25; gun possession, 34, 62–63; history of position,
61–62; implication of, 59–60, 63–64;
loss of authority, 36, 81; perspective
of, 33–36, 95, 109–10; and police
intervention, 34, 35, 94, 95, 97

Vansina, Jan, 173, 176, 207n21

Weapons, 82–85
Weber, Max, 162
Women, 87–89, 118–21, 189. *See also*
Gender

Compositor:	Com-Com
Text:	11/13 Caledonia
Display:	Caledonia
Printer and Binder:	Haddon Craftsmen